# Vegan &
# Vegetarian
# FAQ

## Answers to Your Frequently Asked Questions

COMPILED BY
DAVIDA GYPSY BREIER

NUTRITION SECTION BY
REED MANGELS, PhD, RD

*The* VRg. VEGETARIAN
*Resource Group*

The Vegetarian Resource Group
Baltimore, Maryland

*Please note: The contents of this publication are not intended to provide personal medical or financial advice. Medical advice should be obtained from a qualified health professional.*

Copyright ©2001 The Vegetarian Resource Group

Library of Congress Cataloging-in-Publishing Data
Vegan & Vegetarian FAQ - (1st edition) / Davida Gypsy Breier
Library of Congress Catalog Card Number: 2001130421

ISBN 0-931411-24-6

The Vegetarian Resource Group
PO Box 1463, Baltimore, MD 21203
(410) 366-VEGE; www.vrg.org

All layout and graphic design by Leeking Inc.

Printed in the United States of America

10 9 8 7 6 5 4 3 2 1

# TABLE OF CONTENTS

* Where can I find vegan marshmallows?

* Is kosher gelatin vegan? What is pareve?

* How many people are vegetarian?

* What are the different types of vegetarians?

* How do I become a vegetarian?

* Why do people become vegetarian?

* What about protein? Calcium? Iron?

* Help! My teenager wants to become vegetarian. Is it safe?

* What are the nutritional needs for young vegetarians?

* What is sodium stearol lactylate? What about other hidden ingredients?

* Where can I find out about vegetarian restaurants?

* Where can I find non-leather shoes?

* Where can I find a recipe for...?

* I have food allergies. Can I still be a vegetarian?

* Where can I find vegan donuts?

* How do you pronounce "vegan?"

* Who are some famous vegetarians?

* What is the history of vegetarianism?

* Do you have any idea what I can eat at fast food restaurants?

* Is there one official symbol that denotes a vegetarian product?

* I'm confused. I've seen what appears to be a dairy symbol on some kosher products, but I can't find any mention of dairy in the ingredients. Is there hidden dairy?

* Where can I find vegan bowling shoes?

* Where can I find ballet shoes?

∗Do you have a source for non-leather orthopedic shoes?

∗Do you know where I can get earmuffs made out of faux fur?

∗What about animal ingredients in soap and shampoo? What do I look for?

∗Where can I find cruelty-free contact lens solution?

∗Are there vegan flu vaccines?

∗I was just wondering if you know where I can buy vegetarian/animal rights/anti-meat t-shirts, patches, pins, etc.?

∗What about dogs and cats? Can they be vegetarian?

∗Like most college students I have limited funds. Do you have any suggestions for a healthy vegetarian diet without spending all my money?

∗Is it true that Krispy Kreme doughnuts are vegan?! I've found that when I ask food employees sometimes they don't know or don't feel like checking whenever something contains animal products. How can I find out for sure?

∗Is photographic film really made out of cow bones? Is there an alternative?

∗How can I find out which over-the-counter and prescription medications have animal products in them?

∗I'd rather not use birth control that tests on animals or has animal derived products. Does anything like this exist???

∗What about genetically modified foods (GMOs)? Can organic foods have GMOs?

∗How many animals are killed a year for food in the US?

∗Many of my patients are from Mexico. Where can I find information about vegetarianism in Spanish?

∗Can I be a vegan and an athlete?

∗How do I find out about local vegetarian groups in my area?

∗There isn't a local vegetarian group in my area. What can I do?

∗A few of my friends commented on the connection between vegetarianism and religion. Where can I learn more?

∗In your magazine you mentioned ethical businesses, but what I want to know is who would that be? How can we know which companies are not privately owned, so that we can invest in companies who share the same values as we do, being vegetarian, concerned about animal welfare, and the environment? Got any names of companies?

* I just can't see dating a carnivore. Where can I go to meet other vegetarians?

* Do you know of any carpet or upholstery shampoos that do not contain any animal products and are not tested on animals?

* Do you know of any charities/soup kitchens/hunger organizations that are vegetarian (i.e. Meals on Wheels)?

* I'm doing a college paper on factory farms. I'd like to include a bunch of narratives on how cows are slaughtered to hook the reader's attention. Where should I look for source material?

## CHAPTER 3 NUTRITION Page 47

* Do you know where I can find a vegetarian food pyramid?

* What is the nutritional breakdown of quinoa?

* How can I get omega 3 and 6 by way of food and not supplements and vitamins?

* I'm thinking of being vegan but my family insists I won't get enough B-12. Is this true?

* Are there any adverse effects of taking too much B-12? I have been taking 1000 mcg sublingual each morning for the past 5 days.

* How much iron do I need as a vegetarian? How much is too much?

* How do I go about finding a vegetarian-friendly dietitian?

* I have recently developed diabetes. Can I continue being a vegetarian?

* Can you suggest any vegan vitamins?

* How do I properly combine my protein?

* I read your information regarding calcium. Would almonds be a good source of calcium or do they have too much oxalic acid?

* Do vegetarian women have different health needs than male vegetarians?

* I'm a vegetarian athlete and I want to gain some weight. How do I start?

* Where can I get a comprehensive list of nutritional facts for a teen to follow? For example, a 15 year-old girl who swims 2+ hours per day needs how much protein, calcium, etc.? Is there such a reference available?

* I am 52 years old and four years ago I had a stroke and heart attack. Would a vegetarian diet help me or have I waited too long?

*I need information about vegetarianism for a group of seniors. What do you have?

*I am a vegetarian and have joint pain. Are things like glucosamine and chondroitin considered okay?

*I was recently referred to another physician by the doctor I was seeing. He told me he had several vegan patients who had joint problems. He told me that vegan foods lacked an amino acid needed to produce collagen. Have you heard of this?

*I've been a vegetarian for the past 4 years and recently I noticed significant amounts of hair loss. Can you tell me other than protein, could I be low in certain nutrients?

*I'm a vegetarian and I find my hair and nails do not grow quickly. What am I missing in my diet to make my hair and nails grow?

*I heard that being a vegetarian could cause a birth defect during pregnancy. Is this true? I'm really worried.

*I need impartial scientific studies that show a connection between a vegetarian diet and disease prevention, where do I look?

*I've become vegetarian recently and I'm gaining weight, not losing it! Help?

*I've begun losing weight since I became vegetarian. What should I be eating to maintain my physique?

*What can I do about the gas I've experienced since I switched to a vegetarian diet?

*I find I have a gas and bloating problem when I eat soy. Is this common?

*What is your opinion of the book which pushes blood types as determining whether somebody should be vegetarian or not?

*Over the years, I have read articles describing the deleterious effects from eating casein (dairy protein) and all other forms of animal protein (including fish)...We believe that casein and other animal proteins potentially cause calcium to leech out of the bones, thus causing bone-density loss. But we need empirical evidence in order to convince our friend.

*After repeated attempts at conception, my friend's nutritionist had her add meat - often red - at least once a week. I've been trying to conceive as well and as a vegetarian am worried if this is causing a problem.

*Do vegetarians need to be concerned about vitamin A?

* Has *Vegetarian Journal* addressed the DHA issue? I've read several articles which make it sound important for vegetarians.

* I read an article about men who avoid milk having significantly lower rates of prostate cancer. Do you have any information on this?

* Do you know of any resources specific to vegetarian/vegan lifestyle and dialysis/kidney disease?

*What is amylase?

*What is Royal Jelly?

*Why avoid honey?

*What is stearic acid?

*What about those ingredients that sound like they are from milk, such as lactic acid, lactose, and lactate?

*What is calcium lactate? Is it vegan?

*What is the difference between vitamin D-2 and D-3?

*What are agar-agar and guar gum?

*Is caramel color vegan?

*What is aspartic acid?

*What is glutamic acid?

*What is niacin?

*Does "lecithin" come from beans, such as soybeans, or is it from an animal?

*What are dextrose and maltodextrin?

*Is gluten vegan?

*What is gelatin made from?

*Is maple syrup processed with lard?

*What is aspic?

*Is glycerine safe for vegetarians?

## DIPS AND SAUCES

* Tofu Dill Dip
* Southwestern Red Bean Sauce
* Black Bean and Mango Sauce
* Cindy's Eggless Mayonnaise

## SOUPS

* Potato and Kale Chowder
* Lentil Chowder

## DISHES

* Spinach Pie
* Broccoli and Lemon Sauce
* Fourth of July Garbanzo Bean Burgers
* Tempeh Stuffed Potatoes
* Sweet Potato Kugel
* Stuffed Cabbage
* Vegetable Pot Pie
* Spicy Sautéed Tofu with Peas
* Quick Sloppy Joes
* Sweet Potato Slaw
* Tofu Balls
* Mushroom and Hazelnut Snacking Balls
* Fabulous Fajitas
* Phad Thai
* Noodles with Spicy Peanut Sauce
* Davida's Spicy Garlic Noodles and Tofu

## DESSERTS

* Sophisticated Poached Pears
* Soy Whipped Cream
* Chocolate Pudding
* Karen's Creamy Rice Pudding
* Festive Macaroons
* Heavenly Chocolate Cupcakes
* Macaroons II
* Eggless Banana Pancakes
* Romanian Apricot Dumplings
* Don't Tell the Kids It's Tofu Cheesecake
* Corn and Nut Bread
* Oatmeal Cookies

## ADDITIONAL RECIPES:

* Vegan marshmallows
* Vegan cakes
* Soy milk
* Rice and Almond milks
* Making Tofu
* Using Tofu
* Soy Yogurt
* Wheat Gluten
* Using TVP

✳What is seitan?

✳Where can I buy seitan?

✳What is tempeh?

✳What is TVP?

✳Where can I buy TVP?

✳What is tofu? What do I do with it?

✳What is vegetarian mince? I recently bought a cookbook authored by the late Linda McCartney and she mentions mince in quite a few recipes.

✳Where can I find vegetarian cheeses? What about vegan cheeses?

✳What is brewers yeast (a.k.a. nutritional yeast)? How is it made?

✳Where can I buy nutritional yeast?

✳I'd like to keep certain holiday traditions, but lose the meat. What can I use instead?

✳Where can I buy "mock" tuna?

✳Where can I mail order vegetarian products from?

✳Where can I shop online?

✳Is there such a thing as vegetarian gelatin?

✳I am looking for alternatives to dairy products. What do you suggest?

✳Is there such a thing as vegan eggnog?

✳I just found out gummy bears are made with gelatin! Is there a veggie bear available?

✳Do you know of a vegan chewing gum?

✳Where would I find a salmon substitute?

✳Where can I find vegan candles?

✳I've been vegan for a few months, but I really miss chocolate. Where can I find some dairy-free chocolate?

## CHAPTER 7 COOKING AND BAKING                        Page 128

✳What can I do about cooking on holidays? Thanksgiving? Passover? Christmas?

✳I'm 17 and have been vegetarian for 7 months and I have now made the choice to go vegan. The thing is every time I try to cook with tofu it doesn't work. It's like this magical block of stuff that is supposed to magically transform itself into something yummy. What can I do to make it work? I'm eating pre-made products, but I'd like to give tofu another try.

∗ I am trying to duplicate the "meaty" texture of tofu as I find it in Asian restaurants/recipes. I have frozen it, pressed it, and tried both fresh and store-bought brands - all to no avail. I would be grateful to anyone who can describe how one gets that texture.

∗ What is the best or correct way to drain tofu?

∗ Can anyone tell me how to make tofu cream cheese?

∗ I am trying exclude dairy from my diet but I am having a tough time figuring out how to replace everything I used to eat. Can soymilk be used the same as milk or do I have to use less or more to make the equivalent? Also, I already miss my cream soups. Is there a replacement for cream?

∗ I recently cut out dairy from my diet, but I miss my recipes that call for buttermilk. What can I do to make these recipes, but without the dairy?

∗ I really love the taste of mayonnaise but have had to cut it out of my diet due to ethical and health reasons. What can I do to replace this for my sandwiches?

∗ What can I use to replace butter in my recipes?

∗ What can I use as an alternative to white sugar?

∗ We are trying to make soup mixes and are having trouble finding dried carrots. Can this be done in our oven at home?

∗ Do you know of a culinary program that would be acceptable for a vegetarian?

∗ What type of resources do you offer for food service?

∗ What about parties and cooking for large groups of people?

∗ How do I replace egg yolks and whites?

∗ How do I make a vegan cake?

∗ Where can I find a vegan wedding cake?

∗ Can one become ill from eating raw or undercooked potato?

## CHAPTER 8 TRAVEL AND RESTAURANTS Page 140

∗ Is there a guidebook to vegetarian restaurants available?

∗ Is there a book of natural foods stores available?

∗ I just moved to a small town where there are no local health food stores, any ideas?

* Where can I find out about vegetarian restaurants online?

* Do you have any tips for traveling with veggie kids?

* We are looking for some ideas for cheap eats while on a cross-country road trip. We will have a camping stove and a hot pot.

* I'm going to be traveling to Europe. Where do I start?

* I'm going to be traveling to Europe and Asia, and I need translations to show waiters and chefs in several different languages.

* Do you have any vacation ideas for vegetarians?

* I'm very interested in learning about all the different veggie B&B's throughout the U.S. Does anyone know of a guide to this sort of thing?

* Do you know of any restaurants that will accommodate vegans in Israel?

* Within 3 weeks I will be travelling around in Zambia. What are the possibilities for vegetarian food?

* I'm going to Disneyland with my family. Will I be able to eat there?

* Are there any vegetarian restaurants in Cancun, Mexico?

* Any advice for travelers going to Central and Latin America?

* I'm traveling to the Dominican Republic very soon. What is the possibility of getting vegan (or even vegetarian) food there?

* I'm going to be traveling to Manchester, England. Will I find anything to eat?

* Where can I find out about vegetarian spas?

* I would like to find a travel agent that understands my needs as a vegetarian traveler. Do you know if such a person exists?

* The idea of a dude ranch where I could get vegan meals is probably an oxymoron, but my husband would like to vacation at a dude ranch and I am a vegan. Any suggestions?

* How do I deal with airline meals?

* This summer I'm going on a three-week trip to Japan with my Japanese class. In Japan, they don't eat much red meat, but they do eat fish, and I am a vegetarian. Is it considered rude to not eat everything on your plate? What should I do?

* What types of resources and advice do you have for vegetarian families?

12

✳ What resources do you have for pregnant women?

✳ Do you have any recommendations for books on vegetarian or vegan pregnancies?

✳ Is there such a thing as vegan prenatal vitamins?

✳ Can I feed my infant adequately with a soy formula?

✳ I'm concerned about the phytoestrogens in soy formula. Is this safe to feed my son?

✳ Can I make my own rice milk infant formula?

✳ How do I get my kids to drink soymilk instead of cow's milk?

✳ I am breastfeeding and it seems that whenever I eat vital wheat gluten (seitan) my daughter gets very fussy (gas?), crying and waking at night... I was wondering if you have anything in your resources that could make a connection from her fussiness to the wheat gluten via breastmilk?

✳ My daughter is raising her infant son on a vegan diet. Should I be worried?

✳ How do you deal with peer and family pressure?

✳ How can I meet other vegetarian and vegan parents?

✳ Can I make my own vegan baby foods?

✳ My vegetarian child is having a hard time eating at school. What can I do to encourage the school to incorporate more vegetarian foods for the kids?

✳ How should the request to add more vegetarian menu options be made? Verbally, written, by committee, at school board or PTA meeting, etc.

✳ What's a realistic timeframe that a change like this can be made in?

✳ But where does a school get vegetarian information and products?

✳ Would these methods/rules be different for a student in a private school?

✳ After reading the article on your site called "Vegetarianism in Educational Settings" I was thinking how wonderful it would be if there was a vegetarian school. Do you know if such a school exists ?

✳ I want to become a vegetarian but I hate tofu and beans. Is there any thing else I can eat to keep me healthy? And I forgot that I needed to state that I am only 12 years old. Also I looked at your site and it says mostly tofu and beans so please don't just send me a page of your site to read. (Unless it says other than to eat tofu and beans.) Thanks again!

✳ I have a 6 year old daughter who I am pretty easy with when it comes to dairy and sweets outside of our home. (We are vegan at home.) When my daughter goes to my parents' house and they are eating meat she begs them for chicken or on Thanksgiving turkey. Every time I turned my back on Thanksgiving someone was giving her turkey, which she begged them for. I got really upset and yelled at them and her. Am I wrong or do you think I should let her make her own decision at this age?

∗Please send me more information about your annual essay contest. I'm 17.

∗Although I had grand ideals of an organic, natural foods existence for my kids, I realistically need to know what fast foods we can eat?

∗My 7-year-old son wants to be a vegetarian. He is even passing up McDonalds! So I, as a mother, need to know more about this. I plan on making the whole family eat less meat, and still compensate for my son. What are some good books for us to read?

∗I have a granddaughter in second grade and became a vegetarian when she was four after seeing the movie *Babe*. She is feeling isolated and I would like to hook her up with a vegetarian pen pal. Can you help?

∗Besides the <u>Soup to Nuts</u> and <u>I Love Animals and Broccoli</u> books, are there any resources for teaching preschoolers about vegetarianism?

## CHAPTER 10 SOY                                             Page 168

∗I'm still not clear on soy. Is it a bean or what? How can I include some soy-based foods on my menu? How can I "sell" it to my omnivore customers, so it's worth my while to have it on the menu?

∗I've heard conflicting opinions on the use of soy products to relieve hot flashes and other discomforts of menopause. What do you think?

∗I am interested in using soy as a natural estrogen replacement in my diet. My question is this: is the estrogen in soy heat-sensitive, i.e. in cooking, does it hold up under cooking temperatures? Is there research to back this up?

∗Is it true that eating soy products can suppress the thyroid?

∗What's this I hear about tofu making people senile?

∗I just read your article about the processing of TVP. My question is, are the other soy products questionable too? I recently reviewed an article about soy. Can you respond to some of the following statements based on what I read in the article?

∗I'm confused. One minute all I hear about is soy's benefits and the next it is being treated like a toxin. What gives?

# FOREWORD

This book consumed my thoughts for months. I would be at a concert and start working on it in my mind. Two-hour drives floated by in a sea of questions. I dreamt of it constantly, wishing I had a way to record all of my nocturnal manuscripts. I questioned every answer, double-checking my sources and my source's sources.

And despite all that, I know that I haven't answered every question. This nags at me. This is where you, the reader, have an obligation to keep questioning. I'm not about to stop asking questions and trying to find answers, and neither should you. If you have a question pertaining to vegetarianism, veganism, and related issues, please write, phone, or e-mail The Vegetarian Resource Group (PO Box 1463, Baltimore, MD 21203; (410) 366-VEGE; vrg@vrg.org).

Never stop asking questions and challenging accepted conventions.

Davida Gypsy Breier
Baltimore, MD

# Acknowledgements

Thanks to Charles Stahler and Debra Wasserman for providing this opportunity to learn and thus share. Thanks to Reed Mangels, PhD, RD, Suzanne Havala, MS, RD, and Nancy Berkoff, RD, for their superb information and advice. Thanks to Jeannie McStay, Drew Nelson, Jessica Dadds, and Sarah Blum, who have all aided in so many different ways.

Extra special thanks to Janette, Earl, Patrick, Patti, Ken, Richard, Andy, DB, Tracy, Lydia, and Mrs. Drizen, all of whom helped make this possible.

Thank you to the following volunteers who proofread parts of the manuscript: Bobbi Pasternak, Erik Blum, Jennifer Femia, Sarah Blum, Sheri Runtsch, Stephanie Schueler, Susan Petrie, Susan Weinstein, and especially William P. Tandy, who patiently reviewed the whole thing.

For Ewa, Mica, Smokey, Johnny, and all the others who remind me why on a daily basis.

# INTRODUCTION

Being a vegetarian is all about questioning. Why is it okay to rush one animal to the veterinarian to save its life and take another animal to the slaughterhouse to become dinner? Is meat harmful to my health? What about the land usage and agricultural waste associated with livestock farming? These are but a few of the questions that lead people to vegetarianism.

Once there - then what - a whole new set of questions! What do I eat? Will I get enough protein? Can I raise my kids' vegetarian? What about hidden ingredients? We've listened to the needs of countless individuals who write to The Vegetarian Resource Group (VRG) asking for help. This book is the culmination of the many questions and frustrating lack of answers vegetarians routinely encounter. Hopefully <u>Vegan & Vegetarian FAQ</u> will be helpful to everyone from the novice vegetarian to the life-long vegan to Aunt Sally who is convinced that you are going to starve to death. If we haven't answered your question by the time you've finish the book, please write and ask!

What makes this "lifestyle guide" to vegetarianism different is that it is written based on queries from real people. We are answering the questions people obviously want answers for. While it was written with the assistance of several health professionals, it is not purely a nutritional guide. Instead, we've tried to answer some of the questions that you will encounter on a daily basis, like where to find non-leather shoes and vegetarian fast food. The book will also lead you to sources for additional information if you are interested in learning more.

I've encountered individuals who seem to try and make vegetarianism an exclusive, difficult club. It is not. Being vegetarian is actually very simple. It is the act of <u>not</u> doing something. By not eating meat, you are actively helping animals, your health, and the planet. This book is meant to make being a vegetarian even easier.

**Note**: In many cases websites are referenced for further information. This is due to the increasing access to the Internet and the wide spectrum of information available internationally. Many public libraries offer free use of computers with web access. If you need additional information or are unable to access the Internet, please write or call VRG and we will try and help.

# CHAPTER 1

# VRG's Most Frequently Asked Questions

I began to see the need for this book somewhere around the 8$^{th}$ time in a week I answered the vegan marshmallow question below. The first FAQ I wrote began as a few questions on The Vegetarian Resource Group (VRG) website to help guide people to the answers they sought. And then it took on a life of its own and began growing and growing. By the beginning of 2001, the VRG website was seeing almost 100,000 new visitors a month and correspondingly, the inquiries poured into vrg@vrg.org. There were so many questions that people had about the vegetarian lifestyle. The FAQ was initially Internet based, thus websites are provided for reference or as sources for additional information. In many cases VRG also offers printed brochures or materials, and as you'll see mentioned, you can write (VRG, PO Box 1463, Baltimore, MD 21203), phone (410-366-8343), or e-mail (vrg@vrg.org) to request copies. This chapter deals with the questions that popped up with the greatest frequency.

## WHERE CAN I FIND VEGAN MARSHMALLOWS?

Bad news. Emes was the only manufacturer of vegan marshmallows and they have discontinued producing them. Another company may begin producing them, so don't give up hope. If we hear of anything we will report it in

*Vegetarian Journal, VRG-News,* and on the VRG website. For now, there is a recipe adapted from <u>The Joy of Cooking</u>, by Lisa T. Bennett online at www.fat-free.com/recipes/condiments/marshmallows.

## IS KOSHER GELATIN VEGAN? WHAT IS "PAREVE"?

Kosher gelatin can be made from fish bones, beef, Japanese insinglass, agar agar, carrageenan, and Irish moss. According to the September/October 1989 issue of *Viewpoint,* a magazine from the National Council of Young Israel, "a tiny minority of rabbis permit pork gelatin as a kosher product!" Contrary to assumptions, it is also considered kosher to use animal-derived gelatin with dairy products. Unless it is specified as being derived from a non-animal source, such as agar agar and carrageenan, it is very possible that kosher gelatin is animal-derived.

The general meaning of "pareve" refers to foods that are neither milk nor meat, and many people assume this means that the product is vegetarian. However, pareve certified ingredients can contain animal products, such as fish and eggs. Kosher law is very complex and the bones and hides used in gelatin production, even if they are not kosher slaughtered, can be considered pareve by some koser certifying agencies. "Getting Into the Thick of Things, Which Gelatin is Kosher?" an article from the February 2001 issue of *Kashrus Magazine,* explains the many complexities surrounding kosher gelatin. According to the article,

> *"[Horav Moshe Feinstein] writes that hides are not considered meat (to prohibit its mixture with milk) by Torah Law, but they are prohibited by Rabbinic Law. If they are dried and processed, the gelatin that comes out is not included in this Rabbinic prohibition. Therefore, gelatin produced from the hides of kosher-slaughtered animal may be intentionally used with milk, provided that the hides are cleaned to remove any meat residue."*

## HOW MANY PEOPLE ARE VEGETARIAN?

In 1994 and 1997, VRG conducted Roper Polls and in 2000 we conducted a Zogby poll to determine the number of adults in the US who are vegetarian. In previous polls the numbers varied from 1.2% (1977-78 US Dept. of Agriculture

Food Consumption Survey) to 7% (*Vegetarian Times*, 1992). Part of the reason for the discrepancy is how the question is worded. When asked if they consider themselves vegetarian, many people will reply yes, even if they occasionally eat meat. This leaves the definition of vegetarian in the hands of the person answering the question. When VRG conducted the Roper Polls, the question was phrased as, "Please call off the items on this list, if any, that you **never** eat: Meat (beef, pork, veal, lamb, etc.). Poultry. Fish/Seafood. Dairy Products. Eggs. Honey. Eat Them All. Don't Know." Please note that the key word was never. The numbers would be very different if the word never was omitted.

In both the 1994 and 1997 polls, the number of adult vegetarians was about 1% of the population. Vegans accounted for roughly one-third to one-half of the vegetarian population.

## 1997 Sample Poll Results

|  | Total | Male | Female | Northeast | West |
|---|---|---|---|---|---|
| Never eat red meat | 5% | 4% | 6% | 4% | 8% |
| Never eat poultry | 2% | 2% | 3% | 2% | 4% |
| Never eat fish | 4% | 3% | 5% | 4% | 5% |
| Eat none of the above | 1% | 1% | 1% | under 1% | 2% |

In 2000, VRG conducted a Zogby poll, asking the exact same question. This time the population of adult vegetarians was 2.5%. Based on Census figures, this means there are 4.8 million non-institutionalized vegetarian adults in the United States. The percentage of vegans in the vegetarian population remained the same.

## 2000 Sample Poll Results
**Please tell me which of the following foods, if any, you never eat?**

2.5% Meat, poultry, fish
4.5% Meat
4.5% Poultry
9.0% Fish/Seafood
3.7% Dairy Products
6.7% Eggs
15.4% Honey
0.9% Don't eat any of the foods on the list (vegans)

*(Note: The margin of sampling error is +/- 3.3%. Per Zogby, there would be a +/- 9% margin of sampling error when looking at subgroups of 100 people.)*

# 2000 Sample Poll Results (continued)

## NEVER EAT MEAT
### 4.5% Total of those surveyed

7.5% East
3.5% South
1.9% Central Great Lakes
6.1% West
10.4% Ages 18-29
3.4% Ages 30-49
6.4% Ages 18-24
8.6% Ages 25-34
8.8% Large City
1.2% Small City
4.5% Suburbs
2.3% Male
6.6% Female

## NEVER EAT MEAT, POULTRY, OR FISII (Vegetarians)
### 2.5% Total of those surveyed

3.5% East
1.8% South
1.3% Central Great Lakes
4.2% West
6.0% Ages 18-29
2.3% Ages 30-49
0.7% Ages 50-64
1.6% Ages 65 plus
3.7% Ages 18-24
5.6% Ages 25-34
1.8% Ages 35-54
1.6% Ages 55-69
1.4% Ages 70 plus
5.4% Large City
0.4% Small City

## NEVER EAT MEAT, POULTRY, OR FISH (Vegetarians) cont.

2.0% Suburb
2.2% Rural
1.6% White
9.4% Latino
3.5% Afro-American
8.1% Asian
1.7% Male
3.2% Female

## NEVER EAT ANY FOODS LISTED (Vegan)
### 0.9% Total of those surveyed

1.9% East
1.9% Large City

VRG was also curious about the numbers of young vegetarians. The first teen poll we conducted was in 1995 and the second in 2000. The children and young adults polled were asked the same question as the adults: "Please call off the items on this list, if any, that you never eat: Meat. Poultry. Fish/Seafood. Dairy Products. Eggs. Honey."

The overall average showed that a little over 1.5% of 8-17 year-olds were vegetarian in 1995. In 2000, 2% of 6-17 year-olds were vegetarian and 0.5% of kids were vegan.

## 2000 Sample Teen Poll Results

|  | 6-7 year-olds | 8-12 year-olds | 13-17 year-olds |
|---|---|---|---|
| Do Not Ever Eat: |  |  |  |
| MEAT | 8% | 7% | 5% |
| POULTRY | 3% | 6% | 3% |
| FISH/SEAFOOD | 14% | 19% | 16% |
| NONE OF THE ABOVE | 1% | 2% | 2% |

Another interesting trend is the high demand for vegetarian meals when eating out, which far exceeds the number of vegetarians. A VRG poll Zogby conducted in 1999 showed that about 5.5% of the population always order a dish without meat, fish or fowl and over half of the population (57%) sometimes, often, or always orders a vegetarian item.

For additional information on the polls quoted above, visit www.vrg.org/nutshell/faq.htm#poll. For international figures, try www.ivu.org/articles/stats.html.

## WHAT ARE THE DIFFERENT TYPES OF VEGETARIANS?

* Vegetarian: does not eat meat, fish, or fowl.

* Lacto-Ovo Vegetarian: does not eat meat, fish, or fowl. Eats dairy and egg products.

* Ovo-Vegetarian: does not eat meat, fish, fowl, or dairy products. Eats egg products.

✻ Lacto-Vegetarian: does not eat meat, fish, fowl, or eggs. Eats dairy products.

✻ Vegan: does not eat any animal products including meat, fish, fowl, eggs, dairy, honey, etc. Most vegans do not use any animal products such as silk, leather, wool, etc. as well.

## HOW DO I BECOME A VEGETARIAN?

There are several ways to make the change. Do whatever feels more comfortable for you. Like other types of cooking, vegetarianism can be simple or complicated, expensive or inexpensive. You can use foods that need to be bought in a natural foods store or are easily available at your local supermarket.

There are many common recipes that are easily made veggie/vegan, or already are: spaghetti and other pasta dishes, burritos, tacos, tostadas, mashed potatoes, three bean salad, pancakes, French toast, waffles, grilled cheese sandwiches, hummus, grilled veggies, oven-roasted veggies, rice, etc. Another way to make the change would be to start exploring other cuisines or methods of cooking (go for Chinese, Thai, Indian, etc.) that exclude meat in many dishes to begin with. Some people like to try both approaches. You may find yourself so excited by all your new choices and flavors that you'll never even miss the meat.

You could also try substituting tofu, seitan, or other meat alternatives for the meat in your usual dishes. Most supermarkets carry tofu and other meat substitutes in the produce section. Check the frozen section, near the breakfast foods, for veggie burgers, veggie crumbles, links, and patties (also see the Vegetarian Recipes and Products sections on pages 87 and 117).

*The American Dietetic Association Position Paper on Vegetarian Diets* (1997) helps clarify the nutritional needs of vegetarians. The position statement is as follows: *"It is the position of The American Dietetic Association (ADA) that appropriately planned vegetarian diets are healthful, are nutritionally adequate, and provide health benefits in the prevention and treatment of certain diseases."* To read a full copy of the paper, go to www.vrg.org/nutrition/adapaper.htm or call (410) 366-VEGE or write The VRG, PO Box 1463, Baltimore, MD 21203 and request a copy be mailed to you. To view it on the ADA site, go to www.eatright.org/adap1197.html.

If you are looking for books to help get you started, consider Simply Vegan (Debra Wasserman and Reed Mangels, PhD, RD), The Vegetarian Way (Virginia Messina, MPH, RD and Mark Messina, PhD), and Becoming Vegetarian (Vesanto Melina. MS, RD and Brenda Davis, RD).

There is a wealth of nutrition information on the VRG website. The Nutshell Section is at www.vrg.org/nutshell, and there you will find many of our brochures and guides. Our Nutrition Section, at www.vrg.org/nutrition, offers answers to more specific dietary questions. Also look at "Heart Healthy Diets: The Vegetarian Way" on our website at www.vrg.org/nutshell/heart.htm (or see the Vegetarian Nutrition chapter on page 47). For printed brochures and materials, just write (PO Box 1463, Baltimore, MD 21203), phone (410) 366-8343, or e-mail (vrg@vrg.org). Your request and additional information will be mailed to you.

## WHY DO PEOPLE BECOME VEGETARIAN?

Among the many reasons for being a vegetarian are health, ecological and religious concerns, dislike of meat, compassion for animals, belief in non-violence, and economics. People often become vegetarian for one reason, be it health, religion, or animal rights, and later adopt some of the other reasons as well. According to a *Vegetarian Journal* reader survey conducted in 1998, 82% of readers "are interested in vegetarianism because of health, 75% because of ethics, the environment, and animal rights, 31% because of taste, and 26% because of economics." To read more, go to www.vrg.org/journal/vj98jan/981coord.htm. The Viva Vegie Society in New York distributes *"101 Reasons Why I'm a Vegetarian,"* which offers a wide variety of concerns and issues regarding vegetarianism. You can order a copy for $2 (The VivaVegie Society, Prince St. Station, P.O. Box 294, New York, NY 10012) or view it on the web at www.vivavegie.org.

## WHAT ABOUT PROTEIN? CALCIUM? IRON?

### Protein
Reed Mangels, PhD, RD, VRG nutrition advisor, states in Simply Vegan, *"Vegetarians easily meet their protein needs by eating a varied diet, as long as*

*they consume enough calories to maintain their weight. It is not necessary to plan combinations of foods. A mixture of proteins throughout the day will provide enough 'essential amino acids'."*

Almost all foods, except for alcohol, sugar, and fats are good sources of protein. Vegan sources include: potatoes, whole wheat bread, rice, broccoli, spinach, almonds, peas, chickpeas, peanut butter, tofu, soymilk, lentils, and kale.

For more information, read *Position of The American Dietetic Association on Vegetarian Diets*, Simply Vegan (Debra Wasserman and Reed Mangels, PhD, RD), The Vegetarian Way (Virginia Messina, MPH, RD and Mark Messina, PhD), and Becoming Vegetarian (Vesanto Melina, MS, RD and Brenda Davis, RD). Also see page 205 for a chart on good sources of protein. For more detailed information, read the chapter on protein in Simply Vegan or view it online at www.vrg.org/nutrition/protein.htm.

## Calcium

Calcium, needed for strong bones, is found in dark green leafy vegetables, tofu made with calcium sulfate, and many other foods commonly eaten by vegans. High-protein diets appear to lead to increased calcium losses. Calcium requirements for those on lower protein, plant-based diets may be somewhat lower than requirements for those eating a higher protein, flesh-based diet. However, it is important for vegans to regularly eat foods that are high in calcium and/or use a calcium supplement.

Good sources of calcium include calcium-fortified soy or ricemilk, collard greens, blackstrap molasses, tofu, calcium-fortified orange juice, soy yogurt, and turnip greens. Also see page 207 for a chart on good sources of calcium.

For more detailed information, read the chapter on calcium in Simply Vegan or view it online at www.vrg.org/nutrition/calcium.htm.

## Iron

Dried beans and dark leafy green vegetables are especially good sources of iron: better, on a per-calorie basis, than meat. Iron absorption is increased markedly by eating foods containing vitamin C along with foods containing iron. Vegetarians do not have a higher incidence of iron deficiency than do meat eaters.

Good sources of iron include soybeans, blackstrap molasses, lentils, tofu, quinoa, kidney beans, and chickpeas. Also see page 209 for a chart on good sources of iron.

For more detailed information, read the chapter on iron in <u>Simply Vegan</u> or view it online at www.vrg.org/nutrition/iron.htm.

For additional information about nutrition-related questions, turn to page 47.

✦

## Help! My teenager wants to become vegetarian. Is it safe?

Yes, a vegetarian diet can be perfectly safe for teenagers. VRG offers a brochure that directly addresses the special needs of teen vegetarians. The *Vegetarian Nutrition for Teenagers* brochure is available online at www.vrg.org/nutrition/teennutrition.htm or you can request a paper copy be mailed. Also, in addition to the nutritional information you'll find online, we developed a section of the website just for young adults - www.vrg.org/family/kidsindex.htm. There you'll find details about our annual essay contest, online groups just for vegetarian teens, and information especially useful for young activists.

✦

## What are the nutritional needs for young vegetarians?

This is the opening paragraph of *Feeding Vegan Kids,* by Reed Mangels, PhD, RD:

> *Many members of The Vegetarian Resource Group are glowing testimony to the fact that vegan children can be healthy, grow normally, be extremely active, and (we think) smarter than average. Of course it takes time and thought to feed vegan children. Shouldn't feeding of any child require time and thought? After all, the years from birth to adolescence are the years when eating habits are set, when growth rate is high, and to a large extent, when the size of stores of essential nutrients such as calcium and iron are determined.*

You can access *Feeding Vegan Kids* on our website at www.vrg.org/family. Our *Tips for Parents of Young Vegetarians* is also helpful. Please e-mail (vrg@vrg.org) us requesting an attached text copy or call with your mailing address for a paper copy. You might also want to read over *Raising Vegan Children* for information, as well as the articles "Wholesome Baby Foods from Scratch" and "Healthy Fast Food for Pre-Schoolers." These are online at www.vrg.org/family.

For nutritional concerns about very young children *Vegan Nutrition in Pregnancy and Childhood,* by Reed Mangels, PhD, RD and Katie Kavanagh-Prochaska, RD is available. You can request a paper copy or access it online at www.vrg.org/nutrition/pregnancy.htm. VRG can also provide your healthcare provider with a copy of the *Pediatric Manual of Clinical Dietetics* chapter on *Nutrition Management of the Vegetarian Child.*

Simply Vegan offers chapters on pregnancy and feeding vegan children. Another popular title for vegetarian parents and parents-to-be is Pregnancy, Children, and the Vegan Diet, by Michael Klaper, MD.

Also see the Veggie Kids chapter on page 152.

## What is Sodium Stearoyl Lactylate? What about other "hidden" ingredients?

According to The Vegetarian Resource Group's *Guide to Food Ingredients,* by Jeanne-Marie Bartas:

**Sodium Stearoyl Lactylate** - *An animal-mineral (cow or hog-derived, or milk), or vegetable-mineral. It is a common food additive often used to condition dough or to blend together ingredients which do not normally blend, such as oil and water. Our guide reports it as May Be Non-Vegetarian. Archer Daniels Midland Co., a manufacturer of sodium stearoyl lactylate reports that their product is of vegetable origin; the lactic acid is produced from microbial fermentation and the stearic acid, from soy oil. Sodium is a mineral which is added.*

The *Guide to Food Ingredients* is very helpful in deciphering ingredient labels. It lists the uses, sources, and definitions of common food ingredients. The guide also states whether the ingredient is vegan, typically vegan, vegetarian, typically vegetarian, typically non-vegetarian, or non-vegetarian. The guide is available from VRG for $4 (see page 269).

Also see the Food Ingredient chapter on page 72 and the Handy Chart to Food Ingredients on page 234.

## WHERE CAN I FIND OUT ABOUT VEGETARIAN RESTAURANTS?

There are many vegetarian and vegetarian-friendly restaurants listed in Vegetarian Journal's Guide to Natural Foods Restaurants in the US and Canada. It is available for $16. For more information about the restaurant guide go to page 270 or visit the website at www.vrg.org/catalog/guide.htm.

Tofu Tollbooth, by Elizabeth Zipern and Dar Williams, is a guide to natural foods stores in the US. It is available through VRG for $17. It is published by Ardwork Press and the ISBN is 1-886101-06-X.

You can also check out the websites for many all-vegetarian restaurants on our links pages at www.vrg.org/links/restaurant.htm.

Also see the Travel and Restaurants chapter on page 140.

## WHERE CAN I FIND NON-LEATHER SHOES?

VRG publishes *A Shopper's Guide To Leather Alternatives*, an eight-page guide to vegan mail-order and retail companies, as well as other companies offering non-leather options. It lists everything from boots to baseball gloves to wallets to dress shoes. The paper version of the guide is available for $4 from VRG or it can be accessed online at www.vrg.org/nutshell/leather.htm.

## WHERE CAN I FIND A RECIPE FOR...?

VRG publishes several cookbooks including Simply Vegan, Conveniently Vegan, Meatless Meals for Working People, The Lowfat Jewish Vegetarian Cookbook, Vegan Handbook, Vegan Meals for One or Two, Vegan in Volume and more. You can access our recipe sections online at www.vrg.org/recipes and www.vrg.org/journal.

There are also good vegetarian recipe websites online:

✳ FATFREE: The Low Fat Vegetarian Recipe Archive - www.fatfree.com

✳ International Vegetarian Union Recipes - www.ivu.org/recipes

✳ Veggies Unite! - www.vegweb.com

Also see our links to recipe websites at www.vrg.org/links/#VegRecipes. Turn to page 87 for some popular recipes and resources.

## I HAVE FOOD ALLERGIES. CAN I STILL BE A VEGETARIAN?

There is a cookbook that might be of assistance, as well as an organization that might be able to help.

The Food Allergy network is one of the best resources for information on food allergies. They have a number of handouts on foods which contain possible allergens and recipes which can be used. They can also answer specific questions pertaining to food allergies. Contact them at: The Food Allergy Network, 10400 Eaton Place, Suite 107, Fairfax, VA 22030-2208; www.foodallergy.org.

Vegetarian Cooking for People with Allergies might also be of interest. It is published by Book Publishing Company (ISBN 1-57067-045-5). The book specifies which recipes are appropriate for people with various food allergies, especially wheat and soy. It is available from VRG for $15.

If you are looking for specific food alternatives try contacting Ener-G Foods, Inc. They produce wheat-free breads, pastas, Ener-G Egg Replacer, flours, and other products for people with special needs. Contact: Ener-G Foods, Inc., 5960 First Ave. S, Seattle, WA 98108; (800) 331-5222, (206) 767-6662; Fax: 206-764-3398; www.ener-g.com.

# CHAPTER 2

# VEGETARIANISM IN DAILY LIFE

Living as a vegetarian is a great equalizer. No matter where you live or what your lifestyle is, there's the chance we've all had some similar experiences. Have you been served a meal with meat in it at a restaurant or been given a decidedly non-vegetarian gift from a well-meaning friend or family member? These are the bumps in the road that are hard to avoid. This chapter deals with those basic questions that confront vegetarians from the time they wake up to the time they go to sleep.

## WHERE CAN I FIND VEGAN DONUTS?

Pangea, a store that sells only vegan items, carries several types of donuts (*editor's note - the soy "yogurt" ones are especially good*). Contact Pangea online at www.pangeaveg.com or request a paper catalog from Pangea, 2381 Lewis Ave., Rockville, MD 20851; (301) 816-9300.

Natural foods markets often carry vegan donuts or will order some upon request. Whole Foods Markets have added a few vegan desserts to their bakery in some locations. Two manufacturers to look for are Baking for Health and Vegan Sweets. For information about vegan sweet treats and more check out the Vegetarian Products links page on the VRG website at www.vrg.org/links/products.htm.

# Vegan & Vegetarian FAQ

## HOW DO YOU PRONOUNCE "VEGAN?"

The most common pronunciations are "VEE-gun" and "VAY-gun." It can be pronounced differently in various regions. The word "vegan" was coined in England, and in most US vegetarian and vegan groups we use the British "vee-gun."

## WHO ARE SOME FAMOUS VEGETARIANS?

Sir Paul McCartney (musician), Fiona Apple (vegan musician), James Cromwell (actor, *Babe*), Lindsay Wagner (actress, *The Bionic Woman*), Fred Rogers (entertainer, "Mr. Rogers"), The B-52's (musical group), Cassandra Peterson (actress, a.k.a. "Elvira"), Casey Kasem (voice of "Scooby Doo," "Top 40"), John Harvey Kellogg (cereal maker), George Bernard Shaw (writer), Alice Walker (writer, The Color Purple), Linnea Quigley (actress, *Return of the Living Dead*), Pythagoras (ancient Greek philosopher), Steve Jobs (founder of Apple Computers), and Leonardo DaVinci (Renaissance artist). PETA, The International Vegetarian Union, and *Vegetarian Times* all have additional information about famous vegetarians.

## WHAT IS THE HISTORY OF VEGETARIANISM?

Vegetarianism goes back thousands of years, if not longer. The term "vegetarian" was first used in 1847. Prior to that, vegetarians in western cultures were referred to as "Pythagoreans," after the ancient Greek philosopher who advocated vegetarianism. The history of vegetarianism across the globe depends on cultural ideologies. Some cultures have a long-standing tradition of vegetarianism, while others still consider it an oddity. There are several books that offer some of the history, including A Heretic's Feast, by Colin Spencer and The Vegetarian Sourcebook, by Keith Akers. The International Vegetarian Union website has a nice overview of the history of vegetarianism throughout the world at www.ivu.org/history.

## DO YOU HAVE ANY IDEA WHAT I CAN EAT AT FAST FOOD RESTAURANTS?

We publish *Vegetarian Menu Items at Restaurants and Quick Service Chains*, which lists the vegetarian and vegan menu items at many chains. It also mentions the non-vegetarian items, such as fries made with beef fat, chicken broth in sauces, and gelatin in unexpected places. This 32-page guide is available from VRG for $4. (Go to page 198 to see a quick guide of what's available at fast food restaurants.)

## IS THERE ONE OFFICIAL SYMBOL THAT DENOTES A VEGETARIAN PRODUCT?

There are regulations in the United Kingdom (enforced by the Trading Standards Offices) regarding products labeled as vegetarian. Unfortunately, there are no such regulations for labeling in the US, and consumers are forced to trust manufacturers, who may or may not understand what vegetarian means. The best approach is learn about various ingredients and their sources.

For information about the Vegetarian Society of the UK symbol, visit their website at www.vegsoc.org. In the US, there is a company now offering the use of a vegan symbol (*see right*) for a nominal charge to other natural products manufacturers. For further details, contact Edward & Sons Trading Company, Inc. at PO Box 1326, Carpinteria, CA 93014; (805) 684-8500.

## I'M CONFUSED. I'VE SEEN WHAT APPEARS TO BE A DAIRY SYMBOL ON SOME KOSHER PRODUCTS, BUT I CAN'T FIND ANY MENTION OF DAIRY IN THE INGREDIENTS. IS THERE HIDDEN DAIRY?

There are several possible explanations. It is possible that a dairy component is masked by a non-specific ingredient (such as natural flavors) or is part of the manufacturing process (i.e. whey used as a fermentation medium). The ingredients might be non-dairy, but the equipment might also be used to produce items with dairy in them. In some cases the equipment would be completely washed between batches. However, with other products the production lines might not be completely cleaned. Different certifying agencies have different requirements in order to denote whether a product is pareve (see page 21) or dairy.

For additional information on this issue go to the Orthodox Union (OU) website at www.ou.org/kosher/dairy.htm.

## WHERE CAN I FIND VEGAN BOWLING SHOES?

VRG investigated non-leather bowling shoes, but we were unable to find a manufacturer. However, one of our members did. She informed us of Dexter, a company that produces bowling shoes. They primarily sell leather shoes, but also make non-leather shoes as well. Their website is www.dextershoe.com, or phone (888) 8DEXTER. Best Bowling is a retailer that carriers Dexter shoes. They can be reached at www.bestbowling.com or (877) 789-2378.

## WHERE CAN I FIND VEGAN BALLET SHOES?

This was a tough one, but non-leather ballet shoes were found...in Australia! Vegan Wares offers ballet slippers in a charcoal microfiber or natural canvas, in sizes for women and children. Vegan Wares is owned and operated by vegans, providing alternatives to leather products. They offer shoes, boots, briefcases, wallets, dog collars, and ballet slippers. They will even make-to-order shoes! You can order online from their website - www.veganwares.com or write 78 Smith St., Collingwood, 3066 VIC Australia.

## DO YOU HAVE A SOURCE FOR NON-LEATHER ORTHOPEDIC SHOES?

The Relax line of Arcopedico shoes are made from synthetic materials and contain no animal leather. Call (800) 449-2918, or visit their website at www.arcopedicoshoes.com.

Also, Pedor's offers a shoe with a neoprene forefoot, which stretches to accommodate forefoot abnormalities. There is no leather used in the shoe. For more information, call (800) 750-6729 or visit www.pedors.com.

## DO YOU KNOW WHERE I CAN GET EAR MUFFS MADE OF FAKE FUR?

You can get fake fur ear muffs from Fabulous Furs. They make only faux fur products. Call (800) 848-4650; write 601 Madison Ave., Covington, KY 41011; or visit www.fabulousfurs.com. One VRG member said she found some at WalMart and other discount retailers.

## WHAT ABOUT ANIMAL INGREDIENTS IN SOAP AND SHAMPOO? WHAT DO I LOOK FOR?

If you are accustomed to reading food labels, you will soon learn the similarities of reading personal care product ingredient labels.

For soaps, the most common animal-based ingredients are tallow (rendered cattle and sheep fat) derivatives, such as sodium tallowate. Another possible animal-based ingredient is glycerin, which can also be vegetable-based. Most companies will specify if it is vegetable-based.

The National Anti-Vivisection Society has a guide to personal care products, Personal Care with Principle, which lists animal-derived ingredients. It also lists companies that produce cruelty-free products as well as companies that test on animals. For more information, contact NAVS at 53 W. Jackson Blvd., Ste. 1552, Chicago, IL 60604; (800) 888-NAVS or (312) 427-6065; www.navs.org/index.cfm.

The International Vegetarian Union has a list of animal-derived ingredients from the 1992 edition of Personal Care with Principal online at www.ivu.org/faq/animal_derived.html. It isn't 100% accurate, but is a good place to start educating yourself about various ingredients.

Another excellent source for learning how animal by-products are used is to read meat industry materials. According to "When is a Cow More Than A Cow?" a website that promotes the uses of beef cattle by-products (http://www.telusplanet.net/public/jross/beefprod.htm), the following are just some of the products that can include cattle-derived ingredients:

> Ice cream, pints, cosmetics, crayons, plastics, deodorants, textiles, detergents, shaving cream, fabric softeners, floor wax, toothpaste, glue, insecticides, violin strings, hydraulic brake fluid, airplane lubricants, car polishes, asphalt, cement blocks, industrial cleaners, explosives, printing ink, fertilizers, high gloss paper for magazines, and paper whitener.

In early 2001, Hormel and General Motors announced that Hormel would begin supplying General Motors with a binding agent made from animal-based collagen. This would be used to form sand molds, which create casts for metal parts. The binder, GMBond, will be made from pork and turkey products.

It is practically impossible to be completely pure and free of animal products in your daily life, but it is possible to set personal standards and do the best you can to steer clear of those products that can be easily avoided. As demand increases there will be more and more cruelty-free products.

## WHERE CAN I FIND CRUELTY-FREE CONTACT LENS SOLUTION?

Clear Conscience has created a cruelty-free, non-irradiated, multi-purpose contact lens solution and a sterile saline solution. For more information, contact Clear Conscience at (800) 595-9592 or www.clearconscience.com.

## ARE THERE VEGAN FLU VACCINES?

Vaccine materials are generally grown on egg-based media. According to pathologist Dr. Jerry Marcus, "As far as I can ascertain, there is no such thing as a vegan flu shot. Nobody I spoke to could envision a flu vaccine being made which would be vegan."

This question, as with other questions contained in the book, brings up the issue of setting personal standards and doing the best you can within the framework of current societal conditions.

## I WAS WONDERING IF YOU KNOW WHERE I CAN BUY VEGE-TARIAN/ANIMAL RIGHTS/ANTI-MEAT T-SHIRTS, PATCHES, PINS, ETC.?

VRG offers a few bumperstickers, buttons, and a t-shirt. Just write, e-mail, or phone to request a catalog. These items are also online at www.vrg.org/catalog. Pangea has both an online and paper catalog; contact them at 2381 Lewis Ave., Rockville, MD 20851; (800)-340-1200; www.pangeaveg.com. They are a great resource for vegan and vegetarian activists.
Also try:
   ✱ PETA: 501 Front St., Norfolk, VA 23510; (757) 622-PETA; www.peta-online.org
   ✱ Fund For Animals: 200 West 57th St., New York, NY 10019; (212) 246-2096; www.fund.org
   ✱ Vegan Street: www.veganstreet.com

## WHAT ABOUT DOGS AND CATS? CAN THEY BE VEGETARIAN?

Dogs are omnivorous, just as humans are, so a well-planned vegetarian diet can be nutritionally adequate. Cats are carnivores, so a healthy vegetarian diet is much more difficult. The Vegetarian Society of the United Kingdom has some fact sheets on vegetarianism for companion animals. You will find them online at www.vegsoc.org/info/dogfood1.html and www.vegsoc.org/info/catfood.html. Animal Protection Institute (API) also offers information about pet foods, their ingredients, and alternatives. This information is available as a booklet and on their website under the "Companion Animals" section. Contact API at P.O. Box 22505, Sacramento, CA 95822; (800) 348-7387; www.api4animals.org.

38

# LIKE MOST OTHER COLLEGE STUDENTS, I HAVE LIMITED FUNDS. DO YOU HAVE ANY SUGGESTIONS FOR A HEALTHY VEGETARIAN DIET WITHOUT SPENDING ALL MY MONEY?

You might consider a quick and easy cookbook, such as <u>Meatless Meals for Working People</u>, which offers many inexpensive, simple meals (www.vrg.org/catalog/meatless.htm). You might find the article, "Veggie Viewpoint: Eating at College" by Caroline Pyevich, helpful. You can request a copy, or view it online at www.vrg.org/journal/vj97jan/971coll.htm.

Our *30 Day Menu For Those Who Don't Like to Cook* is often helpful for students who don't have full cooking facilities. It is online at www.vrg.org/nutshell/30daymenu.htm.

The university cafeteria should offer some vegetarian options, and there are many ready-made vegetarian frozen and boil-in-the-bag meals now available at supermarkets. If the cafeteria is finding it difficult to add more vegetarian meals, we offer brochures and assistance specific to food service, such as *Foodservice Update, The Quantity Recipe Packet,* and <u>Vegan in Volume</u> (see page 267).

You could learn to make some simple meals that require one pan and some water, such as couscous, rice, pasta, or noodles, all of which cook quickly and easily. "Just add water" soups and pastas are another option. Tortillas, marinated tofu, and hummus make easy sandwiches, and so does good old peanut butter-and-jelly. Also consider fruit, bagels, popcorn, pretzels, and nuts for snacks in between classes.

# IS IT TRUE THAT KRISPY KREME DONUTS ARE VEGAN? I'VE FOUND THAT WHEN I ASK FOOD EMPLOYEES, SOMETIMES THEY DON'T KNOW OR DON'T FEEL LIKE CHECKING WHETHER SOMETHING CONTAINS ANIMAL PRODUCTS. HOW CAN I FIND OUT FOR SURE?

This myth has come up around the VRG offices several times, so we requested an ingredient list. The donuts are not vegan; they contain eggs, milk, whey, and possibly a few non-vegetarian ingredients.

Regrettably, store employees don't always have the correct information. One of the best ways to find out is to politely ask. You might wish to explain that you are vegan/vegetarian and what that means. If the person is unable to answer your questions, ask to speak with someone who might be better acquainted with the ingredients, or ask for a phone number for the company or management. Very often, chain restaurants have an ingredient listing on their websites or can easily mail you one upon request. Take the opportunity to commend the restaurant for having vegan items, or, perhaps, encourage them to make some changes to include more options for their vegetarian and vegan clients. VRG has additional resources that you can provide or refer them to if they are interested in learning more.

## IS PHOTOGRAPHIC FILM REALLY MADE OF COW BONES? IS THERE AN ALTERNATIVE?

Yes, film and photographic papers are still made using gelatin. Unfortunately, a cruelty-free alternative has yet to be produced. Some people have opted to switch to digital cameras to avoid using photographic film.

## HOW CAN I FIND OUT WHICH OVER-THE-COUNTER AND PRESCRIPTION MEDICATIONS HAVE ANIMAL PRODUCTS IN THEM?

There are a few common inactive ingredients that may be listed on the packaging. These include lactose, various stearates, gelatin (especially in capsules), and glycerin (often in liquids). Unfortunately, there isn't any one list that addresses this problem, nor, in most cases, is there an easy way of knowing with certainty what is included in over-the-counter and prescription medications. It is possible that an ingredient that may cause an allergic reaction (i.e., milk, shellfish, or egg) may be noted as such.

Many medications, such as Premarin and certain types of insulin, have specific animal bases. PETA and The Physician's Committee for Responsible Medicine (PCRM) have additional information on the issue of Premarin. Contact PETA at 501 Front St., Norfolk, VA 23510; (757) 622-PETA; www.peta-online.com and

PCRM at 5100 Wisconsin Ave., Suite 404, Washington, D.C. 20016; (202) 686-2210; www.pcrm.org.

## I'D RATHER NOT USE BIRTH CONTROL THAT TESTS ON ANIMALS OR HAS ANIMAL-DERIVED PRODUCTS. DOES ANYTHING LIKE THIS EXIST???

For information about vegan contraceptive products, check out the Vegan Society of the UK's website at www.vegansociety.com/info/info02.html. In the US, Kimono condoms, which are made without animal testing or casein (a milk-derivative commonly used during processing), are available through Pangea and various natural foods markets.

## WHAT ABOUT GENETICALLY-MODIFIED FOODS (GMO)? CAN ORGANIC FOODS HAVE GMO'S?

The law for organic standards and the inclusion of GMO's in the US was finalized in late 2000. The final ruling prohibits the use of GMO's in foods carrying an organic label. For the latest information, go to the United States Department of Agriculture's (USDA) National Organic Program website at www.ams.usda.gov/nop. Other countries have recognized this as a much larger issue and have different standards. For example, many shops in the UK have lists of foods and products made or grown with and without GMO's. You may want to take a look at the Mothers for Natural Law website at www.safe-food.org, as well as Monsanto's site at www.monsanto.com.

## HOW MANY ANIMALS ARE KILLED IN THE US EACH YEAR FOR FOOD?

Commercial cattle slaughter during 1999 totaled 36.1 million head, up two percent from 1998. Dairy cows accounted for 7.3 percent of the total, heifers 32.8%, and calves slaughtered totaled 1.28 million head, down 12 percent from a year ago. Commercial hog-slaughter totaled 101.5 million head, up one percent from 1998. Commercial sheep-and-lamb slaughter totaled 3.70 million head, down three percent from 1998. Iowa, Kansas, Nebraska, and Texas accounted for over 50 percent of the United States commercial red meat production in 1999. (USDA Livestock Slaughter Report, March 2000)

In 1999, the total number of chickens slaughtered numbered approximately 8.3 billion. Of that number 8.1 billion were broilers (young chickens) and 175 million were hens (egg layers). Twenty-three million ducks and 265 million turkeys were slaughtered. (USDA Poultry Slaughter Report, April 2000)

## MANY OF MY PATIENTS ARE FROM MEXICO. WHERE CAN I FIND INFORMATION ABOUT VEGETARIANISM IN SPANISH?

Three of our core brochures are available in Spanish. Copies can be requested by mail, phone, or e-mail. Our Spanish version of *Vegetarianism in a Nutshell, Una Dieta Vegetariana*, is online at www.vrg.org/nutshell/vegetariana.htm. Our teen vegetarian information, *Guía Alimenticia Vegetariana para los Jóvenes*, is at www.vrg.org/nutshell/jovenes.htm and *Una Dieta Sana Para Un Corazón Sano* is at www.vrg.org/nutshell/corazon.htm.

We also have information in Japanese and Polish. The Japanese information can be accessed at www.vrg.org/nutshell/index.htm. For a copy of our teen brochure in Polish, call, e-mail, or mail a request. For information in additional languages, The International Vegetarian Union offers links and resources at www.ivu.org. If you are interested in volunteering to translate one of our brochures into a another language, please call (410) 366-8343, write PO Box 1463, Baltimore, MD 21203, or e-mail vrg@vrg.org.

## CAN I BE A VEGAN *AND* AN ATHLETE?

You can easily be a vegetarian or vegan athlete. Read our article on *Athletes and Vegetarianism*, by D. Enette Larson, PhD, MS, RD, LD on page 224. It can also be accessed online at www.vrg.org/nutshell/athletes.htm. Another good reference is "Vegetarian Diet for Exercise and Athletic Training and Performing: An

Update," also by D. Enette Larson, PhD, MS, RD, LD, from the Spring 1997 issue of *Vegetarian Dietetics*. It is online at www.andrews.edu/NUFS/ vegathletes.htm.

Jane Black was a former vegan weightlifter who won her class and received the Best Lifter trophy for her age group (40-44) at the Master's World Weightlifting Championships in Canada in 1996. To read more about her, go to www.vrg.org/ journal/vj2000jan/2000janjaneblack.htm. Ruth Heidrich is a vegan tri-athlete and breast cancer survivor. There is information about her at www.vegsource. com/heidrich.

The International Vegetarian Union has a whole page of links to sports-related articles at www.ivu.org/articles/sport.html, as well as a list of famous athletic vegetarians at www.ivu.org/people/sports.

## HOW DO I FIND OUT ABOUT LOCAL VEGETARIAN GROUPS IN MY AREA?

VRG maintains a database of local and national groups and may be able to provide contact information about a group in your area. Contact VRG at vrg@vrg.org or (410) 366-8343, Monday-Friday, 9 a.m.-5 p.m. EST.

Vegetarian groups with websites are listed on the VRG website at www.vrg.org/ links/local.htm. You will find links to local groups on these webpages.
* www.ivu.org/global
* www.greenpeople.org/vegetarian.htm
* www.navs-online.org/fraffil.html

## THERE ISN'T A LOCAL VEGETARIAN GROUP IN MY AREA. WHAT CAN I DO?

Start one of your own! Just send a request to vrg@vrg.org or call (410) 366-8343 (Monday-Friday, 9 a.m.-5 p.m. EST) for a copy of our brochure *Starting a Vegetarian Group* and related materials. It provides some suggestions and ideas on how to get started. You can also access the brochure online at www.vrg.org/activist.

## A FEW OF MY FRIENDS COMMENTED ON THE CONNECTION BETWEEN VEGETARIANISM AND RELIGION. WHERE CAN I LEARN MORE?

Many religions have branches which follow vegetarian diets, or in some cases exclude certain meats. These include Jain, Buddhist, Seventh-day Adventist, Hindu, Hare Krishna, Sikh, Muslim, and Jewish ideologies.

The Christian Vegetarian Association has created a pamphlet titled *Answers to Questions about Vegetarianism for Christians.* One copy is available free of charge, and bulk orders are accepted. For more information, visit veg.faithweb.com or write PO Box 201791, Cleveland, OH 44120.

Dr. Richard Schwartz has created a website that covers issues concerning Judaism and vegetarianism. There are simple fact sheets, FAQ, recipes, links to more in-depth articles, and an online course. To learn more go to jewishveg. vegsource.com.

For more information about vegetarianism and religion, please visit the many articles and links on the International Vegetarian Union website at www.ivu.org/religion.

## IN *VEGETARIAN JOURNAL* YOU MENTIONED ETHICAL BUSINESSES, BUT WHAT I WANT TO KNOW IS WHO THEY WOULD BE? HOW CAN WE KNOW WHICH COMPANIES ARE NOT PRIVATELY-OWNED, SO THAT WE CAN INVEST IN COMPANIES WHO SHARE THE SAME VALUES AS WE DO, BEING VEGETARIAN, CONCERNED ABOUT ANIMAL WELFARE, AND THE ENVIRONMENT? GOT ANY NAMES OF COMPANIES?

According to business professor Wayne Smeltz, PhD, *"When making socially-conscious investment decisions, you must first determine your value priorities as well as your financial risk tolerance. Because of consolidation, there are few pure players in the vegetarian food segment. One possible investment is Hain Celestial Group (HAIN:NASDAQ). Its primary products are natural foods and Celestial Seasonings Tea. Take note that Heinz holds a stake in the company. Other possibilities are the natural food retailers Whole Foods Markets*

*(WFMI:NASDAQ) and Wild Oats Markets (OATS:NASDAQ). Riskier investors may consider Gardenburger (GBUR:NASDAQ) or Tofutti (TOF:AMEX). Depending upon value priorities some investors may consider Kellogg (K:NYSE) who has recently bought Worthington Foods and Kashi Cereal.*

*"As you can see, even in this specialized niche, some of these companies may have products or practices that may conflict with one's value priorities. You will need to research each company to assess your ethical and investment comfort."*

## I JUST CAN'T SEE DATING A CARNIVORE. WHERE CAN I GO TO MEET OTHER VEGETARIANS?

VRG's website has a page with links to several websites with vegetarian/vegan personal ads and singles newsletters. They can be found at www.vrg.org/links/#Social. Also, consider volunteering at a local animal shelter, vegetarian group, or similar organization. You might meet some people with common concerns there.

## DO YOU KNOW OF ANY CARPET OR UPHOLSTERY SHAMPOOS THAT DO NOT CONTAIN ANY ANIMAL PRODUCTS AND ARE NOT TESTED ON ANIMALS?

ECOS makes several types of cleaners that are often available at natural foods stores (44 Greenbay Rd., Winnetka, IL 60093; (800) 335-ECOS; www.ecos.com). You could also try: Sun and Earth (125 Noble St., Norristown, PA 19401; (800) 596-SAFE; www.sunandearth.com).

According to Clean & Green, by Annie Berthold-Bond, you can make your own foam cleaner for upholstery by mixing 1/4 cup of vegetable oil-based liquid soap with 3 tablespoons of water. Whip together, pull the foam off the top, and apply to upholstery.

## DO YOU KNOW OF ANY CHARITIES/SOUP KITCHENS/HUNGER ORGANIZATIONS THAT ARE VEGETARIAN (I.E. MEALS ON WHEELS)?

Food Not Bombs is one, that has chapters all over the country. According to one Food Not Bombs website, there are *"over 175 autonomous chapters sharing vegetarian food with hungry people and protesting war and poverty throughout the Americas, Europe and Australia. The first group was formed in Cambridge, Massachusetts in 1980 by anti-nuclear activists. Food Not Bombs is an all volunteer organization dedicated to nonviolence."* (http://home.earthlink.net/~foodnotbombs/)

For more information contact:
Food Not Bombs, PO Box 32075, Kansas City, MO 64171; (800) 884-1136.
You can also access many Food Not Bombs websites through a contact list found online at www.scn.org/activism/foodnotbombs/contacts.html.

VRG has published several "Veggie Actions" in *Vegetarian Journal* about organizations incorporating vegetarianism into their assistance efforts, such as Soycows in Russia and The Maryland Salem Children's Trust. Also, VRG helped develop a vegetarian meal plan for Meals on Wheels. If working with a soup kitchen, Meals on Wheels, or other charity to integrate more vegetarian items into their program interests you can write, phone, or e-mail to request information.

## I'M DOING A COLLEGE PAPER ON FACTORY FARMS. I'D LIKE TO INCLUDE A BRIEF NARRATIVE ON HOW COWS ARE SLAUGHTERED TO HOOK THE READER'S ATTENTION. WHERE SHOULD I LOOK FOR SOURCE MATERIAL?

A great source is Slaughterhouse by Gail Eisnitz. You should be able to get it from a library or bookstore. She includes quotes from workers about the assembly line that are beyond horrifying. You can also order a copy from The Humane Farming Association, PO Box 3577, San Rafael, CA. 94912; (415) 771-CALF; www.hfa.org.

# CHAPTER 3

# VEGETARIAN NUTRITION

This chapter covers questions that go beyond the basics of vegetarian and vegan nutrition. One of the best nutrition resources for vegetarians and vegans is Simply Vegan, by Debra Wasserman and Reed Mangels, PhD, RD. It contains not only comprehensive nutrition information, but also recipes, practical tips, and sources for vegan products. For more information about this publication, turn to page: 265. You can also consult the nutrition section of the VRG website at www.vrg.org/nutrition. Other excellent resources on vegetarian nutrition are The Vegetarian Way, by Virginia and Mark Messina and Becoming Vegetarian, by Vesanto Melina, MS, RD, Brenda Davis, RD, and Victoria Harrison, RD.

Many of the answers in this chapter were provided by Reed Mangels, PhD, RD, nutrition advisor for VRG, co-author of Simply Vegan, and past chair of The American Dietetic Association's Vegetarian Nutrition Dietetic Practice Group. We've also consulted with Suzanne Havala, MS, RD, another of our nutrition advisors and author of Being Vegetarian, Good Foods, Bad Foods: What's Left to Eat, and Simple, Lowfat, and Vegetarian and previously the primary author of *Position of the American Dietetic Association: Vegetarian Diets* (1988 and 1993 versions).

## Do you know where I can find a vegetarian food pyramid?

There is a vegetarian food pyramid as part of the *Position of the American Dietetic Association: Vegetarian Diets*. You can view a copy online at www.vrg.org/nutrition/adapyramid.htm or request a paper copy. It is also on the ADA website at www.eatright.org/gifs/adap1197.gif. These guidelines are appropriate for both vegetarians and vegans.

There is a vegan food pyramid in <u>Becoming Vegan</u>, by Brenda Davis, RD, and Vesanto Melina, MS, RD. It is also available online at www.nutrispeak.com/veganfoodguide.htm.

Another vegetarian pyramid is available from Health Connection, 55 West Oak Ridge Dr., Hagerstown, MD 21740; (800) 548-8700; www.healthconnection.org.

## What is the nutritional breakdown of quinoa?

The USDA has an online database that shows the nutritional content of common (and not-so-common) foods. It can be accessed at www.nal.usda.gov/fnic/cgi-bin/nut_search.pl.

## How can I get omega 3 and omega 6 fatty acids by way of food and not supplements and vitamins?

There is an excellent article about *Essential Fatty Acids in Vegetarian Nutrition,* by Brenda Davis, RD, in the Summer 1998 issue of *Vegetarian Dietetics*. You can also read the article online at www.andrews.edu/NUFS/essentialfat.htm as part of The American Dietetic Association's Vegetarian Nutrition Dietetic Practice Group (ADA VNDPG) articles collection at Andrews University.

Vegan sources of omega 3 fatty acids include flax seeds, walnuts, and soybeans and oils from these foods. Omega 6 fatty acids are found in sunflower and sesame seeds, walnuts, corn, and soy products.

# I'M THINKING OF BECOMING VEGAN, BUT MY FAMILY INSISTS I WON'T GET ENOUGH B-12. IS THIS TRUE?

The adult recommended intake for vitamin B-12 is very low. Vitamin B-12 comes primarily from animal-derived foods. A diet containing dairy products or eggs should provide adequate vitamin B 12. Fortified foods, such as some brands of nutritional yeast and soymilk, and some soy analogs, are good non-animal sources. Check labels to discover other products that are fortified with vitamin B-12. Tempeh and sea vegetables may contain vitamin B-12, but their content varies and is unreliable. To be on the safe side, if you are one of the few people who do not consume dairy products, eggs, or fortified foods regularly, you can take a non-animal derived supplement. Much research still needs to be done on vitamin B-12 requirements and sources. (Note: Grape Nuts, previously reported to be a good source of B-12 for vegans, has been reformulated and now contains lanolin-derived Vitamin D.)

According to <u>Simply Vegan</u>, *"Vitamin B-12 is needed for cell division and blood formation. Plant foods do not contain vitamin B-12 except when they are contaminated by microorganisms. Thus, vegans need to look to other sources to get vitamin B-12 in their diet. Although the minimum requirement for vitamin B-12 is quite small, 1/1,000,000 of a gram (1 microgram) a day for adults, a vitamin B-12 deficiency is a very serious problem leading ultimately to irreversible nerve damage. Prudent vegans will include sources of vitamin B-12 in their diets. However, vitamin B-12 deficiency is actually quite rare even among long-term vegans."* To read more go to: www.vrg.org/nutrition/b12.htm or see page 265 for ordering information.

# ARE THERE ANY ADVERSE EFFECTS OF TAKING TOO MUCH B-12? I HAVE BEEN TAKING 1000 MCG SUBLINGUAL EACH MORNING FOR THE PAST 5 DAYS.

No harmful effects have been reported with high intakes of vitamin B-12 from food or supplements in healthy people. However, there is no reason to take more than the recommended level of vitamin B-12 (2.4 micrograms for men and non-pregnant women age 14 years and older) unless additional amounts are recommended by your physician.

Reed Mangels, PhD, RD

## HOW MUCH IRON DO I NEED AS A VEGETARIAN? HOW MUCH IS TOO MUCH?

The current recommendations for iron for <u>vegetarians</u> are 14 milligrams per day for men and women post-menopause; 20 mg for women using oral contraceptives; and 33 mg for pre-menopausal women. The upper limit for iron (amount that is likely to cause almost no risk for almost all people) is 45 milligrams per day for adults.

For more detailed information, read the chapter on iron in <u>Simply Vegan</u>, or view it online at www.vrg.org/nutrition/iron.htm. Also see page 209 for a chart on good sources of iron.

Too much iron can be a serious problem for some people. *"Hemochromatosis, an iron overload syndrome, afflicts about one in every 200 to 500 Americans. This is a genetic disorder that causes the body to absorb large amounts of iron that it does not need. Excess iron gets stored in the liver, heart, and pancreas, where it often goes undetected until mid-life when iron levels reach 5 to 50 times normal amounts. The initial symptoms, fatigue, achy joints, and weakness, are sometimes misinterpreted as iron deficiency."*

From *Are You Getting Enough Iron, or Perhaps, Too Much?*, By Eve Shatto Walton, RD, LDN. To read more, request a copy, or view it online at www.vrg.org/journal/iron.htm.

## HOW DO I GO ABOUT FINDING A VEGETARIAN-FRIENDLY DIETITIAN?

VRG maintains a database of vegetarian and vegan-friendly dietitians and other health professionals. Call, write, or e-mail for information.

You may also want to consult The American Dietetic Association website, www.eatright.org, where you'll find a database of dietitians. You are able to specify nutritional or medical concerns to narrow your search. In Canada try www.dietitians.ca.

## I HAVE RECENTLY DEVELOPED DIABETES. CAN I CONTINUE BEING A VEGETARIAN?

There is an article in the Winter 1999 issue of *Vegetarian Dietetics*, "Can Type 2 Diabetes Be Managed Effectively with a Vegetarian Diet," which states, *"Consumption of a low fat, plant-based diet, coupled with regular exercise, can possibly reduce the risk of developing type 2 diabetes. A plant-based diet, rich in legumes and slowly digested grains, may improve glucose tolerance and insulin sensitivity and facilitate the successful management of type 2 diabetes."*

The Vegetarian Way, by Virginia Messina, MPH, RD and Mark Messina, PhD, has an excellent section on diabetes and a vegetarian diet. It can be ordered on the VRG website at www.vrg.org/catalog/vegway.htm.

## CAN YOU SUGGEST ANY VEGAN VITAMINS?

VRG recommends seeing a registered dietitian or health care professional before taking any vitamins. That said, the most vegan-friendly vitamin source we've found is from Freeda Vitamins, Inc. Freeda's can be contacted at 36 East 41st St., New York, NY 10017; (212) 685-4980; www.freedavitamins.com.

Also, Edward & Sons debuted a vegan children's chewable multi-vitamin in early 2001. Contact Edwards & Sons, PO Box 1326, Carpinteria, CA 93014; (805) 684-8500.

## HOW DO I PROPERLY COMBINE MY PROTEIN?

*"Frances Moore Lappe, in her book Diet for a Small Planet advocated the combining of a food low in one amino acid with another food containing large amounts of that amino acid. This got to be a very complicated process, with each meal having specific amounts of certain foods in order to be certain of getting a favorable amino acid mix. Many people got discouraged with the complexity of this approach. Actually, Lappe was being overly conservative to avoid criticism from the 'Nutrition Establishment.' She has since repudiated strict protein*

*combining, saying 'In combatting the myth that meat is the only way to get high quality protein, I reinforced another myth. I gave the impression that in order to get enough protein without meat, considerable care was needed in choosing foods. Actually it is much easier than I thought.'"*

(Diet For a Small Planet, 10th anniversary edition, 1982 and Simply Vegan, 2000, page 144).

Many nutrition authorities, including The American Dietetic Association, have determined that intentional protein combining is not necessary. Research has shown that proteins from a variety of plant foods eaten throughout the day provide adequate amino acids without the need for careful planning at each meal. Protein should not be a concern for most Americans, vegetarians included. The average American takes in close to two times as much protein as he or she needs.

Reed Mangels, PhD, RD

## I READ YOUR WEB PAGE REGARDING CALCIUM. WOULD ALMONDS BE A GOOD SOURCE OF CALCIUM OR DO THEY HAVE TOO MUCH OXALIC ACID?

Almonds are not an especially great source of calcium. This is both due to their fairly low calcium content and the low amount of calcium which is absorbed from almonds. A one-ounce serving of almonds has 80 milligrams of calcium (compare that to 300 milligrams in one cup of calcium-fortified soymilk or cow's milk) and about 21% of this is absorbed, resulting in about 17 milligrams of calcium our body can use from one ounce of almonds. Compare this with 4 ounces of calcium-set tofu which has 80 milligrams of absorbable calcium, or 1/2 cup of turnip greens which has 51 milligrams of absorbable calcium, and you'll see that almonds provide some calcium, but not a lot.

Reed Mangels, PhD, RD

## DO VEGETARIAN WOMEN HAVE DIFFERENT HEALTH NEEDS THAN MALE VEGETARIANS?

Vegetarian men and women need the same nutrients (as do non-vegetarians). We all need things like calcium, iron, selenium, zinc, vitamins, etc. There is no nutrient that has been discovered at this point that women need but men don't (or vice versa). The amounts of nutrients needed will vary depending on lots of factors including gender and body size. For example, women need more iron than men because menstruating women lose iron regularly (see page 27). Men need a bit more thiamine and riboflavin because the need for these nutrients goes up as caloric intake goes up, and men, in general, take in more calories than women do. Men and women appear to need about the same amount of calcium.

Reed Mangels, PhD. RD

## I AM A VEGETARIAN WEIGHTLIFTER AND I WANT TO GAIN SOME WEIGHT. HOW DO I START?

Diets for weight gain, just like those for weight loss, are pretty individualized. There is no magic formula for gaining weight for weightlifters or for anyone else; it's just a matter of eating more calories. But your caloric needs will depend a lot on how much you weigh now and how much you work out. Also, if you do other types of exercise like aerobic exercise (and you should; weight lifting is just one part of a healthy exercise program), you'll be burning extra calories, which figures into the equation as well. Therefore, no one "diet for weight gain" is going to meet the needs of every weightlifter.

If you are maintaining your weight now, you might try adding several hundred calories or so a day to your menus and then keep increasing caloric intake until you are gaining weight at an appropriate rate. To do this, try adding more nutrient-dense foods to your menus, such as cooked dried beans, dried fruits, nut butters, and some added fats, such as vegetable oils. Remember to aim for a balanced diet based on whole foods - lots of whole grains, beans, fruits, vegetables, nuts, seeds, soy products, etc. - and increase your portion sizes and number of servings to boost calorie intake. You don't need any special foods or supplements to do this.

Virginia Messina, MPH, RD

WHERE CAN I GET A COMPREHENSIVE LIST OF NUTRITION-
AL FACTS FOR A TEEN TO FOLLOW? FOR EXAMPLE, A 15-
YEAR-OLD GIRL WHO SWIMS 2+ HOURS PER DAY NEEDS...?
HOW MUCH PROTEIN, CALCIUM, ETC.? IS THERE SUCH A
REFERENCE AVAILABLE?

The best reference I've seen for teen vegetarian nutrition information is Virginia and Mark Messina's book The Vegetarian Way. It has sample menus, tables of foods which are good sources of various nutrients, etc.

I'll try to provide a short answer for some of your questions. Protein needs of someone who is swimming 2+ hours a day would be between 0.45 and 0.68 grams per pound of the person's weight. So if a teen girl weighed 120 lbs and was swimming 2+ hrs per day, she'd need between 54 and 82 grams of protein daily. The recommended intake of calcium for teens is 1300 milligrams daily. There are many tables of food composition which can be used to check a teen's diet for adequacy, or a registered dietitian could be consulted. Simply Vegan also lists how much protein, calcium, and other nutrients are in many vegetarian foods.

Here is one daily food guide for vegetarian teens which was developed by the Vegetarian Nutrition Dietetic Practice Group of The American Dietetic Association:

8-10 (or more) servings of grains, breads, and cereals (1 slice bread, ½ cup cooked grain=1 serving)
1-2 servings (1/2 cup per serving) of dried beans or meat analogs
1-2 servings of nuts or nut butters (2 Tbsp. per serving)
3 servings (1 cup per serving) of calcium-fortified soymilk or cow's milk
2 servings (1/2 cup each) of leafy green vegetables
3 servings (1/2 cup each if cooked or 1 cup each if raw) of other vegetables
3-4 servings of fruit (1/2 cup or 1 piece, 4 oz juice=1 serving)
4-5 servings of fats and oils (1 tsp. oil, margarine or 1 Tbsp. dressing, mayo=1 serving)

Reed Mangels, PhD, RD

# I AM 52 YEARS OLD AND FOUR YEARS AGO I HAD A STROKE AND HEART ATTACK. WOULD A VEGETARIAN DIET HELP ME OR HAVE I WAITED TOO LONG?

It's not too late! Several studies have shown that low-fat, low-saturated fat vegetarian diets have been very helpful for people who have severe heart disease. They have also helped to reduce blood pressure in people with hypertension. For information on heart healthy vegetarian diets, see our website (www.vrg.org/nutshell/heart.htm) or write, phone, or e-mail to request information.

Here's a summary of one study on vegetarian diets in heart disease that appeared in *Vegetarian Journal* ("Scientific Update" May/June 1999).

*Lifestyle Changes, Including a Vegetarian Diet, Help Reverse Heart Disease*

*Nine years ago, Dr. Dean Ornish made medical history when he reported that he had placed patients with moderate to severe heart disease on a regimen which included a 10% fat whole foods vegetarian diet, aerobic exercise, stress management training, smoking cessation, and group psychosocial support. These subjects followed this regimen for one year and were then compared to similar subjects who received more standard medical care (25-30% fat diet, medications as needed). The subjects who followed the vegetarian diet and made other changes had a reduction in blockage of their arteries, had less chest pain, and had lower LDL cholesterol levels. Some (35) subjects of the study were followed for a total of five years and these results were recently reported.*

*20 of the original 28 subjects continued with Ornish's program and 15 of 20 subjects continued usual medical treatment and agreed to be followed. In the subjects who made significant lifestyle changes, fat intake was 8.5% of calories, dietary cholesterol was negligible, and subjects continued with their exercise regimen. Although some subjects gained back some of the weight they had lost initially, they maintained a weight loss of close to 13 pounds. No subjects on Ornish's regimen required lipid-lowering drugs; all control subjects who continued with the study required these medications.*

*The subjects on Ornish's regimen continued to have improvement in arterial blockage while significantly more arterial blockage occurred in the group receiving conventional treatment despite use of lipid lowering drugs. More than twice as many cardiac events (like heart attacks, angioplasty, bypass surgery, and death) occurred in the group receiving conventional treatment compared with subjects following the vegetarian diet and making other lifestyle changes.*

*While this was a small group of subjects, results were certainly promising. An intensive lifestyle change such as was offered by Ornish and colleagues may be both life-improving and life-saving for those with moderate to severe heart disease.*

*Ornish D, Scherwitz LW, Billings JH, et al. Intensive lifestyle changes for reversal of coronary heart disease. JAMA 1998; 280: 2001-2007.*

*Ornish DM, Brown SE, Scherwitz LW, et al. Can lifestyle changes reverse coronary atherosclerosis? The Lifestyle Heart Trial. Lancet 1990; 336: 129-133.*

Reed Mangels, PhD, RD

## I NEED INFORMATION ABOUT VEGETARIANISM FOR A GROUP OF SENIORS. WHAT DO YOU HAVE?

*A Senior's Guide to Good Nutrition,* by Suzanne Havala, MS, RD, FADA offers very useful information. We've included this article in the appendix on page 212. It can also be accessed online at www.vrg.org/nutrition/seniors.htm.

VRG also offers another article by Suzanne Havala, MS, RD, FADA, *New York Department on Aging Tests VRG/Meals on Wheels Vegetarian Menus at 25 Sites,* from *Foodservice Update* (online at www.vrg.org/fsupdate/fsu974/fsu974newyork.htm). There is a 4-Week Menu Set in the booklet available as well (online at www.vrg.org/fsupdate/fsu974/fsu974menu.htm). To obtain a copy of the *Meals on Wheels/Senior's Guide to Good Nutrition* brochure, write, phone, or e-mail VRG.

## I AM A VEGETARIAN AND HAVE JOINT PAIN. ARE THINGS LIKE GLUCOSAMINE AND CHONDROITIN CONSIDERED OKAY?

Glucosamine is extracted from the shells of crabs and other crustaceans and chondroitin is made from cow trachea or shark cartilage (Center for Science in the Public Interest's *Nutrition Action Healthletter*, October 2000).

There was an article in the Autumn 1998 issue of *Vegetarian Dietetics* on "Vegetarian Diets in the Treatment of Rheumatoid Arthritis" that might be of interest to you. It is accessible online at www.andrews.edu/NUFS/arthritis.html.

I WAS RECENTLY REFERRED TO ANOTHER PHYSICIAN BY MY DOCTOR. HE SAID HE HAD SEVERAL VEGAN PATIENTS WHO HAD JOINT PROBLEMS (SOMETHING I AM TRYING TO OVER-COME MYSELF). HE TOLD ME THAT VEGAN FOODS LACKED AN AMINO ACID NEEDED TO PRODUCE COLLAGEN. I ASKED HIM IF HE MEANT ONE OF THE 8 ESSENTIAL AMINO ACIDS AND HE SAID NO. HE WENT ON TO ADD THAT I COULD GET THIS AMINO ACID BY EATING PLANKTON (NOT ANY OLD SEAWEED), SOMETHING THAT SHOULD BE IN ANY BIG HEALTH FOOD STORE. WELL, I LIVE NEAR SEVERAL VERY WELL STOCKED HEALTH FOOD STORES & CO-OPS AND NOBODY EVER HEARD OF SELLING PLANKTON. HAVE YOU HEARD OF THIS?

The only thing that I can think of are two supplements that are reported to ease arthritis pain - glucosamine and chondroitin (derived from crabs and crustaceans and cow trachea and shark cartilage, respectively. See question above.). While they can be found in some foods, they are usually taken as supplements. Neither of these are amino acids, but they are non-vegan products recommended for arthritis treatment. Another possibility are omega-3 fatty acids. These are fats, not amino acids, but increased consumption has been linked to a reduction in symptoms of arthritis. One common omega-3 fatty acid is DHA (docosahexaenoic acid).

As an aside, I've read a few studies that found a vegan diet relieved some arthritis symptoms. This seems to contradict the idea that something is lacking in a vegan diet and leads to joint pain.

Reed Mangels, PhD, RD

# I'VE BEEN A VEGETARIAN FOR THE PAST 4 YEARS AND RECENTLY NOTICED SIGNIFICANT AMOUNTS OF HAIR LOSS. CAN YOU TELL ME, OTHER THAN PROTEIN, COULD I BE LOW IN CERTAIN NUTRIENTS?

Suzanne Havala, MS, RD, answered this question in "Nutrition Hotline" for the November/December 1998 issue of *Vegetarian Journal*:

*"When diet is the cause of thinning hair, the most likely culprit is a sudden change in weight. The medical term for this is Telogen Effluvium. The hair follicles synchronize their growth cycles and a greater number of them reach the "falling out" stage (telogen) at the same time. The hair does grow again, though not necessarily all of it. Rapid weight loss or any physical or emotional stress can cause this.*

*"Some people lose a substantial amount of weight when they switch to a vegetarian diet, particularly if they were overweight in the beginning. Other times, a person may lose weight simply because he/she isn't eating enough. It's the "iceberg lettuce salad" syndrome: when some people decide to make the switch to a vegetarian diet, they know what they don't want to eat, but they haven't quite determined what they can eat. They haven't mastered the skill of vegetarian meal planning. Consequently, they exist on iceberg lettuce salads and not much else. No wonder they lose weight!*

*"If you are getting enough calories to meet your energy needs, and you are eating a reasonable variety of foods on your vegetarian diet, it's not likely that this is an issue contributing to hair loss. However, if you are a "junk food" vegetarian or are simply not getting enough food, then deficiencies of zinc, protein, biotin, and essential fatty acids might be the cause of hair loss or sparsely-growing hair.*

*"Your hair loss may be coincidental with your switch to the vegetarian diet. An especially stressful event (a divorce, illness, profound grief) can cause hair loss, as can hormonal changes, such as those that accompany pregnancy or childbirth. Again, these stresses could cause Telogen Effluvium, as mentioned earlier. Medical problems, such as hypothyroidism, can also cause your hair to thin. A significant number of women also experience a male-pattern thinning of the hair that happens gradually as they age, although some may find an increase in the rate of thinning over a specific time period.*

*"If you are eating reasonably well, it's likely that your problem is due to a genetically-determined pattern of thinning, stress, or a medical issue, rather than the vegetarian diet per se. You should check with your health care practitioner to rule out these possible causes."*

## I AM A VEGETARIAN AND I FIND MY HAIR AND NAILS DO NOT GROW QUICKLY. WHAT AM I MISSING IN MY DIET TO MAKE MY HAIR AND NAILS GROW?

It's unlikely that the growth rate of your hair and nails is linked to your diet (and contrary to the old myth, gelatin certainly doesn't increase the growth or strength of nails!). Instead, any slowing of the growth rate of your hair and nails is probably due to a natural change in your metabolism or the functioning of hair follicles and nails. As people age, the quality of their hair and nails often changes as well. For example, hair may thin or become finer, and nails may become thicker and more brittle. Keeping your hair and nails moisturized, avoiding excessive exposure to heat from hair dryers and curling irons, and wearing gloves in cold or harsh weather can help preserve nails and hair and minimize damage that may cause breakage. You're better off focusing on these factors, rather than diet in this case. (Also see answer on page 58.)

Suzanne Havala, MS, RD

## I HEARD THAT BEING A VEGETARIAN COULD CAUSE A BIRTH DEFECT IN MALE BABIES. IS THIS TRUE? I'M REALLY WORRIED.

Reed Mangels, PhD, RD addressed this issue in "Scientific Update," *Vegetarian Journal* Sept/Oct 2000:

*Hypospadias is a birth defect of the penis which occurs in about 1 out of 300 newborn male babies. While the cause of this defect has not been determined, it has been seen more commonly in sons of women who became pregnant later in life and in sons of women who used hormone-containing medicines during pregnancy. A study in Britain examined the role of maternal nutrition in the* development of hypospadias. Close to 8,000 boys were studied, 51 of whom had hypospadias. The results were surprising. Mothers who followed a vegetarian diet during pregnancy had a higher risk of giving birth to a boy with hypospadias. Was this simply coincidence? Possibly. This is one study, involving a relatively small number of vegetarians (321); of whom 7 had sons with hypospadias. Was there something unique about the women who were vegetarians and whose sons had hypospadias? We don't know. Of the boys who had hypospadias, 44 were sons of non-vegetarians. What factors caused hypospadias in these boys? Although iron supplements and influenza early in pregnancy may have had some effect, there are many unanswered questions. The researchers who conducted this study hypothesized that vegetarians ate more soy foods and thus were exposed to more phytoestrogens and that this led to their increased risk of having a son with hypospadias. There is little basis for this conclusion since there was no significant association between the use of soymilk and other soy products and development of hypospadias. The researchers plan to measure levels of nutrients, phytoestrogens, and pesticides in blood from women who participated in this study to try to determine specific factors which could have increased a woman's risk of having a child with hypospadias. At this point, it seems premature to attribute increased risk of hypospadias to use of a vegetarian diet in pregnancy.

North K., Golding J, The ALSPAC Study Team. A maternal vegetarian diet in pregnancy is associated with hypospadias. BJU International 2000; 85:107-111.

## I NEED IMPARTIAL, SCIENTIFIC STUDIES THAT SHOW A CORRELATION BETWEEN A VEGETARIAN DIET AND DISEASE PREVENTION, WHERE DO I LOOK?

The studies listed below may be helpful. Seventh-day Adventists (SDA) recommend vegetarian diets. However, not all SDAs are vegetarian, although they may have lower levels of meat consumption since their religion frowns on the use of meat. Studies of SDAs may help answer your question.

Reed Mangels, PhD, RD

A cohort of 27,529 SDA adults was followed for 20 years. After adjusting for cigarette smoking, meat consumption was positively associated with overall mortality in males, coronary heart disease mortality in males and females, and mortality from diabetes in males. The consumption of animal products was not related to breast cancer mortality in females, stroke mortality in either sex, or rectal cancer mortality in males or females. A suggestive, but not significant, positive association existed between meat consumption and ovarian cancer mortality and prostate cancer mortality.

*Snowdon DA. Animal product consumption and mortality because of all causes combined, coronary heart disease, stroke, diabetes, and cancer in Seventh-day Adventists. Am J Clin Nutr 1988; 48:739-48.*

A 20-year study of SDAs in California found a significant progressive increase in relative risk of death from coronary disease and diabetes across meat use categories (no meat, meat 1-3 days per week, meat 4+ days per week) in males and females, and in death from all causes in males.

*Phillips RL, Snowdon DA. Mortality among Seventh-day Adventists in relation to dietary habits and lifestyle. In Ory RL, ed. Plant Proteins: Applications, Biological Effects, and Chemistry. Washington, DC: American Chemical Society, 1986, pp 162-74.*

In a 21-year follow-up of over 27,000 SDA vegetarians and non-vegetarians, non-vegetarians had higher age-specific all cause mortality rates. Differences remained after adjusting for age, sex, and smoking history.

*Kahn RH, Phillips RL, et al. Association between reported diet and all cause mortality: twenty-one year follow-up on 27,350 adult Seventh-day Adventists. Am J Epidemiol 1984;119:775-87. (cited in Dwyer, Am J Clin Nutr 1988; 48:712-38.)*

Black Seventh-day Adventists (SDA) were classified as vegetarians (VEG, n=66), semi-vegetarians (SEMIVEG, 1-3 servings of animal flesh per week, n=56), and non-vegetarians (NONVEG, n=45). A significantly lower percentage of VEG were confirmed to be hypertensive compared with the other two groups. The VEG's had lower blood total cholesterol, LDL-cholesterol, and triglyceride levels than the NONVEG's. SEMIVEG's had intermediate levels. These blood values are used to assess risk for premature cardiovascular disease. The three groups had similar nondietary habits including frequency of exercise, and use of alcohol and tobacco. This suggests that diet was the major influence on blood pressure and lipid levels.

Melby CL, Toohey ML, Cebrick J. *Blood pressure and blood lipids among vegetarian, semivegetarian, and nonvegetarian African Americans. Am J Clin Nutr 1994; 59:103-9.*

Reed Mangels, PhD, RD

## I'VE RECENTLY BECOME VEGETARIAN AND I'M GAINING WEIGHT, NOT LOSING IT! HELP?

There are several things which may be going on. In the first place, just changing to a vegetarian diet does not insure weight loss, even if you're not replacing meat with milk and cheese. You may actually be eating more food and more calories than you were before you became vegetarian. You could try writing down everything you eat and drink for several days, including amounts of food. Then look up how many calories are in what you ate in a book (check with your library) or on the web (see page 48) with calorie values for foods. A simple way to estimate how many calories you need to maintain your weight is to change your weight in pounds to kilograms by dividing by 2.2. Multiply this by 21.6 and then multiply by 1.4 if you are mostly occupied in light activity (move around some of the time) or by 1.5 if you are moderately active (workout for an hour 4-5 times a week). This number is an estimate of how many calories you need. If you eat more calories than you expend, you will be gaining weight.

Finally, another possibility is that you may feel bloated due to excessive use of salt. Many foods (like soups and veggie burgers) can be high in sodium and cause your body to retain water, feel bloated, and actually lead to a higher weight. Check the labels of the foods you commonly use to learn their sodium content.

Another possibility to explain the bloating is that your body is just not used to the higher fiber content of a vegetarian diet. If you are eating a lot of beans and fruits and vegetables, you may be producing more gas than you used to. This usually disappears after a few weeks. Try chewing your food well and avoiding other sources of gas, such as carbonated beverages.

Reed Mangels, PhD, RD

## I'VE BEGUN LOSING WEIGHT SINCE I BECAME VEGETARIAN. WHAT SHOULD I BE EATING TO MAINTAIN MY PHYSIQUE?

Vegetarian diets can be bulky if they are heavily dependent on low calorie vegetables (greens, tomatoes, carrots, green beans, etc.). You may need to eat a greater proportion of starchy vegetables (dried beans, potatoes, corn, etc.) and fewer of the low calorie varieties. For instance, instead of minestrone soup, you'd take potato soup or split pea soup; instead of a tossed salad, you might eat potato salad (made with soy mayonnaise). You could also try eating more often. If you're seriously short on calories, you could also increase your fat intake somewhat by incorporating more vegetable oils and fatty plant foods such as peanut butter, almond butter, avocado, nuts, sunflower seeds, and so on.

Suzanne Havala, MS, RD


Try adding high calorie/low bulk foods for weight gain (like some fat, nuts, nut butters, dried fruits, or soy products). Also, there are a few eating tips to try, such as eating small frequent meals and waiting to eat really bulky low caloric foods like salads until you've eaten other higher calorie foods at that meal. These are general suggestions for weight gain and may not work for everyone. I'd also suggest a visit to a registered dietitian who can better plan a diet in keeping with your needs. Also, consult with your physician to see if there is any underlying medical reason for your weight loss. This is especially important if there has been recent, unplanned weight loss (as opposed to having always been thin).

Reed Mangels, PhD, RD


## WHAT CAN I DO ABOUT THE GAS I'VE BEEN EXPERIENCING SINCE I SWITCHED TO A VEGETARIAN DIET?

Gas and bloating can be alleviated, in part, by physical activity. If you have a problem with gas, getting regular exercise can greatly diminish the symptoms. For example, taking a long walk after dinner each night, or being vigorously physically active during the day playing basketball, racquetball, swimming, bike riding, and so on.

Of course, you can also eat less of or avoid specific foods if you find that you have a particular problem with them.

Take some solace in the fact that for most people, eating a high fiber diet over the long run reduces problems with gas as the body adjusts to the increased fiber load.

Suzanne Havala, MS, RD

## I FIND I HAVE A GAS AND BLOATING PROBLEM WHEN I EAT SOY. IS THIS COMMON?

This may be your body's reaction to a very rapid change in diet. Try backing off the soy products a bit (maybe 1 serving a day to start) and then gradually add in more servings. See if one product is especially problematic. This varies from person to person. Try to do all that you can to reduce gas production from other sources: chew your food well and eat slowly, avoid carbonated drinks and chewing gum, try not to eat when you're stressed. I think that with time, this problem will resolve itself.

Reed Mangels, PhD, RD

## WHAT IS YOUR OPINION OF THE BOOK WHICH PUSHES BLOOD TYPES AS DETERMINING WHETHER SOMEBODY SHOULD BE VEGETARIAN OR NOT?

Reed Mangels, PhD, RD addressed this issue in "Nutrition Hotline," *Vegetarian Journal* May/June 1999 -

*Diets that are based on blood types propose that those with one blood type (type A, for example) should be vegetarian while those with other blood types must eat meat or eliminate wheat and other grains. Following the correct diet for your blood type is alleged to help maintain optimal health and weight, avoid many infections, and fight back against life-threatening illnesses. Is there any truth to these claims?*

Advocates of this type of diet often explain the minute details of the foods, supplements, medications, and exercise regimens which should be followed by people with each blood type, but fail to scientifically document the effectiveness of their recommendations. Many of the claims that are made are not backed up by published research. For example, depending on your blood type, you may be presented with detailed lists of foods that are highly beneficial, neutral, or to be avoided. How were these lists generated? Has any research been published showing adverse health effects from use of foods that should be avoided? No studies are presented to support what appear to be speculations.

Numerous studies have shown that vegetarians live longer than non-vegetarians and have lower risk of a number of chronic diseases. These studies are likely to be based on people from all blood type groups. It certainly seems that a vegetarian diet has benefits for those studied, regardless of their blood type. Similarly, studies like those of Dean Ornish appear to demonstrate the beneficial effect of a vegetarian diet and other lifestyle changes on a number of individuals, and not just those of a certain blood type.

Diets based on blood types should not be used as the basis for dietary change. Statements like "I could never be a vegetarian, I'm type O" are not based on scientific evidence and may even lead people to avoid making dietary changes which could benefit both their health and the health of our planet. Our advice? Stick with a varied, whole foods-based vegetarian diet regardless of your blood type.

Another article to refer to regarding fad diets is *Do Low-Carbohydrate Diets Really Improve Health?*, by David Leonard, MAg, from the May 1999 issue of *Vegetarian Nutrition and Health Letter* from Loma Linda University.

MY WIFE AND I HAVE BEEN VEGANS FOR OVER 20 YEARS AND WE HAVE A FRIEND WHO JUST TURNED 50. SHE JUST HAD A BONE DENSITY SCAN AND THE RESULT WAS THAT SHE HAD A 30% BONE-DENSITY LOSS ALREADY! OVER THE YEARS, I HAVE READ ARTICLES DESCRIBING THE DELETERIOUS EFFECTS FROM EATING CASEIN (DAIRY PROTEIN) AND ALL OTHER FORMS OF ANIMAL PROTEIN (INCLUDING FISH). OUR FRIEND WANTS TO RESEARCH ALL AVENUES BEFORE DECIDING WHAT DIRECTION TO TAKE. WE, OF COURSE,

HAVE TRIED TO INFLUENCE HER TO BECOME A VEGAN AND
TO GET HER CALCIUM FROM LEAFY GREENS. WE BELIEVE
THAT CASEIN AND OTHER ANIMAL PROTEINS POTENTIALLY
CAUSE CALCIUM TO LEECH OUT OF THE BONES, THUS
CAUSING BONE-DENSITY LOSS. BUT WE NEED EMPIRICAL
EVIDENCE IN ORDER TO CONVINCE OUR FRIEND.

Thank you so much for your letter. I can appreciate your concern for your friend and your desire to do something to help her. There are many possible interventions. One that is very important is for your friend to begin (or continue) a regimen that includes weight-bearing exercise. This can lead to some improvement in bone density and certainly can help prevent further bone loss. Also, adequate calcium intake is very important. The specific amount of calcium required is controversial. The current recommendation is for 1200 milligrams a day and this would certainly be a level to strive for. Adequate vitamin D is also important; 10 micrograms per day is the recommendation here.

Plant-based diets are often associated with lower hip fracture rates worldwide. However, osteoporosis does occur in third world countries, just not at the rate seen in Western countries. Factors that may reduce the incidence of hip fracture in these countries include greater physical activity; more sun exposure and therefore higher blood vitamin D levels; and genetics which appears to play an important role. This suggests that Western vegans will have higher calcium needs than people in other parts of the world. You propose encouraging your friend to adopt a vegan diet. Certainly there are many advantages to this type of diet. However, I would not want you to look on it as the one thing that would help your friend. One study has suggested that vegan women, on average, actually have lower bone density than do non-vegetarian women, suggesting that vegans need to emphasize good sources of calcium in their diets. While diets very high in protein, especially animal protein, do cause an increased level of calcium in the urine, a diet that is too low in protein has also been shown to lead to changes in bone metabolism. So, it's important to strive for adequate, but not excessive intakes of protein. Foods like collard greens and kale do supply calcium in a form that is well-absorbed but if these are your main source of calcium, you must be willing to eat generous amounts of these foods. For example, 3-1/2 cups of cooked collard greens would provide around 1200 milligrams of calcium. Other options would be foods fortified with calcium, such as calcium-fortified soymilk or juice, and tofu processed with calcium salts.

You asked for empirical evidence that a vegan diet will be advantageous for your friend. Unfortunately, there is not a very clear picture of the bone health of Western vegetarians and certainly not of vegans. An advantage of the vegan diet is that it is fairly easy to formulate a diet that contains adequate but not excessive amounts of protein. It is certainly possible to get adequate calcium on a vegan diet. This type of diet also appears to be important in reducing the risk of developing heart disease and certain cancers, possibly not a major concern at this point for your friend, but something to think about in the long run.

For more information on this issue, see our chapter on calcium from Simply Vegan or view it on the website (www.vrg.org/nutrition/calcium.htm). You may also wish to read the chapter, *Meeting Calcium Needs on a Plant-Based Diet* in the book, The Vegetarian Way, by Virginia and Mark Messina.

Reed Mangels, PhD, RD

## AFTER REPEATED UNSUCCESSFUL ATTEMPTS AT CONCEPTION, MY FRIEND'S NUTRITIONIST HAD HER ADD MEAT, OFTEN RED, AT LEAST ONCE A WEEK. I'VE BEEN TRYING TO CONCEIVE AS WELL, AND AS A VEGETARIAN I AM WONDERING IF THIS IS CAUSING A PROBLEM?

There is no evidence that a vegetarian diet reduces fertility. There is no dietary requirement for meat. However, meat does provide generous amounts of iron and zinc, so vegetarians need to make sure they have good sources of these nutrients. If you are trying to conceive, it is important to make sure that you are maintaining a healthy diet and that you're not anemic. It is also important to have good sources of folic acid in your diet. Vegetarian diets are typically high in folic acid, which is found in green leafy vegetables, dried beans, and fortified grains. Be sure to take a look at the VRG brochure on vegan pregnancy and children. You can access it online at www.vrg.org/nutrition/pregnancy.htm or write, phone, or e-mail for a copy. For more information on good sources of iron and other nutrients, you can read Simply Vegan, The Vegetarian Way, or visit the nutrition section of the VRG website (www.vrg.org/nutrition).

Reed Mangels, PhD, RD

## Do vegetarians need to be concerned about vitamin A?

The Institute of Medicine recently released new recommendations for a number of vitamins and minerals, including vitamin A. Their report concluded that fruits and vegetables provide the body with half as much vitamin A as previously thought. Some newspaper reports warned that vegetarians might need to eat more dark-colored fruits and vegetables if they rely on these foods for vitamin A and don't get vitamin A from meat, fish, eggs, or vitamin A-fortified milk. This is a strange warning since vitamin A deficiency is very rarely reported in the United States, even among those relying on fruits and vegetables for vitamin A. Is this something to be concerned about? Probably not. Darkly-colored fruits and vegetables (like carrots, sweet potatoes, and apricots) are quite high in beta-carotene. Our bodies make vitamin A from beta-carotene. Even if these foods are only half as effective at supplying vitamin A as we thought, they are still great sources. For example, the new RDA for vitamin A is 900 micrograms per day for men and 700 micrograms per day for women. Since 12 micrograms of beta-carotene are needed to provide the equivalent of 1 microgram of vitamin A, if you only used foods containing beta-carotene to meet your vitamin A requirements, a safe level of beta-carotene would be 8,400 micrograms (700 x 12) for women and 10,800 micrograms (900 x 12) for men. Please note that these are micrograms of beta-carotene NOT vitamin A. A half-cup of cooked carrots provides 6,252 micrograms of beta-carotene, while 1 medium raw carrot provides 5,390 micrograms. A half-cup of sweet potatoes provides 9,488 micrograms of beta-carotene, 2 apricots provides 1,788 micrograms, and a half-cup of broccoli has 959 micrograms. As you can see, eating a couple of servings of dark green vegetables or deep-orange fruits and vegetables daily can easily provide all the vitamin A you need. In addition, some brands of soymilk are fortified with vitamin A. Do vegetarians need to be concerned about vitamin A? No, as long as we eat a variety of fruits and vegetables regularly.

*Food and Nutrition Board, Institute of Medicine. Dietary Reference Intakes for Vitamin A, Vitamin K, Arsenic, Boron, Chromium, Copper, Iodine, Iron, Manganese, Molybdenum, Nickel, Silicon, Vanadium, and Zinc. Washington, DC: National Academy Press, 2000; www.nas.edu.*

Reed Mangels, PhD, RD

# Has Vegetarian Journal addressed the DHA issue? I've read several articles that make it sound important for vegetarians.

DHA stands for docosahexaenoic acid. DHA is a polyunsaturated fatty acid. High levels of DHA are found in our brains and in our retinas (part of the eye) and it appears to be important for both brain function and for vision. DHA is especially important in infants to ensure appropriate brain and retinal development. Vegetarian diets are generally low in DHA since major food sources are fish, animal brains, cow's liver, and eggs (especially eggs from hens fed flaxseed). Vegans generally consume no DHA.

The good news is that we do not have to get DHA from food. Our bodies are able to produce DHA from another fatty acid called alpha linolenic acid. However, we are not very good at doing this and when we eat large amounts of another fatty acid called linoleic acid or trans-fatty acids, our bodies make even less DHA. Studies have shown that vegans and other vegetarians have lower levels of DHA in their blood than do non-vegetarians. We do not know, however, whether or not people who eat little or no DHA are more efficient at using it for mental and visual function. There is no evidence that vegetarians exhibit any symptoms of DHA deficiency. DHA is important in the developing fetus and in early infancy. During pregnancy, DHA appears to be transferred to the fetus through the placenta, even in vegetarians whose DHA intakes are low. Although the level of DHA in human milk from vegans was lower than that of non-vegetarians in one study, it was still higher than that found in cow's milk formula which does not contain DHA.

Additional research is needed on DHA needs of vegetarian and vegan infants, especially premature infants. Premature infants are born with lower levels of DHA. Until more research can be conducted on DHA status of vegetarians, vegetarians can do several things to improve their DHA status. One positive step is to include some foods rich in alpha-linolenic acid which will provide material for your body to make DHA. These foods include flax seed, flaxseed oil, walnuts, soy products (not fat-reduced), and canola oil. Another step is to limit foods rich in linoleic acid like corn, sesame, and safflower oils. You can also try to avoid trans fatty acids that come from partially hydrogenated fats and are found in many commercial crackers, cookies, and margarines. Pregnant and breastfeeding women may need to be especially conscious of these recommendations in order to positively influence DHA status of their infants. Increased maternal DHA has been shown to increase blood DHA levels in infants.

There are DHA supplements on the market, some of which are derived from algae. These have been shown to raise blood levels of DHA in vegetarians but have not been shown to have other beneficial effects. These may be an option for some vegetarians. Some supplements are in the form of gelatin-based capsules with the gelatin possibly derived from animal bones, so if you decide to use DHA supplements, check on what the capsules are made from. Additionally, there is some evidence that significant amounts of DHA will affect immune function. Use of vitamin E supplements along with the DHA supplements may reduce or eliminate the effects of DHA on the immune system.

*J Pediatrics 1992; 120:S71-7.*
*Lipids 1996; 31:S183-7.*
*Am J Clin Nutr 1993; 57:703S-10S.*
*J Immunology 1995; 154:1296-1306*
*New England Journal of Medicine 1989; 320:265-71*
*Am J Clin Nutr 1991; 54:896-902.*

Reed Mangels, PhD, RD

## I READ AN ARTICLE STATING THAT MEN WHO AVOID MILK HAVE SIGNIFICANTLY LOWER RATES OF PROSTATE CANCER. THE ARTICLE REFERRED TO THE WORLD CANCER RESEARCH FUND AND THE AMERICAN INSTITUTE FOR CANCER RESEARCH, SAYING 11 SEPARATE HUMAN POPULATION STUDIES TIED DAIRY CONSUMPTION TO PROSTATE CANCER. DO YOU HAVE ANY INFORMATION ON THIS?

The report referred to in that article was a 600-page book published by the American Institute for Cancer Research (AICR) and the World Cancer Research Fund called Food, Nutrition, and the Prevention of Cancer: A Global Perspective. You can order it directly from the AICR website at www.aicr.org/report2.htm. Here is a summary of their comments with regard to prostate cancer: *"There is as yet no convincing evidence that any dietary factors modify risk of prostate cancer, nor evidence of any probable causal relationships with diet. Diets high in vegetables are possibly protective and regular consumption of fat, saturated/animal fat, red meat and milk and dairy products possibly increase risk. Current evidence suggests that the most effective dietary means of preventing prostate cancer, is consumption of diets high in vegetables and low in fat and saturated/animal fat, red meat, and milk and dairy products."* I hope you will find lots of information in *Vegetarian Journal* and on our website that will help your family move towards a diet that is close to the one recommended by the AICR.

Reed Mangels, PhD, RD

## DO YOU KNOW OF A RESOURCE SPECIFIC TO THE VEGETAR-IAN/VEGAN LIFESTYLE AND DIALYSIS/KIDNEY DISEASE?

The American Dietetic Association's Fact Sheet on *Vegetarian Diets and Renal Disease* can be obtained by contacting The American Dietetic Association (ADA), 216 W. Jackson Blvd., Chicago, IL 60606; (312) 899-0040. You can also access it directly on the VNDPG webpage www.eatright.org/dpg/dpg14.html.

Another excellent source for materials relating to health issues and vegetarian diets are Seventh-day Adventist hospitals. We have a copy of <u>Diet Manual</u>, published by The Seventh-day Adventist Dietetic Association. There is a section on renal diets, as well as other specialized medical diets. For more information, contact The Seventh-day Adventist Dietetic Association, PO Box 75, Loma Linda, CA 92354.

There are additional resources available online from The ADA Vegetarian Nutrition Practice Group at www.andrews.edu/NUFS/vndpg.html.
These are a few of the articles you'll find there: *Phytochemicals: Guardians of Our Health, Factors in Vegetarian Diets Influencing Iron and Zinc Bioavailability, Working With Vegetarian Clients, Dietary Phytoestrogens and Bone Health, The Challenge of Defining Optimal Fat Intake, An Education in Vegetarian Dietetics, Vegetarian Diets During Cancer Treatment, The Writing Life of a Dietitian, Planning Meat-Based Diets as a Vegetarian Dietitian, Functional Foods, Folate and Colorectal Cancer: Is There a Connection?,* and *Making the Change to a Vegetarian Diet.*

# CHAPTER 4

# FOOD INGREDIENTS

The purpose of our food ingredient research is to educate so individuals may make informed decisions about the foods that they eat. Suppliers and ingredients are ever changing. When you are purchasing foods, an exact guarantee of the ingredients is probably not possible. It is very easy to get wrapped up in the microscopic details and ignore larger issues. There is no such thing as a perfect vegetarian or vegan. Vegetarians and vegans will draw their own lines at what they will or won't eat. Do the best you can; it is all any of us can do.

In 1997, VRG first published the *Guide to Food Ingredients* (see page 269) to aid consumers in deciphering ingredient labels. Some of the following answers were provided by research gathered for the guide. The *Guide to Food Ingredients* lists the uses, sources, and definitions of common food ingredients. It also states whether the ingredient is vegan, typically vegan, vegetarian, typically vegetarian, typically non-vegetarian, or non-vegetarian. The guide is available for $4. You can order online at www.vrg.org/catalog/order.htm. You can also order by mailing a check to VRG, PO 1463, Baltimore, MD 21203, or by calling (410) 366-8343, M-F 9-5 (EST), to order with a Visa or MasterCard.

## WHAT IS VITAMIN B-12 DERIVED FROM? ISN'T IT ALWAYS FROM AN ANIMAL PRODUCT?

Vitamin B-12, when used to fortify foods, is generally synthetic or fungal in origin. While it is commonly found in animal products, it is now more readily available in soymilks, meat analogues, Vegetarian Support Formula (Red Star T-6635+) nutritional yeast, and even fortified tofu.

## WHAT ARE "NATURAL FLAVORS?"

According to our research department, the exact definition of natural flavorings and flavors from Title 21, Section 101, part 22 of the Code of Federal Regulations is as follows:

*"The term natural flavor or natural flavoring means the essential oil, oleoresin, essence or extractive, protein hydrolysate, distillate, or any product of roasting, heating or enzymolysis, which contains the flavoring constituents derived from a spice, fruit or fruit juice, vegetable or vegetable juice, edible yeast, herb, bark, bud, root, leaf or similar plant material, meat, seafood, poultry, eggs, dairy products, or fermentation products thereof, whose significant function in food is flavoring rather than nutritional."*

In other words, natural flavors can be pretty much anything approved for use in food. It's basically impossible to tell what is in natural flavors unless the company has specified it on the label. A few of the vegetarian and vegan-oriented companies are doing this now, but the overwhelming majority of food manufacturers do not.

Why do companies "hide" ingredients under "natural flavors?" It's considered a way of preserving the product's identity and uniqueness. Sort of like a "secret recipe" - they worry that if people knew what the flavorings were, then someone would be able to duplicate their product.

So what is a vegetarian to do? Call the company. Ask them what's in the flavorings or ask them if the ingredients are vegetarian or vegan. Chances are they may not be able to tell you, or may be unwilling to tell you.* But the more they hear this question, the more likely they are to become concerned about putting a clarifying statement on their labels. It does work in some cases (remember what happened when enough people wrote to the USDA about the organic standards), although it tends to take awhile. We have already had several large food companies call us concerning their natural flavors and how to word their labels if they use only vegetarian or vegan flavorings. They called because it had come to their attention that this was a concern for vegetarians and vegans.

*Many of the numbers listed on food labels are customer-service call centers staffed by people who can only read from the information provided to them by the company. While it's tempting to get frustrated and yell at them, please don't. It's sort of like taking it out on the stock clerk because you don't like the grocery store's policies.*

## ARE McDONALD'S FRIES MADE WITH BEEF?

From VRG's *Guide to Fast Food* (see page 269):

> *"In February 1997, McDonald's informed us by telephone that the natural flavor in their French fries is a "beef product." At that time, they declined to send us this information in writing. In July 1997, McDonald's sent us a fax stating that "[t]he natural flavor used in French fries is from an animal source." McDonald's reports that the fries are cooked in vegetable oil apart from the meat/seafood products. According to their February 1997 Nutrition Facts brochure, the French fries are cooked in a blend of soybean and corn oils, TBHQ (a synthetic antioxidant), citric acid, dimethylpolysiloxane (a synthetic antifoaming agent), and natural flavor. In November 2000, when contacted for another update to the Guide, no changes were made to this information."*

## IS THE SAME TRUE FOR FRANCHISES IN THE UK?

Fast food companies have different standards based on the wants of the local population and the supplies available. In Canada, the fries can be prepared with beef fat, but that would be considered unacceptable in India. Specifics for the UK were not apparent on McDonald's website, but there are corporate contacts online at www.mcdonalds.com/countries/usa/corporate-/info/contacts/index.html.

## Do you know the origin of thiamine hydrochloride, di-sodium guanylate, and disodium inosinate? They are from a package of TVP.

*Thiamine hydrochloride*: This is vitamin B-1 and is typically vegan. It is typically synthetic.

*Disodium guanylate*: This is a flavor enhancer derived from fungal sources.

*Disodium inosinate*: This is a flavor enhancer, which may be non-vegetarian. Its sources are mineral, animal (meat/fish), vegetable, or fungal.

If it is Textured Vegetable Protein (TVP), the disodium inosinate is probably of vegetable or fungal origin.

## Is wine vegetarian?

In January 1997, *Vegetarian Journal* published an article, *"Why is Wine So Fined?"*, by Caroline Pyevich, about the manufacturing processes involved in wine-making and the animal products that are used in the production. Due to the high interest in this information, this article has been included in the appen dix on page 231. The article can also be accessed online at www.vrg.org/journal/vj97jan/971wine.htm.

Here is an excerpt: *"Some clarifiers are animal-based products, while others are earth-based. Common animal-based agents include egg whites, milk, casein, gelatin, and isinglass. Gelatin is an animal protein derived from the skin and connective tissue of pigs and cows. Isinglass is prepared from the bladder of the sturgeon fish. Bentonite, a clay earth product, serves as a popular fining agent."*

Following are a few wine companies that produce vegan wines (note: some organic wine companies use egg whites as clarifiers):

∗Hallcrest Vineyards at (408) 335-4441. Hallcrest offers mail order. Website: www.hallcrestvineyards.com.

∗Frey Vineyards is distributed across the US. Call and they will let you know where their wine can be purchased locally. Phone: (800) 760-3739; Website: www.freywine.com.

∗Offerings From The Vine produces wine made with fresh fruits and maple syrup, without sulfites, preservatives, or additives. Contact Yafah B. Asiel at (404) 752-5194.

∗LaRocca Vineyards offers organic, sulfite-free wines. Phone: (800) 808-9463; Website: www.laroccavineyards.com.

The Vegetarian Society of the United Kingdom (VSUK) offers additional information on this subject at www.vegsoc.org/info/alcohol.html. VSUK notes that most spirits are acceptable for vegetarians.

## DOES THE SAME GO FOR BEER?

According to the Vegetarian Society of the United Kingdom (VSUK) website (www.vegsoc.org/info/alcohol.html#beer),

*"Cask-conditioned ales need fining to clear the material (especially the yeast) held in suspension in the liquid. This is invariably done by adding isinglass, derived from the swim bladders of certain tropical fish especially the Chinese sturgeon, which acts as a falling suspension. If you were to hold a pint of real ale up to the light and see cloudy lumps swirling around that would suggest that the cask had been recently disturbed and the isinglass shaken up from the bottom. Bottled naturally conditioned beers will not always have been treated with isinglass. Keg Beers and Lagers are pasteurised and usually passed through Chill Filters, as are canned beers and some bottled beers, however a considerable number of breweries still use isinglass to clear their pasturised beers, though sometimes only to rescue selected batches which are considered too hazey. Also occasionally the sometimes animal derived additive Glyceryl Monostearate is used in place of 900 Dimethylpolysiloxane as a foam-control agent in the production of keg beers.*

*"It is sometimes possible to buy barrels of cask-conditioned beer from a brewery before it has been fined. The beer would then have to be left for a considerable time to stand before consumption. To our knowledge, only one pub in England sells unfined real ale on draught: The Cumberland Arms in Byker, Newcastle on Tyne."*

The VSUK list of vegetarian beers is at www.vegsoc.org/info/vegbeers.html. In the US, it seems that some mircobrews either don't use animal clarifiers or are more knowledgeable about their products and can tell you what clarifiers are used.

## WHY WON'T SOME VEGANS EAT SUGAR?

This is because some sugar companies process sugar through a bone char. The bone char decolorizes the sugar. For more information read *"Sugar and Other Sweeteners: Do they Contain Animal Products?"*, by Caroline Pyevich. It is online at www/journal/vj97mar/973sugar.htm. To request a paper copy write, phone, or e-mail VRG.

## WHAT IS FD & C RED #40 AND IS IT VEGAN?

FD & C Red #40 is 99% coal tar derivatives. We don't know of any animal products in it. For years a rumor has claimed that it is made of cochineal or carmine, but that is not true.

## WHAT IS CHEWING GUM MADE OUT OF?

Most chewing gums innocuously list "gum base" as one of their ingredients, masking the fact that petroleum, lanolin, glycerin, polyethylene, polyvinyl acetate, petroleum wax, stearic acid, and latex may be among the components. Because of standards of identity for items such as gum base and flavoring, manufacturers are not required to list everything in their product. According to Dertoline, a French chemical manufacturer, their adhesive "dercolytes" is used as a label and tape adhesive, as well as a chewing gum base. Many brands also list glycerin and glycerol as ingredients on the label. Both of those compounds can be animal-derived. See page 126 for sources of vegan gum.

## WHAT IS COCHINEAL (CARMINE)?

Some red dyes are made from the female cochineal beetle. These are usually labeled as cochineal, carmine, or carminic acid.

## PRE-GELATINIZED WHEAT STARCH IS FROM AN ANIMAL, RIGHT?

According to A Consumer's Dictionary of Food Additives, "When starch and water are heated the starch molecules burst and form a gelatin."

According to The Dictionary of Food Ingredients it is a starch that has been created by swelling wheat in cold water. It is also known as gelatinized wheat starch.

According to Food Chemistry, "Pre-gelatinized flour is made from ground cereals....and is sometimes blended with guar flour or alginates."

It appears to be a completely vegetarian product.

## WHAT IS SODIUM STEAROYL LACTYLATE?

It is an animal-mineral (cow or hog-derived, or milk) or vegetable-mineral common food additive. It is often used to condition dough or to blend together ingredients that do not normally blend, such as oil and water. Our *Guide to Food Ingredients* reports it "may be non-vegetarian." Archer Daniels Midland Co., a manufacturer of sodium stearoyl lactylate, reports that their product is of vegetable origin; the lactic acid is produced from microbial fermentation and the stearic acid, from soy oil. Sodium is an added mineral.

## WHAT ARE "E" NUMBERS?

There are different words for various food ingredients across the world. In Europe, some food ingredients are noted as "E" numbers. According to The International Vegetarian Union FAQ about food ingredients, vegans and vegetarians will want to avoid:

E120 - cochineal (red food coloring made from crushed beetles)
E542 - edible bone phosphate
E631 - sodium 5'-inosinate
E901 - beeswax
E904 - shellac
E920 - L-cysteine hydrochloride

Ingredients with the following "E" numbers may be animal derived: 101, 101a, 153, 203, 213, 227, 270, 282, 302, 322, 325, 326, 327, 333, 341a, 341b, 341c, 404, 422, 430, 431, 432, 433, 434, 435, 436, 470, 471, 472a, 472b, 472c, 472d, 472e, 473, 474, 475, 476, 477, 478, 481, 482, 483, 491, 492, 493, 494, 495, 570, 572, 627, and 635.

To read more, go to The International Vegetarian Union FAQ about food ingredients at www.ivu.org/faq/food.html.

## WHY ARE SOME CHEESES LABELED AS "VEGETARIAN CHEESE?" WHY WOULDN'T CHEESE BE VEGETARIAN? WHAT IS RENNET?

Cheese is often made with rennet or rennin, which is used to coagulate the dairy product. According to the McGraw-Hill Encyclopedia of Science and Technology, rennin, which is an enzyme used in coagulating cheese, is obtained from milk-fed calves. "After butchering, the fourth stomach...is removed and freed of its food content." After this the stomach goes through several steps including being dry-salted, washed, scraped to remove surface fat, stretched onto racks where moisture is removed, then finally ground and mixed with a salt solution until the rennin is extracted. To read more on this topic go to www.vrg.org/nutshell/cheese.htm.

Some cheeses are made with vegetable, fungal, or microbial enzymes. There's a list of vegetarian cheeses on our website at www.vrg.org/nutshell/cheesebybrand.htm.

Also, take a look at Trader Joe's lists: East Coast: www.traderjoes.com/tj/products/brochures/rennet_east.stm and West Coast: www.traderjoes.com/tj/products/brochures/rennet_west.stm.

## WHAT IS CASEIN?

It is the principle protein in milk. It is found in many soy cheeses, as it helps the soy cheese to melt more like dairy-based cheese. It is also used to make plastics, adhesives, and paints. It is considered vegetarian, but not vegan.

## WHAT IS WHEY?

Whey is the watery material that remains after most of the protein and fat have been removed from milk during the cheese-making process. It is also the liquid that rises to the top of yogurt and heated milk. It is typically vegetarian, but not vegan.

## DO YOU THINK WHEY IS VEGETARIAN? IT IS USUALLY A BY-PRODUCT OF THE CHEESE MAKING PROCESS. A LOT OF CHEESE MANUFACTURERS USE MICROBIAL RENNET, BUT MANY USE ANIMAL RENNET. SINCE THE ENZYME CAUSES THE LIQUID MILK TO COAGULATE, DOES THE ENZYME STAY IN THE SOLID? IS THAT THE "CHEMICAL PROCESS?" THE RESULT WOULD BE THE CHEESE HAS THE ENZYME IN IT AND THE WHEY DOES NOT. DO YOU HAVE A DEFINITIVE ANSWER?

To give you the short answer first, VRG's *Guide to Food Ingredients* states that whey is "typically vegetarian." However, this is a bit of a gray area question. Rennet acts as a catalyst, promoting a chemical reaction without being used up in the process. The rennet is responsible for separating the curds (what will become cheese) and whey. The end product of whey will not have the rennet in it, but it is part of the production method.

Another example of an ingredient used in the process, but not found in the final product is when whey is used as the fermentation medium for vegetable-based lactic acid. The final product can be considered dairy-free because the whey is not considered present in the final form of lactic acid.

## WHAT ARE ENZYMES? ARE THEY VEGETARIAN?

They are proteins or conjugated proteins added to foods as modifiers. They can be animal, vegetable, bacterial, or fungal. Those used in cheese-making are often animal-derived. Those used in breadmaking are often fungal. Examples of enzymes are: lactase (fungal), lipase (animal or fungal), papain (vegetable), pectinase (fruit), protease (animal, vegetable, bacterial, or fungal), rennet (animal), and trypsin (animal).

## DOES GUACAMOLE CONTAIN GELATIN?

Some processed kinds found in the supermarket do, but fresh guacamole often does not contain it.

## WHAT IS CYSTEINE?

VRG's research indicates that a common source of cysteine is human hair. Also known as L-cystine, cysteine is a necessary amino acid, which can be produced by the human body. It is a common ingredient in breads.

## WHAT IS CELLULOSE? IS IT ANIMAL-DERIVED?

According to VRG's *Guide to Food Ingredients,* cellulose gum is vegan. It comes from a vegetable or synthetic source. It is the principle component of plant cells and is used to prevent ice crystallization in foods.

## WHAT ARE MONO- AND DIGLYCERIDES?

Monoglycerides and diglycerides are common food additives used to blend together certain ingredients, such as oil and water, which would not otherwise blend well. The commercial source may be either animal (cow- or hog-derived) or vegetable or synthetic. They are often found in bakery products, beverages, ice cream, chewing gum, shortening, whipped toppings, margarine, and confections. According to our *Guide*, they "may be non-vegetarian." Archer Daniels Midland Co., a large manufacturer of monoglycerides, reports that they use soybean oil.

## WHAT IS AMYLASE?

Amylase is an enzyme that breaks down starch into a simpler form. It can be derived from bacterial, fungal, or animal (pig-derived) sources. It is typically vegan.

## WHAT IS ROYAL JELLY?

Royal jelly is a substance produced by the glands of bees and used as a source of B vitamins, minerals, and amino acids. It is considered vegetarian, not vegan.

## WHY AVOID HONEY?

Many vegans choose not to consume anything from an animal, including insects. For production methods and ethics concerns please read the *Vegetarian Journal* article "Busy Bees: Honey Production and Agricultural Pollination." This article is online at www.vrg.org/journal/vj96nov/bee.htm or a paper copy can be requested, by writing, phoning, or e-mailing VRG.

## WHAT IS STEARIC ACID?

Stearic acid is used as a binder in foods and its source may be either animal or vegetable. It is found in vegetable and animal oils, animal fats, cascarilla bark extract, and in synthetic form. It is used in butter flavoring, vanilla flavoring, chewing gum and other candy, and fruit waxes. It may not be vegetarian.

## WHAT ABOUT THOSE INGREDIENTS THAT SOUND LIKE THEY ARE FROM MILK, I.E. LACTIC ACID, LACTOSE, AND LACTATE?

If it's lactate or lactic acid, it's generally not from dairy (exception - stearol lactate due to the stearic acid). "Lac" ingredients are usually produced by a fermentation process using cornstarch or beet sugar. Lactose is always from dairy. Most ingredients made with calcium are vegan (i.e. calcium carbonate, calcium phosphate, calcium sulfate). The exceptions are calcium caseinate and calcium stearate.

## WHAT IS CALCIUM LACTATE? IS IT VEGAN?

It should be a vegan ingredient. It is a calcium salt of lactic acid. According to our research, domestically-made lactic acid is produced without whey as the fermentation medium. It is typically vegan. Archer Daniels Midland Co. reports that they use only hydrolyzed cornstarch as the fermentation medium. Purac America, Inc., says that they use only beet sugar. However, with imported products, such as some olives, the source of the lactic acid is unknown.

## WHAT IS THE DIFFERENCE BETWEEN VITAMIN D-2 AND D-3?

D-2 (ergocalciferol) is derived from yeast, while D-3 (cholecalciferol) is derived from lanolin (from sheep) or fish. D-2 and D-3 are both used to fortify milk and other dairy products. Some D-3 vitamin supplements are made with fish oil. D-3 can also be produced by plants and fungi, but this isn't as common as using lanolin or fish as a source.

## WHAT ARE AGAR-AGAR AND GUAR GUM?

Both are thickening agents. Agar (also known as agar-agar) is a vegetable gum obtained from seaweeds. Guar gum is a common and versatile vegetable gum. Agar and guar gum are vegan products.

## IS CARAMEL COLOR VEGAN?

Caramel color is a common food coloring and flavoring that is usually derived from corn. It is also derived from other vegetable sources, and is considered vegan. It is used in soft drinks, baked goods, candy, ice cream, meats (to impart a brown color), and also as a flavoring.

## WHAT IS ASPARTIC ACID?

Aspartic acid is an amino acid needed by humans, and can be produced by the body. It is considered typically vegetarian and its commercial source is generally bacterial or fungal.

## WHAT IS GLUTAMIC ACID?

Glutamic acid is an amino acid generally used as a flavor enhancer. Its commercial source is generally vegetable-based and it is considered typically vegetarian.

## WHAT IS NIACIN?

Niacin (also known as nicotinic acid, nicotinamide, niacinamide, or vitamin B-3) is a B vitamin that is important in the normal functioning of the nervous system. Its commercial source is synthetic, and it may also be found in liver, yeast, meat, legumes, and whole cereals. It is typically vegan.

## DOES "LECITHIN" COME FROM BEANS, SUCH AS SOYBEANS, OR IS IT FROM AN ANIMAL?

Lecithin is found in egg yolks, the tissues and organs of many animals, and some vegetables, such as soybeans, peanuts, and corn. Lecithin is commonly used in foods that are high in fats and oils in order to make dissimilar substances, such as oil and water, blend and/or stay blended. The *Guide to Food Ingredients* list it as typically vegetarian. Archer Daniels Midland Co., a major manufacturer of lecithin, extracts it from soybeans. Soy is the standard for lecithin in the food industry these days.

## WHAT ARE DEXTROSE AND MALTODEXTRIN?

Dextrose has a vegetable source, but may be processed through a bone char filter (see sugar question on page 77). It is a simple sugar, which functions as a sweetener in foods and drinks. The *Guide* lists it as typically vegan.

Maltodextrin has a vegetable source. It is a modified food starch, which may be used to give body to foods. *The Guide to Food Ingredients* lists it as vegan.

## IS "GLUTEN" VEGAN?

Gluten is a mixture of proteins from wheat flour. It is a vegan product. You will often see it referred to as wheat gluten or seitan.

## WHAT IS GELATIN MADE FROM?

Gelatin is made from the bones, skins, hoofs, and tendons of cows, pigs, fish and other animals. It is animal protein used especially for its thickening and gelling properties. It is a non-vegetarian product. It is often used in candies and Jell-O™. Also, see page 21 for information on kosher gelatin.

## Is maple syrup processed with lard?

Maple syrup can be treated with a very small amount of animal fat, butter, or cream to reduce foaming. Most modern producers use synthetic compounds in order to reduce foaming during production. It is typically vegan. Spring Tree, Maple Groves, and Holsum Foods all report that their maple syrups do not use an animal-derived defoaming agent.

## What is aspic?

It is a clear viscous material typically made of stock and gelatin (bones, skins, hoofs, and tendons of cows, pigs, fish, and other animals).

## Is glycerine safe for vegetarians?

Glycerine can be animal, vegetable, or synthetic. It is commonly animal-based, or a blend of animal and vegetable oils. Even kosher glycerine can be animal-based. Asking particular companies about their food ingredients is often the only way to find out if the source is animal or vegetable.

# CHAPTER 5

# RECIPES

VRG publishes several cookbooks including <u>Simply Vegan</u>, <u>Conveniently Vegan</u>, <u>Meatless Meals for Working People</u>, <u>The Lowfat Jewish Vegetarian Cookbook</u>, <u>No Cholesterol Passover Recipes</u>, <u>Vegan Handbook</u>, <u>Vegan Meals for One or Two</u>, <u>Vegan in Volume,</u> and more (see page 265 for information about the books). Vegetarian Journal, VRG's bi-monthly magazine, also features recipes in every issue (see page 266). You can access our recipe sections online at www.vrg.org/recipes and www.vrg.org/journal.

You can also go to the search engine of your choice and type in "vegetarian recipes" and you will discover thousands of websites.

The following are a few recipes we've found to be popular.

*Note: Contrary to popular opinion, many vegans enjoy sweet treats; thus many of the recipes listed below are for tasty vegan desserts.*

# DIPS AND SAUCES

**FROM SIMPLY VEGAN**
## TOFU DILL DIP
## (SERVES 5)

1 cucumber, peeled
1 pound tofu
1 teaspoon dill weed
2 Tablespoons lemon juice
1/4 cup fresh parsley or 1 Tablespoon dried parsley
1/2 teaspoon garlic powder
Salt to taste

Place all of the ingredients into a food processor or blender and blend until creamy. Serve with raw vegetables and crackers.

Total Calories per serving: 77     Fat: 5 grams     Protein: 8 grams
Carbohydrates: 3 grams     High in iron

**FROM THE ARTICLE "USING THE OL' BEAN,"** *VEGETARIAN JOURNAL* **(JANUARY/FEBRUARY 2001) BY NANCY BERKOFF**
## SOUTHWESTERN RED BEAN SAUCE
## (YIELD: 2-1/2 CUPS OR FIVE 1/2 CUP SERVINGS)

Serve this colorful sauce over rice, white or black beans, cut corn, or grilled veggies. It can also be used as an ingredient in soups or in casseroles instead of tomato sauce or tomato juice.

1-1/2 cups cooked or canned red beans, drained
1/2 cup fresh tomatoes (see details below)
2 Tablespoons diced red onion
4 fresh chilies, seeded and chopped
1 clove garlic, minced
2 Tablespoons orange juice concentrate
2 Tablespoons vinegar

2 Tablespoons water
Vegetable oil spray
3/4 cup diced fresh pineapple

Place beans in a large bowl and set aside.

Blacken tomatoes, either in the oven at 400 degrees on a baking sheet until peel is blackened, or over an open flame. Peel and chop.

Place tomatoes, onion, chilies, garlic, orange juice concentrate, vinegar, and water in a blender or food processor and blend until smooth.

Spray frying pan, heat, and add pineapple. Sauté until soft (about 5 minutes).

Remove pineapple and add puréed mixture to frying pan. Over high heat, stir puréed mixture for 1 minute.

Add pineapple and puréed mixture to beans and mix to combine. Serve hot.

Note: Canned, drained pineapple may be used if fresh pineapple is not available; this will give a sweeter flavor to the sauce.

Total calories per serving: 142    Fat: 2 grams    Carbohydrates: 27 grams
Protein: 7 grams    Sodium: 5 milligrams    Fiber: 8 grams

## FROM THE ARTICLE "USING THE OL' BEAN," VEGETARIAN JOURNAL (JANUARY/FEBRUARY 2001) BY NANCY BERKOFF
## BLACK BEAN AND MANGO SAUCE
## (SERVES 6)

Served over rice, this makes a wonderful entrée! Or, serve over steamed quinoa, barley, or couscous. This sauce also makes a great basis for a Caribbean chowder; just allow it to cook a bit longer to reduce and add cooked, diced potatoes, cut corn, and green peas.

2 Tablespoons olive oil
2 cups chopped white onions

2 cloves garlic, minced
2 Tablespoons minced bell pepper
2 Tablespoons minced fresh ginger
1 teaspoon ground cumin
4 cups cooked or canned, drained black beans
4 Tablespoons lime juice
1 cup pitted and chopped, fresh, ripe mango

Garnish:
Lime wedges
Chopped green onions
Chopped fresh cilantro

Heat oil in a large frying pan. Add onions, garlic, bell pepper, ginger, and cumin and sauté until onions are soft (about 3 minutes).

Turn heat to low and add beans and lime juice. Sauté for 5 more minutes or until beans are heated. Add the mango and stir and mash for 5 more minutes.

Serve immediately. Garnish with lime wedges, chopped green onions, and fresh cilantro.

Total calories per serving: 231     Fat: 5 grams     Carbohydrates: 38 grams
Protein: 11 grams     Sodium: 18 milligrams     Fiber: 13 grams

FROM NO CHOLESTEROL PASSOVER RECIPES
## CINDY'S EGGLESS MAYONNAISE
## (MAKES 1-1/2 CUPS)

Try this unique almond-based mayonnaise. Use in moderation.

1/2 cup raw almonds
1-1/2 cups boiling water
1 cup oil
Juice of one lemon
1 teaspoon vinegar
1 teaspoon white horseradish

1/4 teaspoon garlic powder

Blend almonds and boiling water together for about 3 minutes. Strain through cheesecloth or muslin.

Pour 1/2 cup of this "almond milk" and 1/2 cup oil into blender. As you blend at high speed, slowly drizzle in the remaining oil. It should start to thicken. Then add the other ingredients and blend one more minute until the consistency of mayonnaise.

WARNING: THIS RECIPE WILL NOT WORK ON A DAMP, HUMID, OR RAINY DAY!

Total calories per 1 Tablespoon serving: 86     Fat: 10 grams     Protein: 1 gram
Carbohydrates: 1 gram

# SOUPS

## FROM THE ARTICLE "VEGETABLE CHOWDERS," *VEGETARIAN JOURNAL* (SEPTEMBER/OCTOBER 2000) BY NANCY BERKOFF
## POTATO AND KALE CHOWDER
## (SERVES 6)

For a creamier texture, add 6 ounces of puréed tofu while the veggies are simmering.

3 pounds unpeeled red or white rose potatoes
1 pound fresh kale
4 quarts water
2 Tablespoons oil
3 cloves garlic, minced
1 teaspoon red pepper flakes
2 Tablespoons diced onions

Cut the potatoes into small chunks and shred the kale. Place potatoes in a large pot and place kale on top. Add the water.

Allow to simmer, stirring occasionally to moisten kale, until potatoes are tender (12-15 minutes).

While veggies are simmering, heat oil in a frying pan. Add garlic, pepper flakes, and onions and sauté. Set aside.

Allow potatoes and kale to continue to simmer until the water is half gone. Add the sautéed veggies. Stir and allow to cook until potatoes fall apart and liquid is thickened. Serve warm.

Total calories per serving: 263    Fat: 5 grams    Carbohydrates: 49 grams
Protein: 7 grams    Sodium: 47 milligrams    Fiber: 5 grams

FROM THE ARTICLE "VEGETABLE CHOWDERS," *VEGETARIAN JOURNAL* (SEPTEMBER/OCTOBER 2000) BY NANCY BERKOFF
LENTIL CHOWDER
(SERVES 6)

An old familiar standby for vegans, but served here with a South Indian twist.

2 Tablespoons oil
1 teaspoon ground cumin
3/4 cup peeled and diced potatoes
1/2 onion, diced
1 teaspoon red pepper flakes
2 cups water
1 cup cooked lentils
1/2 cup thawed frozen peas
1/4 cup diced fresh tomatoes
1 teaspoon garam masala (or 1/4 teaspoon each turmeric, coriander, ground ginger, and white pepper)

Heat oil in large pot. Add cumin and sauté for 15 seconds. Add potatoes and onion and sauté for 2 minutes. Add red pepper flakes and water and bring to a boil. Lower heat, cover, and allow to simmer for 10 minutes.

Add lentils, peas, tomatoes, and garam masala and allow to simmer for 10 minutes or until potatoes are soft and liquid is thickened. Serve warm.

Total calories per serving: 110    Fat: 5 grams    Carbohydrates: 13 grams
Protein: 4 grams    Sodium: 15 milligrams    Fiber: 4 grams

# DISHES

## FROM MEATLESS MEALS FOR WORKING PEOPLE
## SPINACH PIE
## (SERVES 8)

10-ounce box frozen spinach
1-1/2 cups chopped onion
3 cloves garlic, minced
2 Tablespoons oil
3 cups crumbled tofu (soft or silken tofu is best)
1 Tablespoon lemon juice
Salt and pepper to taste
1 pre-made pie crust

Cook spinach according to package directions. Sauté onion and garlic in oil in a large pot over medium heat for 3 minutes. Add spinach, tofu, lemon juice, and seasoning. Preheat oven to 350 degrees. Meanwhile, continue cooking spinach/tofu mixture for 5 minutes. Mix well. Pour into pie crust. Bake at 350 degrees for 15-20 minutes until crust is brown.

Total calories per serving: 180     Fat: 11 grams     Protein: 7 grams
Carbohydrates: 15 grams     Fiber: 1 gram

## FROM THE LOWFAT JEWISH VEGETARIAN COOKBOOK
## BROCCOLI AND LEMON SAUCE
## (SERVES 5)

Make sure you try this quick and easy side dish. The sauce can also be used on other steamed vegetables such as green beans, yellow squash, or cauliflower.

2 pounds broccoli, chopped
1 cup water
Juice of 2 fresh lemons
1/4 cup water
1 Tablespoon cornstarch (or potato starch for Passover)

Steam broccoli over water in a large pot for several minutes until tender.
In a separate pot over medium heat constantly stir lemon juice, water, and cornstarch until the sauce thickens (about 2 minutes). Serve sauce over steamed broccoli while warm.

Total calories per serving: 64    Fat: 0 grams    Protein: 6 gram
Carbohydrates: 14 grams    Fiber: 7 grams

## FROM LEPRECHAUN CAKE AND OTHER TALES
## FOURTH OF JULY GARBANZO BEAN BURGERS
## (MAKES 6 BURGERS)

2 cups pre-cooked or canned garbanzo beans (chickpeas), drained and mashed
1 stalk celery, finely chopped
1 carrot, finely chopped
1/4 cup small onion, peeled and finely chopped
1/4 cup whole wheat pastry flour
Salt and pepper to taste
2 teaspoons vegetable oil

Mix all ingredients except for cooking oil in a bowl. Form 6 flat patties. Fry in
oiled pan over medium-high heat until burgers are golden brown. Turn burgers
over and fry on the other side until done. Serve alone or with tomato sauce,
ketchup, or barbecue sauce.

Total calories per serving: 133    Fat: 3 grams    Protein: 5 grams
Carbohydrates: 23 grams    Sodium: 250 milligrams    Fiber: 2 grams

## FROM CONVENIENTLY VEGAN
## TEMPEH STUFFED POTATOES
## (SERVES 5)

5 baking potatoes (about 3 pounds, scrubbed)
8-ounce package of tempeh, chopped into 1-inch cubes

1 small onion finely chopped
1/8 teaspoon garlic powder
1/8 teaspoon cumin
2 teaspoons oil
1/2 cup boiling water

Preheat oven to 400 degrees. Bake potatoes about 1 hour or until done. Remove from oven.

Meanwhile, in a separate, large non-stick frying pan, sauté tempeh, onion, and seasonings in oil over medium-high heat for 10 minutes.

When the potatoes are done, split them in half lengthwise. Scoop out the cooked potato, leaving a 1/4-inch shell. Mash the potatoes with the water and mix in the tempeh mixture. Stuff the mixture into the potato shell and serve two halves per person immediately. You can also reheat the stuffed potatoes and serve at another time.

Total calories per serving: 332     Fat: 6 grams     Carbohydrates: 60 grams
Protein: 13 grams     Sodium: 19 milligrams     Fiber: 5 grams     High in iron

## FROM NO CHOLESTEROL PASSOVER RECIPES
## SWEET POTATO KUGEL
## (SERVES 12)

6 small sweet potatoes, peeled and grated
3 apples, peeled and grated
1 cup of raisins
1 cup of matzo meal
2 teaspoons cinnamon
1 cup walnuts, chopped (optional)
1 cup fruit juice or water

Preheat oven to 375 degrees. Mix ingredients together. Press into a large baking dish. Bake 45 minutes at 375 degrees until crisp on top. Serve.

Total Calories per serving: 156     Fat: 1 gram     Protein: 2 grams
Carbohydrates: 38 grams

## FROM No CHOLESTEROL PASSOVER RECIPES
## STUFFED CABBAGE II
## (SERVES 6-8)

Small head of cabbage
4 teaspoons of oil
2 small onions, chopped finely
1-1/2 cups matzo farfel or 4 pieces of matzo crushed
1 cup of raisins
2 stalks of celery, chopped finely
2 Tablespoons red dry wine (optional)
2/3 cup apple juice
1/2 cup applesauce
29-ounce can tomato sauce
1 cup water

Steam head of cabbage in water until leaves are soft. Remove cabbage from water, cool, and separate leaves.

In oil sauté onions, farfel, raisins, and celery over medium heat for 10 minutes. Add wine, juice, and applesauce. Simmer 5 more minutes.

Preheat oven to 375 degrees. Place some stuffing on each cabbage leaf and fold ends in. Lay in deep baking dish with folded cabbage ends down. Mix tomato sauce with water. Pour sauce over cabbage so leaves remain moist and don't dry out. Bake at 375 degrees for 30 minutes or until heated through.

Total Calories per serving: 268     Fat: 3 grams     Protein: 4 grams
Carbohydrates: 62 grams

## FROM MEATLESS MEALS FOR WORKING PEOPLE
## VEGETABLE POT PIE
## (SERVES 8)

CRUST: This is a quick crust that can be used in many different recipes. (In a rush, use a store-bought pie crust.)

2 cups whole wheat pastry flour or unbleached white flour
(note: use pastry flour, not regular whole wheat flour)
1/2 teaspoon salt
1/2 cup vegan margarine
1/2 cup water

Mix flour and salt in a bowl. Work in margarine with fingers. Add water, stirring as little as possible to form a ball. Divide into 2 equal balls and roll out to 1/8-inch thickness. Prick pie shells and bake in pie pans at 400 degrees for 10 minutes.

VEGETABLE FILLING:
1/2 cup vegetable broth
1 cup chopped onions
1 cup celery, chopped
1/2 cup carrots, chopped
1-1/4 cups peas (fresh or frozen)

Sauté above ingredients in broth until onions are soft. In a separate bowl, mix the following:

1/4 cup oil
1/2 cup unbleached white flour
1-2/3 cups water
1/2 teaspoon garlic powder
1 teaspoon salt
1/3 teaspoon pepper

Preheat oven to 350 degrees. Add above mixture to sautéed vegetables. Pour into one pie shell and cover with the other pie shell. Bake at 350 degrees until crust is brown (approximately 15-20 minutes).

Total calories per serving: 320    Fat: 18 grams    Protein: 7 grams
Carbohydrate: 34 grams

## FROM SIMPLY VEGAN
## SPICY SAUTÉED TOFU WITH PEAS
## (SERVES 4)

This dish is high in iron, protein, and calcium.

2 pounds tofu, cut into small cubes
1 Tablespoon oil
1/4 cup water
1 teaspoon dill weed
1/2 teaspoon each basil, cumin, turmeric, and curry
2 cloves garlic, minced
2 Tablespoons tamari or soy sauce
1/4 cup nutritional yeast (optional)
10-ounce box frozen peas, thawed
1/2 cup cashew pieces (optional)

Stir-fry all the ingredients except the peas and cashews for 5 minutes over medi-um-high heat. Add peas and cashews and heat 5 minutes longer over low heat. Serve hot.

Total calories per serving: 256    Fat: 15 grams    Protein: 22 grams
Carbohydrates: 14 grams    Sodium: 580 milligrams    High in iron and calcium

## FROM CONVENIENTLY VEGAN
## QUICK SLOPPY JOES
## (SERVES 5)

Serve this dish on whole-wheat buns or over baked potatoes.

Small onion, chopped
2 teaspoons oil
Two 8-ounce packages tempeh, grated
2 teaspoons chili powder
1/2 teaspoon garlic powder
1/4 teaspoon salt
6-ounce can tomato paste
2 cups water

Sauté onion in oil in a large frying pan over medium heat for 2 minutes. Add tempeh and stir-fry 5 minutes longer.

Reduce heat, add remaining ingredients, and simmer 5 minutes. Serve warm.

Total calories per serving: 234    Fat: 9 grams    Protein: 19 grams
Carbohydrates: 24 grams    Sodium: 400 milligrams    High in iron

## FROM THE ARTICLE "COOKING WITH POTATOES," VEGET-ARIAN JOURNAL (MAY/JUNE 2000) BY NANCY BERKOFF
## SWEET POTATO SLAW
## (MAKES SIX 6-OUNCE SERVINGS)

This slaw has a vibrant color and a milder flavor than traditional cabbage slaw. Be sure to use fresh sweet potatoes or yams.

Dressing:
1/4 cup vegan mayonnaise
1/4 cup silken tofu (plain soy yogurt can be used for more "tang")
2 Tablespoons orange juice concentrate
1 Tablespoon lemon juice
1 teaspoon minced fresh garlic
1 teaspoon black pepper

Slaw:
2 1/2 cups shredded raw sweet potato
1/2 cup shredded raw broccoli stalks
1/4 cup walnuts
1/4 cup raisins
2 teaspoons lemon zest
1 teaspoon orange zest

In a nonreactive bowl, combine all dressing ingredients and mix until blended.

In a large bowl, combine all slaw ingredients and toss to combine. Add dressing to slaw and mix until slaw is well coated. Refrigerate, covered, until ready to serve. Will last up to 2 days in the refrigerator.

Total calories per serving: 168     Fat: 8 grams     Carbohydrates: 24 grams
Protein: 3 grams     Sodium: 44 milligrams     Fiber: 2 grams

## FROM THE ARTICLE "NEATBALLS," *VEGETARIAN JOURNAL* (MARCH/APRIL 2001) BY NANCY BERKOFF
## TOFU BALLS
## (Serves 5)

These crunchy, toasty balls also make good burgers. You have the option of frying or baking. Make a double batch and freeze one batch; this makes a great quick dinner. Just heat the tofu balls in tomato or mushroom sauce and serve with rice or pasta or in pita, tortillas, or rolls as a hot "neatball" sandwich.

2 cups drained and crumbled firm tofu
1 clove garlic
1/8 cup minced onions
1/2 cup wheat germ
1/2 cup dry breadcrumbs
1 Tablespoon soy sauce
1/4 cup chopped fresh parsley
1/2 cup minced celery
1/4 cup chopped bell peppers
1/4 cup water or 1/4 cup carrot juice
Oil for frying (about 1/8 cup)

In a large bowl mash tofu until almost smooth. Add all ingredients except water and combine until well mixed. Slowly add water or juice until mixture is thick enough to form balls.

Form into small balls and refrigerate for 30 minutes. Fry in oil until browned or bake (at 350 degrees) for 20 minutes, until heated and browned.

Total calories per serving fried: 290     Fat: 16 grams     Carbohydrates: 20 grams
Protein: 21 grams     Sodium: 321 milligrams     Fiber: 5 grams

Total calories per serving baked: 242     Fat: 11 grams     Carbohydrates: 20 grams
Protein: 21 grams     Sodium: 321 milligrams     Fiber: 5 grams

FROM THE ARTICLE "NEATBALLS," *VEGETARIAN JOURNAL*
(MARCH/APRIL 2001) BY NANCY BERKOFF
## MUSHROOM AND HAZELNUT SNACKING BALLS
(SERVES 6)

The dough from this recipe can be shaped into balls and served as a cold appetizer on a bed of baby greens or cold couscous; pressed into a loaf pan and sliced (as a vegan paté); spread on veggies or crackers; or used as a sandwich spread - your choice!

Vegetable oil spray
1/2 medium onion, chopped
1 cup chopped fresh button mushrooms
2 cloves garlic, minced
1 cup whole hazelnuts (also called filberts)
1/4 cup chopped fresh parsley
1 teaspoon soy sauce
1/2 teaspoon onion powder
2 teaspoons nutritional yeast (see note)
1 teaspoon cracked black pepper

In a medium frying pan, spray vegetable oil and heat. Sauté onions, mushrooms, and garlic until soft (about 4 minutes). Place vegetables and all remaining ingredients in a blender or food processor and blend until smooth. Mixture will be very thick. Form into small balls or patties and refrigerate for at least 30 minutes before serving.

Note: Red Star's Vegetarian Support Formula nutritional yeast is a good source of vitamin B 12. Look for this product in your local natural foods store.

Total calories per serving: 134   Fat: 12 grams   Carbohydrates: 5 grams
Protein: 4 grams   Sodium: 59 milligrams   Fiber: 2 grams

FROM THE ARTICLE "FINGER FOODS," *VEGETARIAN JOURNAL* (MARCH/APRIL 1999) BY NANCY BERKOFF

## FABULOUS FAJITAS
## (SERVES 4)

This recipe takes advantage of the textures and colors of different vegetables.

6 cups thinly sliced bell peppers, assorted colors
1 cup thinly sliced yellow or red onions
Vegetable oil spray
3 cups thinly sliced portabello mushroom caps
2 cloves garlic, minced
1/2 teaspoon red chili flakes
1/2 teaspoon black pepper
3 Tablespoons fresh lime or lemon juice
4 Tablespoons chopped fresh cilantro
8 tortillas, warmed

In a large nonstick frying pan, cook and toss peppers and onions until tender (but still crisp). Set aside.

In same skillet, spray oil, allow to heat, and sauté portabellos and garlic until soft (about 3 minutes). Return peppers and onions to skillet, add chili flakes, pepper, juice, and cilantro. Cook until juice evaporates, about 3 minutes. Serve mixture wrapped in tortillas. Garnish with salsa, guacamole or chopped tomatoes, onions, and fresh chilies.

Total calories per serving: 354    Fat: 6 grams    Carbohydrates: 68 grams
Protein: 11 grams    Sodium: 346 milligrams    Fiber: 7 grams    High in Iron

FROM THE ARTICLE "EATING OFF THE STREETS: FOOD CRUISING IN THAILAND," *VEGETARIAN JOURNAL* (JULY/AUGUST 1999) BY NANCY BERKOFF

## PHAD THAI
## (SERVES 6)

This most popular of Thai dishes is found in sit-down restaurants and at food stalls. We found this dish to be perfect for a hot dinner or served as a cold lunch.

8 ounces rice vermicelli
1 Tablespoon peanut oil (see note below)
1/2 cup diced red or green bell pepper
3 cloves garlic, minced
3/4 cup chopped Roma tomatoes
1/4 cup thinly sliced water chestnuts or fresh jicama
3/4 cup firm tofu, cut into small cubes
2 Tablespoons soy sauce
2 Tablespoons fresh lime or lemon juice
3 Tablespoons chopped fresh cilantro
1/4 cup whole snow peas
2 whole scallions, chopped
1/4 cup peanut granules
1/4 cup soybean sprouts

Boil 3 quarts of water in a large pot. When water boils, turn heat off, add vermicelli, and cook until al dente. Drain and set aside.

In a wok or deep skillet, heat oil. Add pepper and garlic and stir-fry until veggies are soft. Stir in tomatoes, water chestnuts, and tofu, and stir-fry until well-combined, about 3 minutes. Add soy sauce and lime juice and allow to simmer for 2 minutes. Stir in cilantro and snow peas.

Toss vermicelli and veggie combo together. Garnish with scallions, peanuts, and sprouts.

Note: If you are an adept stir-fryer, you can substitute a liberal spray of vegetable oil for the liquid oil. Peanut oil is not essential, but does give an authentic flavor.

Total calories per serving: 300    Fat: 8 grams    Carbohydrates: 52 grams
Protein: 11 grams    Sodium: 423 milligrams    Fiber: 1 gram

## FROM THE ARTICLE "EATING OFF THE STREETS: FOOD CRUISING IN THAILAND," *VEGETARIAN JOURNAL* (JULY/AUGUST 1999) BY NANCY BERKOFF

## NOODLES WITH SPICY PEANUT SAUCE (SERVES 6)

The sauce for this dish can be made a day ahead. Cashews or almonds can be used instead of peanuts.

3/4 cup peanut oil
1 cup raw nuts
1/2 cup brewed black tea
6 cloves garlic, minced
1-1/2 Tablespoons minced fresh ginger
2 fresh chilies, chopped (choose your heat)
1 teaspoon orange juice concentrate
1 Tablespoon tamari
1/4 cup fresh lime or lemon juice
1 teaspoon chili flakes
1 cup cucumber slices
1/4 cup chopped cilantro
1-1/2 pounds noodles, cooked and drained (try rice vermicelli or mung bean noodles)

In a wok or deep skillet, heat oil until almost smoking. Add the nuts and stir until lightly toasted. Remove from heat and drain well. Save the oil.

In a food processor, grind the nuts into a coarse paste. Add a small amount of tea and all the garlic, ginger, and chilies. Grind until blended. Add the remaining tea, juice concentrate, tamari, fresh juice, and chili flakes, and blend again until ingredients are incorporated.

Heat a small amount of the reserved oil in a skillet. Add the sauce and mix quickly until combined.

Place sauce in a serving bowl and garnish with cucumbers and cilantro. Allow each diner to toss the desired amount of sauce with the cooked noodles.

Total calories per serving: 774    Fat: 19 grams    Carbohydrates: 148 grams
Protein: 20 grams    Sodium: 178 milligrams    Fiber: 2 grams    High in Iron

## DAVIDA'S SPICY GARLIC NOODLES AND TOFU (SERVES 2-4)

The core ingredients to this simple, yet filling, dish are just noodles, tofu, garlic, oil, and soy sauce. If you are looking for a quick meal, this can be made in 10 minutes. Also, almost everything can be substituted depending on what you have at hand (i.e. linguini for lo mein noodles; seitan or chopped veggie burger for tofu).

1-2 Tablespoon(s) oil (I prefer sesame oil, wok oil, or garlic oil)
1/2 medium sweet onion, chopped
1 Tablespoon chopped garlic
4 ounces marinated tofu
1 bunch broccoli, florets only, discard stalks
1/2 cup baby corn, drained (optional)
1/2 red pepper, chopped (optional)
8-ounce packet of lo mein noodles
2 Tablespoons soy sauce
Pinch of ginger powder
1 teaspoon garlic-infused vinegar (optional)
1 teaspoon red pepper flakes (optional)
1 teaspoon sesame seeds (optional)

Sauté the onion and garlic in a little of the oil over medium-high heat in a large frying pan. Boil water in a pot for the noodles. In a steamer or separate pan, steam the broccoli for 2 minutes and set aside. Add tofu, red peppers, baby corn, and red pepper flakes to the onion and garlic just before you add the noodles to the boiling water.

Noodles should boil, depending on thickness, for approximately 5 minutes. Drain and add noodles to the frying pan. Add steamed broccoli at this point, along with the remaining oil, soy sauce, vinegar, and sesame seeds. Once noodles and vegetables are moist with the soy sauce and oil mixture it is done.

Variations: Add mandarin orange sauce for sweet and spicy noodles, or add some chili for an extra spicy dish. Other vegetables can be added depending on taste. I like to use green beans, snow peas, corn, water chestnuts, bean sprouts, green peas, and straw mushrooms. Fresh cilantro is a fantastic addition as well.

Total calories per serving: 580     Fat: 12 grams     Carbohydrates: 95 grams
Protein: 24 grams     Sodium: 1038 milligrams     Fiber: 6 grams
High in iron and calcium

# DESSERTS

## FROM VEGAN IN VOLUME
## SOPHISTICATED POACHED PEARS
## (YIELDS 25 PEARS)

20 ounces red dessert wine*
8 ounces strawberry jam
  *(apricot glaze, or mixed berry or apple jam may be substituted)*
4 ounces orange juice
1 ounce orange zest
1/2 ounce lemon zest
2 cinnamon sticks
5 whole cloves
1 ounce ground ginger
25 pears, fresh (5 ounce)

In a braising pan, combine wine, jam, juice, zests, cinnamon, cloves, and ginger. Simmer. Place pears in poaching liquid and simmer until pears are soft, about 20 minutes. Remove pears and allow to cool. Strain poaching liquid. Can be used as a hot sauce by returning to heat and allowing to reduce until thickened. Can be used as a cold garnish by freezing strained liquid, removing from freezer, and chopping, as a pear "ice."

* Note: Port, red Zinfandel, and Muscadet are good wines to use.

Total calories per pear: 147    Fat: 1 gram    Protein: 1 gram
Carbohydrate: 31 grams    Sodium: 3 milligrams

## FROM SIMPLY VEGAN
## SOY WHIPPED CREAM
## (MAKES ENOUGH TO TOP ONE PIE)

1/4 cup soymilk
1/2 cup oil
1 Tablespoon maple syrup
1/2 teaspoon vanilla extract

Place soymilk and 1/4 cup oil in a blender. Blend at highest speed and slowly drizzle in remaining 1/4 cup oil. Blend in syrup and vanilla. Add a little more oil, if necessary, to thicken. Chill and serve.

Note: This recipe does not work well on damp, rainy days.

Total calories per serving (1/6 recipe): 175    Protein: 1 gram    Fat: 18 grams
Carbohydrates: 3 grams    Sodium: 5 milligrams    Fiber: 0 grams

## FROM SIMPLY VEGAN
## CHOCOLATE PUDDING
## (SERVES 3)

1-1/2 cups soymilk
3 Tablespoons cornstarch
1/4 teaspoon vanilla
1/4 cup maple syrup
1/4 cup cocoa powder
2 bananas, sliced (optional)

Whisk all the ingredients (except the bananas) together in a pot. Cook over medium heat, stirring constantly until pudding thickens.

Remove pot from stove. Stir in sliced bananas, if desired. Chill for at least 15 minutes before serving.

Variation: Replace chocolate powder with non-dairy carob powder.

Total calories per serving: 198    Protein: 7 grams    Carbohydrates: 36 grams
Fat: 4 grams    Sodium: 155 milligrams    Fiber: negligible

**FROM SIMPLY VEGAN**
## KAREN'S CREAMY RICE PUDDING
## (SERVES 8)

2 cups pre-cooked rice
1-1/2 teaspoons cinnamon
1 Tablespoon vanilla extract
1 cup raisins
1/2 cup slivered almonds (optional)
3-4 cups soymilk

Mix all the ingredients together in a pot. Simmer until the mixture begins to thicken (15-20 minutes), stirring occasionally.

Remove from stove and serve hot or cold.

Total calories per serving: 175    Protein: 5 grams    Carbohydrates: 34 grams
Fat: 3 grams    Sodium: 53 milligrams    Fiber: 2 grams

**FROM NO CHOLESTEROL PASSOVER RECIPES**
## FESTIVE MACAROONS I
## (MAKES ABOUT 20)

These delicious, eggless macaroons should be eaten in moderation.

2 cups shredded coconut
4 ripe bananas, mashed
1/4 cup cocoa
1/2 cup walnuts, chopped

Preheat oven to 350 degrees. Blend ingredients together. Form pyramids on a cookie sheet. Bake at 350 degrees for 20 minutes.

Total calories per macaroon: 89    Fat: 5 grams    Protein: 1 gram
Carbohydrates: 11 grams

FROM SIMPLY VEGAN
# HEAVENLY CHOCOLATE CUPCAKES
## (MAKES 18)

1 cup molasses
1/2 cup soymilk
2 cups non-dairy, dark chocolate chips
6 Tablespoons soy margarine
1 teaspoon vanilla extract
4 Tablespoons cornstarch
2 cups unbleached white flour
1 teaspoon baking soda
1/2 cup soymilk

Preheat oven to 275 degrees. Combine molasses, soymilk, and chips in a small pan. Heat on low, stirring occasionally, until chips melt. Remove from heat and add margarine, stirring until it softens. Add vanilla and cornstarch to mixture and stir. Add flour, baking soda, and soymilk. Mix ingredients well.

Lightly oil 18 muffin cups and divide the batter among them, filling each cup about half full. Bake for 20 minutes at 375 degrees. Cool cupcakes before removing from tins.

Variations: Replace chocolate chips with non-dairy carob chips, or add 3/4 cup chopped walnuts to batter before baking.

Total calories per cupcake: 231     Protein: 3 grams     Carbohydrates: 34 grams
Fat: 11 grams     Sodium: 119 milligrams     Fiber: 1 gram

## FROM <u>NO CHOLESTEROL PASSOVER RECIPES</u>
# MACAROONS II
## (MAKES ABOUT 10)

This is a simple eggless macaroon recipe. Eat in moderation.

1 cup shredded coconut
2 ripe bananas, peeled and mashed

Preheat oven to 350 degrees. Mix ingredients together. Spoon onto oiled baking pan and shape into pyramids. Bake at 350 degrees for 20 minutes.

Total calories per macaroon: 68     Fat: 3 grams     Protein: 1 gram
Carbohydrates: 10 grams

## FROM <u>MEATLESS MEALS FOR WORKING PEOPLE</u>
# EGGLESS BANANA PANCAKES
## (SERVES 2)

1/2 cup rolled oats
1/2 cup flour
1/2 cup cornmeal (white or yellow)
1 Tablespoon baking powder
1-1/2 cups water
2 to 3 bananas, peeled and sliced or mashed
2 teaspoons oil

Mix all the ingredients except oil, together in a bowl. Pour about 1/4 cup of the batter into oiled, preheated frying pan. (The batter will make 4 pancakes). Fry over low heat on one side until lightly browned, then flip over pancake and fry on the other side until done.

Variations: Add raisins, blueberries, or chopped apples to batter.

Total calories per serving: 482     Protein: 12 grams     Carbohydrates: 97 grams
Fat: 8 grams     Fiber: 9 grams     High in calcium and iron

## FROM THE LOWFAT JEWISH VEGETARIAN COOKBOOK
# ROMANIAN APRICOT DUMPLINGS
## (SERVES 8, 3 DUMPLINGS EACH)

Although this dessert is not easy to prepare, it's so good that it's worth the effort. You can substitute different fruit such as peaches.

4 pounds potatoes, peeled and chopped
10 cups of water
1/2 teaspoon of salt
1/2 cup maple syrup
2 cups whole wheat pastry flour
6 ripe apricots, pitted
1 teaspoon oil
2 teaspoons cinnamon

Cook potatoes in salted water in large pot over medium heat until tender. Drain and cool, saving liquid to use later. Mash potatoes once (not too much). Stir in maple syrup. Slowly add flour to make a dough that's not too thick, but not too sticky either.

Chop apricots into quarters. Take a handful of dough and flatten with your palm. Put chopped apricot quarter in center of dough. Roll dough into ball, covering apricot. Repeat process to make approximately 24 dumplings.

Bring potato water that was set aside earlier back to a boil. Add oil. Place six dumplings into boiling water. Dumplings are done when they float to the top of the pot. Remove from boiling water and strain them in a colander. Repeat this process four times. Sprinkle dumplings with cinnamon and serve warm.

Total calories per serving: 363    Fat: 1 gram    Protein: 8 grams
Carbohydrate: 82 grams

FROM VEGAN IN VOLUME
# DON'T TELL THE KIDS IT'S TOFU CHEESECAKE
## YIELD: 2 NINE-INCH PIES; 10 SLICES EACH

This recipe is very versatile and can be used for everyday or holidays. Top with seasonal fruit for extra color.

CRUST:
2 pounds Graham cracker crumbs*
4 ounces maple syrup
1/2 ounce orange extract

*Note: be sure to choose vegan graham crackers that do not contain honey to make the crumbs.

FILLING:
2 pounds silken tofu
3 ounces orange juice concentrate, thawed
2 ounces apple butter
1/2 ounce orange zest
1 ounce cornstarch (dissolved in 3 ounces of soy or rice milk)

Preheat oven to 350 degrees. In a mixing bowl combine crumbs, syrup, and orange extract until crumbs are moistened. Divide between two 9-inch layer pans, and press firmly into pans. Bake 5 minutes and allow to cool.

In blender, combine remaining ingredients until smooth. Pour into crust and bake for 30 minutes, or until top is slightly browned. Cool and refrigerate until firm and set, about 2 hours.

VARIATION: If desired, press crust into individual muffin tins to create "personal" cheesecakes.

Total calories per serving: 259     Fat: 6 grams     Protein: 6 grams
Carbohydrate: 45 grams     Sodium: 280 milligrams

**FROM THE ARTICLE "*A-MAIZE-ING* ENDINGS WITH CORN,"**
***VEGETARIAN JOURNAL* (JULY/AUGUST 2000)**

# CORN AND NUT BREAD
## (MAKES 8 SERVINGS FROM A 2-QUART BAKING DISH)

1 cup white cornmeal
1 cup boiling water
1 cup soymilk
2 teaspoons lemon juice
1/3 cup soft tofu
3 teaspoons vegetable oil
3 Tablespoons softened vegan margarine
4 ounces cooked corn
1 teaspoon salt
2 teaspoons baking powder
1/2 teaspoon baking soda
1/2 cup finely ground nuts
Vegetable oil spray

Preheat oven to 375 degrees.

Place cornmeal in a bowl, pour water over, and allow to soften (about 2 minutes). Blend milk, lemon juice, tofu, and vegetable oil together and add to cornmeal. Combine well. Add in the margarine and corn and stir well.

Stir together the salt, baking powder, soda, and nuts and add to corn mixture. Mix to combine.

Place batter in sprayed 2-quart baking pan or casserole pan. Bake for 45 minutes, or until top is golden brown and knife inserted in middle comes out clean.

Total calories per serving: 184     Fat: 12 grams     Carbohydrates: 17 grams
Protein: 4 grams     Sodium: 559 milligrams     Fiber: 2 grams

## FROM MEATLESS MEALS FOR WORKING PEOPLE
## OATMEAL COOKIES
## (MAKES 40 COOKIES)

1/2 cup vegan margarine
1-1/2 cups (15 ounces) applesauce
1/2 cup molasses or maple syrup
2 large ripe bananas, peeled
1-3/4 cups whole wheat pastry flour
1 teaspoon baking soda
1 teaspoon baking powder
1 teaspoon cinnamon
1 teaspoon nutmeg
3 cups rolled oats
1/2 cup raisins or chopped dates

Preheat oven to 400 degrees. Cream together margarine, applesauce, molasses or maple syrup, and bananas in a large bowl. Add remaining ingredients and mix well. Drop a rounded tablespoon of batter at a time on a lightly oiled cookie sheet. Bake 8 minutes at 400 degrees. Allow to cool before removing from cookie sheet.

Variation: Add chopped walnuts or chopped apples to batter.

Total calories per cookie: 84    Fat: 3 grams    Protein: 2 grams
Iron: 1 milligram    Carbohydrate: 15 grams    Fiber: 1 gram

# ADDITIONAL RECIPES

If you are looking for specific recipes or just want to experiment, there are also good vegetarian recipe websites and databases online:

✱ FatFree: The Low Fat Vegetarian Recipe Archive - www.fatfree.com
✱ The International Vegetarian Union Recipes - www.ivu.org/recipes
✱ Veggies Unite! - www.vegweb.com

The online recipe websites and databases offer links to thousands of recipes, from the standard to the exotic. These are a few we are asked about frequently:

## VEGAN MARSHMALLOWS

There is a recipe for vegan marshmallows online at
www.fatfree.com/recipes/condiments/marshmallows

## VEGAN CAKES

Recipes for vegan cakes can be found online at www.vrg.org/recipes/
vegancakes.htm and www.vrg.org/journal/vj98sep/989party.htm.

## WHERE CAN I FIND VEGETARIAN COOKIE RECIPES?

Try www.fatfree.com/recipes/cookies and
www.vegweb.com/frames/index/sweets/index-frames.shtml.

## MAKING SOYMILK

Try www.fatfree.com/recipes/drinks/soymilk-2 and
www.fatfree.com/recipes/drinks/soymilk.

## RICE AND ALMOND MILKS

Go to www.vegweb.com/frames/index/drink/index-frames.shtml.

## MAKING TOFU
Go to www.ivu.org/recipes/nct/tofu3.html.

## USING TOFU

Try www.vegweb.com/frames/index/tofu/index-frames.shtml and www.fatfree.com/recipes/tofu/.

## SOY YOGURT

There's a recipe at www.ivu.org/recipes/extras/queen-p.html

## WHEAT GLUTEN (SEITAN)

Here are several links to recipes for seitan. All you really need is flour and water to make it. You can add spices and such if you want to but the basic recipe is relatively simple.

www.fatfree.com/recipes/meat-analogues/basic-wholewheat-seitan
www.fatfree.com/recipes/meat-analogues/home-made-seitan
www.fatfree.com/recipes/meat-analogues/seitan-2
www.vegweb.com/frames/index/seitan/index-frames.shtml
www.ivu.org/recipes/net/seitan.html

## USING TVP

There are some recipe ideas at
www.ivu.org/recipes/net/tvp.html
www.fatfree.com/recipes/meat-analogues/
www.vegweb.com/frames/index/tvp/index-frames.shtml

Also see page 240 for a list of suggested cookbooks.

# CHAPTER 6

# VEGETARIAN PRODUCTS

When people first become vegetarian the new foods they encounter, such as seitan and TVP, often sound mysterious and complicated. Then there is the second problem - where to find these new foods! This chapter explains some common vegetarian products and also where one can buy them. Ten years ago, this chapter would have been much slimmer and offered much more obscure sources for purchase. Today, many of the products vegetarians routinely enjoy can be found in neighborhood supermarkets and nearby natural foods stores. As the interest in vegetarianism continues to grow, we see a correlating increase in vegetarian products.

## WHAT IS SEITAN?

Seitan is also known as wheat gluten. It is a protein found in wheat. It is commonly made by mixing whole wheat flour, water, and spices. The starch is removed by rinsing until the gluten is obtained. It is simmered and when done, it can be fried, baked, or used in stew and sandwiches. Turtle Island Foods and Now and Zen both make holiday meat alternatives from seitan (see page 122). It is also used to make mock "cheesesteak," cutlets, mock "poultry," and "beef" stew. Seitan can also be used to make burgers; it is chewier than most other meat alternatives, such as TVP and soy.

117

Try this recipe for seitan by Dez Figueria from <u>Vegan Handbook</u>:

To make 3-1/2 to 5 pounds of gluten from scratch.
1. Mix 12 cups of flour with 7 cups of water until all the flour is moistened. Gather dough into a ball. After the dough begins to hold together, knead twenty minutes. The dough should be smooth and springy.
2. Place dough in a large bowl, cover completely with water and let rest one hour.
3. Place a large bowl of cool water in the sink. Adjust faucet so that a continuous trickle of cool water runs into the bowl.
4. Break off an apple-sized piece of dough and put it in the water in the bowl, stretch and squeeze the dough in the water so that the milky starch begins to separate. It takes about 15 minutes of washing for each piece of dough. Keep replacing water in bowl, keeping the dough under water as much as possible. Properly developed gluten is slightly iridescent and feels squeaky. When washing is complete, the rinse water should be clear.
5. Place the washed gluten in a container of cold water. Repeat step 4 until all gluten has been washed.
6. Raw gluten can be boiled for 20 minutes in water or a flavored broth, roasted slowly in broth, shaped into patties and fried, ground, and pan fried, or mixed with peanut butter and tomato paste and baked. Boiled gluten can also be frozen and thawed for a different texture.

**Flour**: Any wheat flour will produce gluten (except self-rising). My flour of choice is stone ground, whole, hard red winter wheat from Arrowhead Mills, preferably Tascosa, or other hard red winter wheat varieties. Refined, bleached white flour probably has the lowest yield. It is okay to mix several different types of flour. Any type of wheat flour you have on hand will make gluten.

Stone ground whole wheat flour has the bran still in it, which adds dimension to the gluten texture and fiber to your diet. Some of the bran will be lost in the washing process. Another good flour to try is red durum which produces a golden creamy gluten.

Protein in wheat flour does vary according to the type of wheat it is made from. Hard spring wheat is about 12 to 18% protein. Hard winter wheat is about 10 to 15% protein.

The complete article this recipe is excerpted from is available in <u>Vegan Handbook</u>, edited by Debra Wasserman. See page 270 for more details.

## WHERE CAN I BUY SEITAN?

Are you looking for a ready-made product or a mix? The Mail Order Catalog offers both. They have a paper and online catalog. You can request a paper catalog by writing PO Box 99, Summertown, TN 38483; (800) 695-2241. The online catalog is at www.healthy-eating.com.

You may also want to check out the Dixie Diners Club. Their webpage is at www.dixiediner.com. Write PO Box 1969, Tomball, TX 77377, or call (800) 233-3668, Ext. 300 for a paper catalog.

Is there a natural foods market near you? They may have many different seitan products, both refrigerated and mixes. Check the refrigerated section near the meat analogs and also the frozen section for products such as Meat of Wheat. Another Internet source is www.nomeat.com. Gluten flour is often in the bulk foods section.

## WHAT IS TEMPEH?

Tempeh is made from fermented soybeans and sometimes grains (such as rice or barley) and/or vegetables. The fermentation process binds the beans together and gives tempeh a distinctive, sometimes smoky, flavor.

It is higher in fiber and lower in fat than tofu and has 19 percent of calories as protein. Tempeh can be baked, grilled, deep-fried, or stir fried. Tempeh can also be bought packaged in various flavors. Turtle Island Foods makes drumsticks for their Tofurky holiday package out of tempeh.

## WHAT IS TVP?

Textured vegetable protein, or TVP, is made from soy flour that is compressed until the protein fibers change in structure. It comes dried and it is rehydrated in hot water. TVP is available in different sizes, so if you wanted to make a stew-like dish, you could use the larger chunks, compared to the smaller pieces, which would be good for chili and sloppy joes. TVP is available in most health food stores and may come in bulk, which is cheaper. The T.V.P. Cookbook is available from Book Publishing Company. Also check out the soyfoods website at www.soyfoods.com.

## WHERE CAN I BUY TVP?

Try the bulk bins of your local natural foods store. If they don't carry it, you can try The Mail Order Catalog, which sells TVP and other vegetarian food staples. They have both a paper and online catalog. You can request a paper catalog by writing PO Box 99, Summertown, TN 38483; (800) 695-2241. The online catalog is at www.healthy-eating.com.

## WHAT IS TOFU? WHAT DO I DO WITH IT?

Tofu is a soybean product made from coagulated soymilk. It comes in a variety of textures, from silken, which is good for blending into sauces and dips, to extra firm, which holds up well to stir-frying and baking. There is a wide variety of pre-packaged tofu that are available in different flavors, from Thai to Garlic-Mushroom to Italian. Tofu, depending on how it is used, can be used in place of cheese, dairy, eggs, and meat.

There are two good cookbooks, Tofu Cookery, by Louise Hagler, and Tofu and Soyfoods Cookery, by Peter Goblitz, that offer only tofu and soyfoods recipes. Also, see page 130 in the Cooking and Baking chapter.

Additionally, check out the US Soyfoods Directory website at www.soyfoods.com.

## WHAT IS VEGETARIAN MINCE? I RECENTLY BOUGHT A COOKBOOK AUTHORED BY THE LATE LINDA MCCARTNEY AND SHE MENTIONS THIS MINCE IN QUITE A FEW RECIPES.

Based on Linda's Kitchen (page 186), it appears she is referring to a ground meat substitute. This is traditionally part of British cuisine. There are pre-made vegetarian mincemeat items available in the UK.

If you are in the US, you could try these pre-made products:
    Gimme Lean by Lightlife Foods
    Just Like Ground! by Yves
    Morningstar Farms Ground Meatless
    Nature's Ground Meatless
    Protein Crumbles by Green Giant
    Vegan Crumbles from Natural Touch
You could also try using TVP.

## WHERE CAN I FIND VEGETARIAN CHEESES? WHAT ABOUT VEGAN CHEESES?

There is a list of vegetarian cheeses on our website at www.vrg.org/nutshell/cheesebybrand.htm. Also take a look at Trader Joe's lists: East Coast: www.traderjoes.com/tj/products/brochures/rennet_east.stm and West Coast: www.traderjoes.com/tj/products/brochures/rennet_west.stm

An article in the November/December 2000 issue of *Vegetarian Journal* offers a "Guide to Vegan Cheese, Yogurt, and Other Non-Dairy Product Alternatives" (www.vrg.org/journal/vj2000nov/2000novnondairy.htm). VeganRella, Soymage, and Soy of Joy Instead O'Cheese are some vegan cheese manufacturers.

Crumbled tofu can be substituted for cottage cheese or ricotta cheese in lasagna and similar dishes. Also see page 131 in the Cooking and Baking chapter.

## WHAT IS BREWERS YEAST (A.K.A. NUTRITIONAL YEAST)? HOW IS IT MADE?

Brewer's yeast is not the same as nutritional yeast. Brewer's yeast, as the name implies, was originally used by beer brewers. The commercial source is fungal. Although it is a good source of B vitamins and protein, it may cause allergic reactions in some people.

Nutritional yeast (Saccharomyces cerevisiae) is a food yeast, which comes as yellow flakes or powder and is grown on a molasses solution. It can often be used by those sensitive to other yeasts. It is prized for its cheesy taste and high nutritional content. It is a reliable source of high-quality, easily-assimilated protein and is a source of B-complex vitamins. It is an inactive yeast which means it has no fermenting power, as does the live yeast used in leavening or brewing, rendering it more digestible. Nutritional yeast is not dried torula (candida utilis), a yeast-like organism which is grown on waste-products from the wood pulp industry, nor is it brewer's yeast or baking yeast. None of these products should ever be substituted in recipes calling for nutritional yeast.

Red Star T-6635+ has been tested and shown to contain active B-12. This brand of yeast is often labeled as Vegetarian Support Formula with or without T-6635+ in parentheses following this name. It is a reliable source of vitamin B-12.

***

## WHERE CAN I BUY NUTRITIONAL YEAST?

Many natural foods stores sell nutritional yeast in bulk. Red Star T-6635 Nutritional Yeast can be mail ordered from The Mail Order Catalog (PO Box 99, Summertown, TN 38483; (800) 695-2241; www.healthy-eating.com.) and Pangea (2381 Lewis Ave., Rockville, MD 20851; (301) 816-9300; www.pangeaveg.com).

***

## I'D LIKE TO KEEP CERTAIN HOLIDAY TRADITIONS, BUT LOSE THE MEAT. WHAT CAN I USE INSTEAD?

Here are some holiday meat alternatives...

Field Roast is a vegetarian meat made from grains, vegetables and legumes. It is wrapped in a cotton netting and simmered in small kettle batches. It is made with Washington state grown Pardina and French Green Petite lentils, mushrooms, fresh garlic, onions, and red wine. Field Roast's seasonings and textures are 100% plant-based. Field Roast can be simmered, chopped, minced, sautéed, grilled, and breaded. Contact Field Roast at 1225 S. Angelo St., Seattle, WA 98108; (800) 311-9497; www.fieldroast.com.

Soul Vegetarian Caterers designed a vegan "Holiday Roast Special." The meal includes Vegetarian Stuffed Roast (made with wheat gluten and cornbread), Tofu-Spinach Quiche, Potato Salad, Cole Slaw, BBQ Twists, Vegan Southern Style Macaroni and Cheese, and five kinds of pies and cakes. They can deliver anywhere in the US. For more information, call (202) 291-9244.

Turtle Island Foods also offers a complete Tofurky Vegetarian Feast, which includes a TofuRoast, Tempeh Drummettes, Tofurky 'Giblet' Gravy, and a Wishstix. For more information, contact Turtle Island Foods at PO Box 176, Hood River, OR 97031; (800) 508-8100; www.tofurky.com.

Now and Zen makes the [Un]Turkey, which come in two sizes and is completely vegan. [Un]Turkeys are made of seitan with a "skin" of soy. Now and Zen also makes Hip Whip, a dairy-free whipped topping. It comes in chocolate and vanilla. Other Now and Zen meat alternatives include UnRibs, UnChicken, and UnSteakout. For more information, contact 665 22nd St., San Francisco, CA 94107; (415) 695-2805; www.nowandzen.net.

## WHERE CAN I BUY "MOCK" TUNA?

Worthington has a mock tuna called "Tuno." It is carried in some large grocery stores, such as Trader Joe's in California. The Mail Order Catalog offers it by mail and Internet order. It can also be purchased online at www.nomeat.com.

## WHERE CAN I MAIL ORDER VEGETARIAN PRODUCTS FROM?

The Mail Order Catalog and Pangea both have good products and reputations. Contact them at The Mail Order Catalog (PO Box 99, Summertown, TN 38483; (800) 695-2241; www.healthy-eating.com.) and Pangea (2381 Lewis Ave., Rockville, MD 20851; (301) 816-9300; www.pangeaveg.com). Also try Dixie Diners Club. Their webpage is at www.dixiediner.com. Write PO Box 1969, Tomball, TX 77377, or call (800) 233-3668, Ext. 300 for a paper catalog.

To order direct from manufacturers and to access several catalogs, go to the vegetarian products links page on the VRG site at www.vrg.org/links/products.htm.

## WHERE CAN I SHOP ONLINE?

For meat analogs try www.nomeat.com and www.vegecyber.com. For personal care products, treats, and accessories try Pangea (www.pangeaveg.com) and VegEssentials (www.veganessentials.com). For shoes and other clothing alternatives try the companies linked in our Shopper's Guide to Leather Alternatives (www.vrg.org/nutshell/leather.htm).

To order direct from manufacturers and to access several catalogs go to the vegetarian products links page on the VRG site at www.vrg.org/links/products.htm.

## IS THERE SUCH A THING AS VEGETARIAN GELATIN?

There are several vegetarian gelatin substitutes, such as agar agar, guar gum, and carageenan, all of which are vegetable-based.

Agar agar and carrageenan are derived from seaweed. They should be available at your local natural foods store. Hain makes a flavored vegetarian gelatin. This should be available at a natural foods store as well. The Mail Order Catalog carries a vegetable gelatin called Emes Kosher-Jel K. You may be able to find additional vegetable gelatin through vegetarian online retailers (see above).

## I AM LOOKING FOR ALTERNATIVES TO DAIRY PRODUCTS. WHAT DO YOU SUGGEST?

It depends on whether you are looking for recipes or products to buy. If you are looking for recipes you might find the Uncheese Cookbook, by Joanne Stepaniak, helpful. It offers substitute recipes for many cheeses.

You can make great "mock" sour creams and dips out of tofu. Many vegetarian cookbooks have a recipe or two. See page 88 for a recipe for Tofu Dill Dip.

There are more and more dairy-free products on supermarket shelves. It has become easier to find dairy-free margarine, cheese, and soy, rice, and nut milks.

If you are looking for specific non-dairy substitutions, you can try Tofutti and Galaxy. Tofutti makes many non-dairy alternatives, including cream cheese and sour cream. Their websites are www.galaxyfoods.com and www.tofutti.com.

If you would like to investigate more non-dairy products go to www.vrg.org/links/products.htm.

We've done several guides to non-dairy alternatives and many are online at www.vrg.org/journal/#Food.

## IS THERE SUCH A THING AS VEGAN EGGNOG?

There sure is! WhiteWave produces Silk Soy Egg Nog. It is a seasonal favorite around the VRG office. For more information, go to www.whitewave.com.

If you can't find the product in your area, you can also try a recipe found in Cooking with PETA (Book Publishing Company).

## I JUST FOUND OUT GUMMY BEARS ARE MADE WITH GELA- TIN! IS THERE A VEGGIE BEAR AVAILABLE?

More and more companies are making vegetarian versions. Hain, Planet Harmony, and Edward and Sons all offer vegetarian versions.

Organic Mixed Fruity Jelly Bears are made by Edward & Sons, Trading Co., Inc. The candies are made from whole organic fruits, which are dried to create fruit powders. For more information, contact Edward & Sons at PO Box 1326, Carpinteria, CA 93014; (805) 684-8500.

Planet Harmony can be contacted at Harmony Foods Corp., 2200 Delaware Ave., Santa Cruz, CA 95060; (831) 457-3200; www.harmonyfoods.com.

Hain Food Group, Inc. is at 50 Charles Lindbergh Blvd., Uniondale, NY 11553; (800) 434-4246; www.westbrae.com.

## Do you know of a vegan chewing gum?

Yes, there is a vegan chewing gum available. Speakeasy® Natural Gum Rainforest Chicles is produced by Cloud Nine, a maker of other vegan candies and chocolates. It comes in six flavors: gingermint, wintergreen, cinnamon, tangerine, peppermint, and spearmint. Its primary ingredient is chicle, a tree sap that is hand tapped by chiclero farmers in Guatemala, Mexico, and Brazil. The company notes that this is an environmentally-friendly process, and provides a viable means of income for the farmers and their families. The natural flavors and colors are vegan. For more information, contact Cloud Nine at 300 Observer Hwy., Hoboken, NJ 07033 or call (800)-398-2380.

## Where would I find a salmon substitute?

Sugiyo USA, Inc. has created a vegetarian smoked "salmon." "Smokehouse Flakes" are primarily made of cornstarch, curdlan (a sugar derivative), sugar, and water. The natural flavors used are of vegetable origin. They have individual retail packs and large blocks for foodservice. For more information, contact Sugiyo USA, Inc., 3200 T Ave., PO Box 468, Anacortes, WA 98221; (260) 293-0180.

NoMeat.com (www.nomeat.com) and VegeCyber, Inc. (www.vegecyber.com) also offer a few mock fish products . Chinese and Asian markets and restaurants might also offer faux seafood. If you are vegan, be careful, as many contain whey.

## Where can I find vegan candles?

Based on the growing number of manufacturers present at The Natural Products Expo (an industry trade show), there are more and more soy based candles available. One company is Candleworks. They make candles with a trademarked soy-based wax, Phylawax. Candleworks can be reached at 2920 Industrial Park Rd., Iowa City, IA, 52240; (319) 377-6316; www.candleworks.org. Vegan retailers also offer some candles for sale.

## I HAVE BEEN VEGAN FOR A FEW MONTHS, BUT I REALLY MISS CHOCOLATE. WHERE CAN I FIND SOME DAIRY-FREE CHOCOLATE?

There are more vegan chocolate producers than you would think. Here are a few to try:

*Vegan Splendor, PO Box 163126, Sacramento, CA 95816; (916) 441-4812; www.vegansplendor.com.

*Chocolate Decadance, 1050-D Bethel Drive, Eugene, OR 97402; (541) 689-8737; www.decasa.com.

*Edward & Sons, PO Box 1326, Carpinteria, CA 93014; (805) 684-8500.

*Newman's Own Organics, 246 Post Road East, Westport, CT 06880; www.newmansownorganics.com.

Pangea sells some of the above, as well as Vegan Sweets, Tropical Source, and more. Pangea, 2381 Lewis Ave., Rockville, MD 20851; (301) 816-9300; www.pangeaveg.com.

# Chapter 7

# Cooking and Baking

There are many excellent cookbooks and resources devoted to vegetarian cooking. See page 240 for a list of suggested cookbooks. In this chapter we've assembled some of the more specialized questions, as well as a few helpful tips, such as freezing tofu to change the consistency and making soy "buttermilk."

## What can I do about cooking on holidays? Thanksgiving? Passover? Christmas?

### Thanksgiving:

For Thanksgiving you might want to try VRG's *Thanksgiving Treasures* recipes. You can order a copy of this four-page handout by mailing your request and two first class stamps to: The Vegetarian Resource Group, PO Box 1463, Baltimore, MD 21203.

There are some meat alternatives, such as Tofurky and [Un]Turkey, mentioned on page 122 of the Vegetarian Products chapter that could be used in place of turkey.

You might also want to look through our online recipe section for articles such as *Must Pumpkin Always Be Pie?* by Patti Bess at www.vrg.org/recipes/vjpumpkin.htm.

Don't forget that many traditional Thanksgiving foods are or can be made vegetarian, such as mashed potatoes, breads, corn, cranberry sauce, stuffing, sweet potatoes, and pie.

## PASSOVER AND OTHER JEWISH HOLIDAYS:

For Passover and other Jewish holidays, you might wish to consult our books No Cholesterol Passover Recipes and The Lowfat Jewish Vegetarian Cookbook.

No Cholesterol Passover Recipes includes eggless blintzes, dairyless carrot cream soup, festive macaroons, apple latkes, sweet and sour cabbage, knishes, vegetarian chopped "liver," no-oil lemon dressing, eggless matzo meal pancakes, and much more.

The Lowfat Jewish Vegetarian Cookbook offers eggless challah, hamentashen for Purim, Chanukah latkes, Passover vegetarian kishke, mock chopped "liver," Russian charoset, eggless matzo balls, and Syrian wheat pudding.

Several recipes from each of the books are included in the Recipe chapter on page 87.

To read more about these books, turn to page 268.

## CHRISTMAS:

If you are visiting with meat-eating relatives you might consider bringing vegetarian dishes everyone can enjoy. Tofurky and Now and Zen both sell complete vegan meals that are also rather portable for holiday dinners. Contact information for both companies can be found on page 122.

Additionally, there is a book by Bryanna Clark Grogan, The (Almost) No-Fat Holiday Cookbook: Festive Holiday Recipes, which offers vegan recipes for 18 holidays. It is published by The Book Publishing Company (ISBN 1-570670-09-9).

## I'M 17 AND HAVE BEEN A LACTO-OVO VEGETARIAN FOR ABOUT 7 MONTHS AND I HAVE NOW MADE THE CHOICE TO GO VEGAN. THE THING IS, EVERY TIME I TRY TO COOK

WITH TOFU, IT DOESN'T WORK. IT'S LIKE THIS MAGICAL BLOCK OF STUFF THAT IS SUPPOSED TO MAGICALLY TRANSFORM ITSELF INTO SOMETHING YUMMY. WHAT CAN I DO TO MAKE IT WORK? RIGHT NOW I'M JUST EATING PRE-MADE TOFU AND SOY PRODUCTS, LIKE VEGAN BURGERS AND HOT DOGS, BUT I'D LIKE TO GIVE TOFU ANOTHER TRY.

There are several tricks for making tofu tasty. One of the easiest is to freeze a block (or chunks) of firm tofu in a plastic bag. Defrost it and press the water out with a towel. It should have a chewy, spongy consistency. You can use it in soups or stews and it will absorb more of the broth. Another trick is to fry thin rectangles of tofu in a bit of sesame oil and dip the "tofu fingers" into a soy sauce, sweet orange sauce, or another sauce of your choice. Crumble some tofu and fry it with a bit of garlic and oil to create a filling for burritos. Try marinating it.

If you want to experiment with something like a dip, blend some silken tofu with herbs, a little oil, lemon juice or vinegar, and a sweetener, such as maple syrup.

There are many recipe sites that will offer other suggestions. You might even want to check your local library. There are several books on tofu, and many Asian cookbooks will offer additional cooking methods. There are two good cookbooks, Tofu Cookery, by Louise Hagler, and Tofu and Soyfoods Cookery, by Peter Goblitz, that offer only tofu and soyfoods recipes. Also see pages 88, 99, 98, 100, 102, 105, 112, 115, and 116 in the Recipe chapter.

I AM TRYING TO DUPLICATE THE "MEATY" TEXTURE OF TOFU AS I FIND IT IN ASIAN RESTAURANTS/RECIPES. I HAVE FROZEN IT, PRESSED IT, AND TRIED BOTH FRESH AND STORE-BOUGHT BRANDS — ALL TO NO AVAIL. I WOULD BE GRATEFUL TO ANYONE WHO CAN DESCRIBE HOW ONE GETS THAT TEXTURE.

There are a couple of things to try. You might have had marinated baked tofu or deep-fried tofu. Quick deep-frying of tofu often changes the texture; you might try that technique. You can often find marinated tofu in Asian groceries or health food stores. It has a denser texture and has already been baked. Tofu-Kan and Tofu-Lin are some of the brand names that you might look for. If what you tried was yuba, it is a bit harder to find; you will need to check Asian markets or even try an online retailer. Yuba is basically sheets of bean curd or tofu.

Also, some of the dishes you've had in Asian restaurants may be seitan (wheat gluten), yasai, or healmey rather than the tofu with which you are familiar. There are a number of meat substitutes that are particular to Asian cuisine. If you aren't sure, ask the waitstaff. Perhaps they can even offer a local source.

## What is the best or correct way to drain tofu?

I am assuming you are referring to the practice of "pressing tofu." This information is from Companion Guide to Healthy Cooking by Natalie and Shirley Nigro:

> "Pressing: Pressing tofu makes the entire block uniformly firmer. This is the technique to use if a recipe calls for firm tofu and you happen to have soft tofu in the refrigerator. To press a block of tofu, place it between towels and put a heavy weight (such as a cast iron frying pan, concrete paving blocks, or bricks) on top and let it sit for an hour or so. Storing or cooking pressed tofu in a liquid will undo the effects of the pressing. Pressing silken tofu dries it out and causes it to lose its creamy characteristic and may produce a chicken-like texture"
> (page 193)

## Can anyone tell me how to make tofu cream cheese?

There are two recipes for Tofu Cream Cheese, both light and rich versions, in The Uncheese Cookbook. Joanne Stepaniak, author of the book, offers 191 pages of recipes for dairy-free cheese substitutes and dishes. There are chapters on "Cheezes, Spreads, and Dips" (including Swizz Cheeze, Mostarella Cheeze, Betta Feta, Brie, Tofu Ricotta, and Tofu Cottage Cheeze), "Soups and Chowders," "Fondues and Rarebits," "Sauces, Pestos, and Dressings," "Pizzas, Polentas, and Breads," "Quiches, Casseroles, and Entrees," and "Sweets." The Uncheese Cookbook is available through VRG.

If you are looking for products, you can try Tofutti and Galaxy. Tofutti makes many non-dairy alternatives, including cream cheese and sour cream. Contact:

    ✳Galaxy Foods Company, 2441 Viscount Row, Orlando, FL 32809; (800) 808-2325; www.galaxyfoods.com.

    ✳Tofutti Brands Inc., 50 Jackson Dr., Cranford, NJ 07016; (908) 272-2400; www.tofutti.com.

There are links to more non-dairy products online at www.vrg.org/links/products.htm.

We've done several guides to non-dairy alternatives in *Vegetarian Journal* and many are online at www.vrg.org/journal/#Food.

## I AM TRYING TO EXCLUDE DAIRY FROM MY DIET, BUT I AM HAVING A TOUGH TIME FIGURING OUT HOW TO REPLACE EVERYTHING I USED TO EAT. CAN SOYMILK BE USED JUST THE SAME AS MILK, OR DO I HAVE TO USE LESS OR MORE TO MAKE THE EQUIVALENT? ALSO, I ALREADY MISS MY CREAM SOUPS; IS THERE A REPLACEMENT FOR CREAM?

For most recipes you can use soymilk one to one with cow's milk. If you are using soymilk for something like mashed potatoes, be sure that it is a plain and not a sweetened flavor. Vanilla soymilk is good for baking or for breakfast dishes, such as oatmeal or Cream of Wheat. Soymilk comes in many different varieties. Generally, light or reduced-fat soymilks will be thinner (more like the consistency of skim milk), and original and fortified formulas have a thicker consistency. Some people prefer the taste of rice or nut milks to soy milk. You may want to try a few different kinds to see what you like.

White Wave produces a soy creamer that is perfect in place of dairy cream, especially if you like cream in your coffee. This is also what you might want to use for creamy soups or sauces. For something even thicker, you can try mixing the creamer and plain soy yogurt (such as from White Wave or Wholesoy). Silken tofu can also be used. Brother Ron Pickarski, in his book Friendly Foods, uses nut milks to create creamy soups. He also utilizes puréed cooked starchy vegetables, such as carrots and potatoes, as the thickening agent in his soups.

## I RECENTLY CUT OUT DAIRY FROM MY DIET, BUT I MISS MY RECIPES THAT CALL FOR BUTTERMILK. WHAT CAN I DO TO MAKE THESE RECIPES, BUT WITHOUT THE DAIRY?

Buttermilk can be replaced with soured soy or rice milk. For each cup of buttermilk, use 1 cup soymilk plus 1 tablespoon of vinegar.

## I REALLY LOVE THE TASTE OF MAYONNAISE BUT HAVE HAD TO ELIMINATE IT FROM MY DIET. WHAT CAN I DO TO REPLACE THIS FOR MY SANDWICHES?

You can use a ready-made dairy-free mayonnaise such as Nayonaise, made by Nasoya, or Vegenaise. These should be available in your local natural foods store or supermarket. You can also make your own. Please see the recipe on page 90.

## WHAT CAN I USE TO REPLACE BUTTER IN MY RECIPES?

Willow Run is a soy margarine that comes in sticks and is made by Shedd's Spread. You can also use Spectrum Spread, which is a brand name for a dairy-free and hydrogenated oil-free shortening made from canola oil. You should be able to use this as a one-to-one equivalent to butter. Spectrum also makes organic margarine and shortening. Contact Spectrum Organic Products, Inc., 1304 South Point Boulevard., Suite 280, Petaluma, CA 94952; (800) 995-2705; www.spectrumnaturals.com. For baking, you can also use mashed bananas or applesauce to replace the oil or butter.

## WHAT CAN I USE AS AN ALTERNATIVE TO WHITE SUGAR?

The easiest way to replace white sugar is to use a natural sugar. This should be readily available in large supermarkets and natural food stores. There are many brands, but a few are Sucanat, Florida Crystals, and Sugar in the Raw. Fruit-Source is a granulated sweetener made from juice concentrate and brown rice syrup. FruitSource is also available at natural foods stores.

You can replace sugar also with liquid sweeteners such as maple syrup, brown rice syrup, and molasses. You may have to use a little more brown rice syrup than you would sugar because it is not quite as sweet. Maple syrup and molasses are very sweet, so you might have to cut back the amount. When using liquid sweeteners you may have to play with the ingredients to make them work. You might need to reduce the amount of other liquids in the recipe. For example, use 3/4 cup water rather than 1 cup.

## WE ARE TRYING TO MAKE SOUP MIXES AND ARE HAVING TROUBLE FINDING DRIED CARROTS. CAN THIS BE DONE IN OUR OVEN AT HOME?

According to Chef Nancy Berkoff, RD, "You should be able to find dried carrots in the produce section of many grocery stores. If not, go to www.friedas.com, a specialty produce house. They should be able to direct you to a source."

You can also contact them at Frieda's Inc., 4465 Corporate Center Dr., Los Alamitos, CA 90720; (714) 826-6100.

Chef Berkoff adds, "If you want to make your own carrot chips (smaller pieces would be almost impossible to do at home), peel and wash medium sized carrots. Dry on paper towels. Slice as thinly as possible. Place on an ungreased baking sheet and bake at 250 degrees until the carrots are the degree of dryness you want. Carrots can also be dried in a food dehydrator."

## DO YOU KNOW OF A CULINARY PROGRAM THAT WOULD BE ACCEPTABLE FOR A VEGETARIAN?

Here are a few of which we are aware:
   *The Natural Gourmet Cookery School: 48 W. 21st St., 2nd Floor, New York, NY 10010; (212) 645-5170; www.naturalgourmetschool.com.
   *Naturally Grand Junction Cooking School: 2837 Elm Ave., Grand Junction, CO 81501; (800) 833-1336.

*Institute for Culinary Awakening: 7 Ave Vista Grande, #316, Santa Fe, NM 87505; (505) 466-4597; www.ica-plantchefs.com.

*Galaxy Nutritional Foods has a Veggie Culinary School. For more details, contact Tony Oust at Galaxy, 2441 Viscount Row, Orlando, FL 32809; (800) 808-2325, ext 123; www.veggieforlife.com; toust@galaxyfoods.com.

You might also want to take a look at The Guide to Cooking Schools, by Shaw Guides (PO Box 231295, New York, NY 10023). They have a website with an online database at www.shawguides.com.

Some schools might focus on macrobiotic cooking, which wouldn't be strictly vegetarian (i.e. fish), but would probably be amenable to a vegetarian curriculum. If you are outside of those areas, you could ask local culinary schools whether they offer any veggie courses. Some will accommodate vegetarians. This kind of piecemeal coursework probably would not lead to a certificate or degree. According to Chef Nancy Berkoff, "My suggestion is to hook up with a veggie chef and apprentice with him or her (you can coordinate this with the American Culinary Federation's apprenticeship program.) You and your chef would have to agree to meet the hours and the topics outlined by the ACF, with several supplemental courses given at area community colleges."

Also, in early 2001, Chef Berkoff instituted an online college-level course on vegetarianism. College credit is optional and the course is open to the general public. For more information contact VRG or view the course introduction online at www.vrg.org/berkoff/introduction.htm.

⁂

## WHAT TYPES OF RESOURCES DO YOU OFFER FOR FOOD SERVICE?

We offer a quarterly newsletter, *Foodservice Update*. You can subscribe for $20 a year, or $30 for both *Foodservice Update* and *Vegetarian Journal*. (Outside the US, rates for *Foodservice Update* are $20 per year for Canada and Mexico and $25 a year for all other foreign subscriptions.) You can access some of our past issues of *Foodservice Updates* online at www.vrg.org/fsupdate/index.htm. Back issues can be ordered for $1 each. To subscribe, call (410) 366-8343 with a Visa or MasterCard, send a check or money order drawn on US funds to PO Box 1463, Baltimore, MD 21203, or go to www.vrg.org/journal/subscribe to subscribe online.

VRG's *Quantity Product Listing* lists over 170 companies that offer vegetarian foods in bulk. It is online at www.vrg.org/fsupdate. Paper copies are available for $3.

Vegan in Volume, by Nancy Berkoff, RD, offers recipes and resources for quantities of 25 and over. See below for more details. Chef Berkoff is also teaching an online course, *Introduction to Vegetarian Foodservice and Nutrition*, which is helpful for everyone, from consumers who want to learn more about vegetarian cooking, to institutional food service staff and managers, to restaurateurs who want to please their vegan diners. College credit is optional and the course is open to anyone. The lectures and coursework will follow an academic calendar for those seeking credit, but non-credit students can enroll at anytime.

VRG also offers The Quantity Recipe Packet for $15, or $5 for students. Call, write, or go online (www.vrg.org/catalog/quant.htm) for additional information.

## WHAT ABOUT PARTIES AND COOKING FOR LARGE GROUPS OF PEOPLE?

In January, 2000, we published a cookbook devoted to quantity cooking - Vegan in Volume (272 pages). The author, Chef Nancy Berkoff, is a Registered Dietitian and Certified Food Technologist. Vegan in Volume offers information about catered events, weddings, birthday celebrations, college food service, quantity hospital food (including special diets), restaurant meals, menu ideas for dinner parties, party beverages, and holiday recipes. There are 125 great-tasting and unique vegan recipes. Turn to page 267 for more information and ordering details.

## HOW DO I REPLACE EGG YOLKS AND WHITES?

There are a few alternatives for eggs.
Any of the following can be used to replace eggs as binders:

  * 1 banana for 1 egg (great for cakes, pancakes, etc.)
  * 2 Tablespoons cornstarch or arrowroot starch for 1 egg

∗ Ener-G Egg Replacer (or similar product available in health food stores or by mail order)

∗ 1/4 Cup tofu for 1 egg (blend tofu smooth with the liquid ingredients before they are added to the dry ingredients.)

Chef Nancy Berkoff, RD, suggests using egg replacer and oil to simulate egg yolks. However, "Egg whites are much more difficult, as not too many things have the physical and chemical properties of egg white. You might play with soy flour and water, but you won't get the lightness of an angel food cake or a sponge cake."

The Ener-G Egg Replacer can be ordered directly from Ener-G Foods Inc. 5960 First Ave. S., Seattle, WA 98108; (800) 331-5222; www.ener-g.com. It can also be ordered from Pangea (2381 Lewis Ave., Rockville, MD 20851; (301) 816-9300; www.pangeaveg.com).

## HOW DO I MAKE A VEGAN CAKE?

Here is a recipe from the article *"Let's Party,"* by Lisa Rivero, from the September/October 1998 issue of *Vegetarian Journal.*

## Chocolate Cake
## (Makes two 8" round layers or 12 cupcakes)

### Dry Ingredients:
1 cup whole-wheat pastry flour
1 cup unbleached all-purpose flour
1/4 cup cocoa powder or carob powder
1 teaspoon baking soda
1 teaspoon salt

### Wet Ingredients:
1 cup soymilk or 7/8 cup rice milk
3/4 cup pure maple syrup
1/2 cup hot, well-cooked long-grain brown rice
1/4 cup canola oil
1 teaspoon pure vanilla extract (optional)

Preheat oven to 350 degrees. Oil two 8" round cake pans or 12 cupcake tins; set aside. Whisk together dry ingredients in a large mixing bowl; set aside. Combine wet ingredients in a blender container, and blend until very smooth. Add wet ingredients to dry ingredients, and stir to combine. Pour batter into prepared pans. Bake 20 to 25 minutes for cakes, 15 to 20 minutes for cupcakes, until a toothpick inserted in the middle of the cake or cupcake emerges clean. Cool slightly before turning onto a wire rack. Top with fruit-only raspberry preserves, Easy Chocolate Glaze, or White Frosting (see article for these recipes).

Total calories per unfrosted cupcake: 186
Fat: 6 grams

You can read the rest of the article online at www.vrg.org/journal/vj98sep/989party.htm.

Also see our article "*Can a 'Real' Birthday Cake be Vegan?*" by Judith Grabski Miner. It is online at www.vrg.org/recipes.

## WHERE CAN I FIND A VEGAN WEDDING CAKE?

A good place to start looking is at vegetarian and vegan restaurants near you that have or utilize a vegan-friendly bakery. You can use our book, The Vegetarian Journal's Guide to Restaurants in the US and Canada, as a good starting place to locate restaurants. Also see the travel and restaurant chapter on page 140.

Whether you need a cake for a wedding, your child's birthday party, an anniversary celebration, or an office meeting, the following are some places to start your search.

**Blind Faith** in Evanston, Illinois (847) 328-6875. They also have great vegan corn bread and cupcakes.

**Fire and Water** in Northampton, Massachusetts (413) 586-8336.

**Funks Democratic Coffeehouse and Bistro** in Baltimore, Maryland (410) 276-3865. They are well-known in Baltimore for their vegan chocolate cake.

**Real Food Daily** in West Hollywood, California (310) 289-9910.

**West Lynn Cafe** in Austin, Texas (512) 482-0950.

**Veggie Works** in Belmar, New Jersey (732) 280-1141. Their home-cooked non-meat meat loaf and mashed potatoes aren't to be missed either.

Also, many Whole Foods and other large natural foods stores now offer vegan cakes.

## CAN ONE BECOME ILL FROM EATING A RAW OR UNDER-COOKED POTATO?

According to Chef Nancy Berkoff, RD, "It's true, raw potatoes are very fibrous and difficult for humans to digest. You still get some nutrition, just not all of it. I don't recommend eating raw potatoes. Uncooked potato skin contains some natural chemicals that can become toxic if eaten in large quantities. Cooking actually enhances the nutrient value of potatoes."

Vegetarian
Meals
Served

# CHAPTER 8

# TRAVEL AND RESTAURANTS

One of the best places to start looking for vegetarian travel resources is our Travel Section on the VRG website. You will find a listing of sites, books, and a bulletin board at www.vrg.org/travel. You will also find several City Guides there, including Chicago, Anaheim, Baltimore, and Atlanta. Another very helpful section of our site is the travel links page, where you will find links to vegetarian and vegetarian-friendly tours, travel agents, and lodging. This can be found at www.vrg.org/links/vacation.htm. Also take a look at page 243 for a list of recommended travel books.

## IS THERE A GUIDEBOOK TO VEGETARIAN RESTAURANTS AVAILABLE?

We author The Vegetarian Journal's Guide to Natural Foods Restaurants in the US and Canada. Turn to page 270 for more details. You can also read more about it online at www.vrg.org/catalog/guide.htm.

If you are looking for travel guides for the United Kingdom, Europe, and more you will want to contact Vegetarian Guides Ltd. They publish Vegetarian London, Vegetarian Britain, Vegetarian France, and Vegetarian Europe. They have created a new online shop, www.vegetarianguides.co.uk, or e-mail them at info@vegetarianguides.co.uk.

If you are a vegetarian traveling to Walt Disney World and the Orlando area, Vegetarian Walt Disney World will be invaluable. Contact Vegetarian World Guides at 145 Keener Road, Morgantown, WV 26508; (304) 292-2497; www.vegetarianworldguides.com.

The Artichoke Trail, by James Bernard Frost, is a guide to vegetarian restaurants, organic food stores, and farmers' markets in the US. For more information, contact Hunter Publishing, 130 Campus Dr., Edison, NJ 08818.

## IS THERE A BOOK OF NATURAL FOODS STORES AVAILABLE?

Tofu Tollbooth is a guide to natural foods stores in the US by Elizabeth Zipern and Dar Williams. It is available through VRG or can be ordered from the publishers at Ceres Press/Ardwork Press, PO Box 87, Woodstock, NY 12498. For more details visit www.tofutollbooth.com.

You can also try Healthy Journeys, a 243-page guide, which is available from Charisma Publishing, 175 Heartbreak Hill, Palermo, ME 04354. They also have an online database of the stores at www.healthyjourneys.net.

## I JUST MOVED TO A SMALL TOWN WHERE THERE ARE NO LOCAL HEALTH FOOD STORES - ANY IDEAS?

Sometimes, searching online is your best bet. This site will help you find natural foods stores near you: www.healthyjourneys.net/Default.htm.

There are restaurants and stores here: www.vegeats.com/restaurants.

You might decide that you want to order some hard to find products via mail or Internet catalogs. There are some vegetarian product and retailer websites linked here: www.vrg.org/links/products.htm.

# WHERE CAN I FIND OUT ABOUT VEGETARIAN RESTAURANTS ONLINE?

We have links to vegetarian restaurants at www.vrg.org/links/restaurant.htm.

There are a few online lists and databases here:
* www.VegEats.com.
* www.VegDining.com
* www.happycow.net

Often the best place for information about area restaurants is a local vegetarian group. You will find links to US-based groups on these pages:

* www.vrg.org/links/local.htm
* www.greenpeople.org/vegetarian.htm
* www.navs-online.org/fraffil.html

Also, if you are traveling to Maryland, don't forget to check out our *Maryland Dining Guide.* It lists over 130 vegetarian-friendly restaurants in Baltimore and the surrounding areas (www.vrg.org/travel/mddining.htm).

# DO YOU HAVE ANY TIPS FOR TRAVELING WITH VEGGIE KIDS?

We sure do - try *Traveling with Vegan Children,* by Reed Mangels, PhD, RD. Write, phone, or e-mail to request a copy. Or go to www.vrg.org/journal/vj97may/976trav.htm.

# WE ARE LOOKING FOR SOME IDEAS FOR CHEAP EATS WHILE ON A CROSS-COUNTRY ROAD TRIP. WE WILL HAVE A CAMPING STOVE AND A HOT POT.

You could try couscous, rice, pasta, or noodles, all of which cook quickly and easily. "Just add water" soups and pastas are another option. There are also several Asian-style meals available in grocery stores that just need to be boiled to heat and serve. Tortillas, marinated tofu, and hummus make easy road sandwiches, and so does good old peanut butter-and-jelly. Fruit leather, trail mix, nuts, crackers, pretzels, and tortilla chips are good for snack foods.

## I'M GOING TO BE TRAVELING TO EUROPE. WHERE DO I START?

The best place for international information is The International Vegetarian Union. This Internet-based hub for international links and information is at www.ivu.org. It is an extensive site with contact information for local groups, links to restaurant guides, information about various countries, language translations, recipes, and much more.

You will also want to check World Animal Net at worldanimalnet.org/new.asp where you will find additional local resources.

If you need a guide book, try Vegetarian Europe, by Vegetarian Guides Ltd. VRG carries this and other Vegetarian Guides publications. They can be contacted at Vegetarian Guides Ltd., PO Box 2284, London W1A 5UH, England; www.vegetarianguides.co.uk.

## I'M GOING TO BE TRAVELING TO EUROPE AND ASIA, AND I NEED TRANSLATIONS TO SHOW WAITERS AND CHEFS IN SEVERAL DIFFERENT LANGUAGES. DO YOU KNOW WHERE TO LOOK?

You can go to the International Vegetarian Union at www.ivu.org and look at their pages of translations: www.ivu.org/phrases. They should have information for most major languages.

You can also contact the American Vegan Society, which offers a "Vegan Passport," explaining vegetarianism in several languages. The American Vegan Society, 56 Dinshah Lane, P.O. Box H, Malaga, New Jersey 08328-0908; (609) 694-2887.

www.vegetariantraveler.com offers a series of translations on cards that you present to your waiter or waitress to ensure you get a vegan, lacto, or ovo-lacto meal when you travel abroad.

The book Speaking Vegetarian, published by Pilot Books, is another helpful guide. They can be reached at (800) 797-4568.

## Do you have any vacation ideas for vegetarians?

Our *Vegetarian Vacation Guide* lists vacation spots all over the US, Canada, and Europe, along with some websites to check out. Write, phone, or e-mail VRG to request a copy. It can also be accessed online at www.vrg.org/travel/vacation.htm.

The Vegetarian Traveler (303 pages), by Jed and Susan Civic, is a guidebook for vegetarian, vegan, and environmentally-sensitive travelers. This guide lists almost 300 guest houses, B & B's, motels, hotels, spas, resorts, hostels, retreat centers, and outdoor adventure tours. It has an international focus and includes information for the US, the Caribbean, South America, the UK, and Europe. The Vegetarian Traveler is available through VRG.

## I'm very interested in learning about all the different veggie B&B's throughout the U.S. Do you know of a guide to this sort of thing?

Try looking through our *Vegetarian Vacation Guide* (see previous question).

There is a whole section of B & B's on our travel links page, both domestic and international. The webpage is at www.vrg.org/links/vacation.htm. There is another online guide at about.com at www.bandb.about.com/travel/bandb.

The Vegetarian Traveler, by Jed and Susan Civic, is a guidebook for vegetarian, vegan, and environmentally sensitive travelers. (See above for more information).

## DO YOU KNOW OF ANY RESTAURANTS THAT WILL ACCOMMODATE VEGANS IN ISRAEL?

If you are traveling to Israel, the Guide to Vegetarian Restaurants in Israel is helpful. Visit the VRG website at www.vrg.org/catalog/isguide.htm for details. Also, check with some of the local groups in Israel; you'll find links on the IVU website at www.ivu.org/global/asia/israel.html.

## WITHIN 3 WEEKS, I WILL BE TRAVELLING AROUND IN ZAMBIA, AFRICA. WHAT ARE THE POSSIBILITIES FOR VEGETARIAN FOOD?

The IVU site has a section on Zambia: www.ivu.org/global/africa/zambia.html. Also, The Zambian Society of Vegetarians, P.O. Box 40728 MUFULIRA Fax: + 260 (2) 410 211 might be able to offer some advice.

## I'M GOING TO DISNEYLAND WITH MY FAMILY. WILL I BE ABLE TO EAT THERE?

The map visitors are given as they enter the park indicates which restaurants offer vegetarian options. Fresh fruit is also available. You will also want to look at our *Dining Guide to Anaheim.* Write, e-mail, or phone for a copy. It can also be accessed on the web at www.vrg.org/travel/anaheim.htm.

An article in the February 1998 issue of *Vegetarian Times* suggests that most of the restaurants at Disney World can accommodate vegetarian diners. Some of the restaurants offer vegetarian and vegan options at all times, and some are available upon request. Hopefully this holds true of Disneyland as well.

## ARE THERE ANY VEGETARIAN RESTAURANTS IN CANCUN?

There is a vegetarian restaurant in Cancun, Mexico called 100% Natural, with three locations: Av. Sunyaxchen, Cancun; (98) 843617; Plaza Terramar, Cancun; (98) 831180; and Plaza Kukulkan, Cancun; (98) 852904. There is also a 100% Natural in Playa del Carmen. Natural, at 5th Ave. (next door to Maya Bric Hotel), offers falafel, salads, and smoothies.

## ANY ADVICE FOR TRAVELERS GOING TO CENTRAL AND LATIN AMERICA?

We publish a *Guide to Latin American Resources* that is on our website at www.vrg.org/travel/larg.htm#Restaurants. Paper copies can be requested by mail, e-mail, or phone. We published an article, *"Veggie Dining in Mexico City"* in *Vegetarian Journal* that can be accessed at www.vrg.org/travel/vjmexcty.htm.

The International Vegetarian Union page for Latin America - www.ivu.org/global/latinam/index.html - has some helpful information, and additional links.

## I'M TRAVELING TO THE DOMINICAN REPUBLIC VERY SOON. WHAT IS THE POSSIBILITY OF GETTING VEGAN (OR EVEN VEGETARIAN) FOOD THERE?

You should find some help from the links listed on this page www.ivu.org/global/latinam/dominican.html. Farmers' markets should offer some fresh fruits and vegetables.

## I'M GOING TO BE TRAVELING TO MANCHESTER, ENGLAND. WILL I FIND ANYTHING TO EAT?

You might find the article *"Vegan in the UK"* helpful. There is a list of tips and resources at the end. Write, phone, or e-mail for a paper copy, or read it online at www.vrg.org/travel/ukdavida.htm. Also contact the Vegetarian Society of the UK at www.vegsoc.org.

## WHERE CAN I FIND OUT ABOUT VEGETARIAN SPAS?

Many spas are more than willing to accommodate the dietary requests of their clients. Here are two spas that offer all-vegetarian or almost all-vegetarian accommodations.

Rio Caliente Hot Springs Spa (US Office, spa is in Mexico) - POB 897, Millbrae, CA 94030; (800) 200-2927; www.riocaliente.com.

Spa Atlantis - 1460 S. Ocean Blvd., Pompano Beach, FL 33062; (800) 583-3500; www.spa-atlantis.com.

## I WOULD LIKE TO FIND A TRAVEL AGENT THAT UNDERSTANDS MY NEEDS AS A VEGETARIAN TRAVELER. DO YOU KNOW IF SUCH A PERSON EXISTS?

Adventure Health Travel is an Internet-based travel agency that specializes in spas and fitness, eco-adventure/natural history land and cruise packages, vegetarian travelers, retreats, and hideaways. Contact: PO Box 638, Ashland, OR 97520; (800) 443-9216, www.adventurehealthtravel.com

Also contact Green Earth Travel and ask for or write to Donna Zeigfinger, who specializes in arranging travel plans for vegetarians. Contact: 6505 Democracy Blvd., Bethesda, MD 20817; (888) 2GO-VEGE; www.vegtravel.com.

## THE IDEA OF A DUDE RANCH WHERE I COULD GET VEGAN MEALS IS PROBABLY AN OXYMORON, BUT MY HUSBAND WOULD LIKE TO VACATION AT A DUDE RANCH AND I AM A VEGAN. ANY SUGGESTIONS?

Surprisingly, there are several that will cater to vegetarians and vegans! Here are a few links to places we found doing an online search:

  ∗ Van Eden Ranch Retreat - www.coloradodirectory.com/vanedenranch
  ∗ La Garita Creek Ranch - www.ranchweb.com/lagarita/glance.htm

∗ Pinegrove Dude Ranch - www.pinegrove-ranch.com
∗ Coulter Lake Ranch - www.guestranches.com/coulterlake/lodging.htm
∗ Guest Ranches - www.guestranches.com

## HOW DO I DEAL WITH AIRLINE MEALS?

Airline meals need to be requested at least 24 hours in advance, and even then there's no guarantee that you'll get what you ordered.

According to Simple, Lowfat, and Vegetarian,

*"One large airline catering organization is Sky Chefs. Sky Chefs' Miami facility services American Airlines as well as Mexicana. According to Tom Prior, Production Manager at Sky Chefs' Miami facility, of the approximately 10,000 meals produced at his facility each day, about 1% of those are vegetarian meals that have been requested by passengers. In other words, his facility prepares about 100 vegetarian meals per day, including breakfast, lunch, dinner, and snacks.*

*"Surprisingly, more vegetarian meals are ordered than lowfat, low cholesterol meals (which make up only about 1/2% of the total special meals ordered). "Probably the most frequently ordered special meals are the vegetarian meal, the seafood plate, and the fruit bowl," explained Prior. Most people don't realize that all of these options are available, and the airlines don't necessarily go out of their way to advertise it, since the special meals are costlier to produce. However, many frequent flyers take advantage of the special meal options.*

*"About a year ago, the facility began making all of their vegetarian meals dairy-free and egg-free, or vegan, unless a passenger requests otherwise. Stated Prior, "We've been consolidating some of our diets, and it made more sense to do it that way. Also, most of the people who request vegetarian meals want the vegan option."*

*"Throughout most of the airline industry, the designation VGML is used to denote a standard, animal-product-free vegetarian meal. Those who request a vegetarian meal that includes dairy or egg may see the designation, "DVEG" on their tray when it arrives at their seat. Fruit bowls are also a popular request for vegetarians, especially at breakfast.*

*"Airlines differ in what they serve for vegetarian meals. Some airlines offer only one vegetarian menu, so frequent travelers may notice that every time they fly a certain airline, they get the same dinner meal - pasta primavera, for instance. Other airlines may offer a few menus, sometimes on a rotating basis and sometimes not. American Airlines, for example, uses four different vegetarian meals. So, passengers are likely to see any of these four on any given flight; they may get the same meal two or three times in a row, or they might get a different meal on each of four flights.*

*"The meals may vary by region, as well, especially on international flights or flights that are frequented by certain cultural groups. For instance, vegetarian meals on flights from the US to London, or elsewhere in Europe, are likely to be "Asian-vegetarian" - a curried lentil and rice dish, for instance - which would be more familiar to some vegetarian international travelers. On the other hand, vegetarian meals served on flights in the domestic market are more likely to be Western-style vegetarian meals - pasta primavera or chili-stuffed peppers.*

*"Mike Agius is Executive Chef for the Sky Chefs' Miami facility. According to Agius, it isn't feasible or practical for travelers to get much information ahead of time about what specifically is going to be on the menu for special meals on any given flight. The reservation clerks don't have this information readily available to them, and in some cases, such as when a caterer is being supplied with frozen meals from another source, even they don't know precisely what is being delivered for any given day. Mike suggests, "If you aren't sure that you'll like the meal being served on a certain flight, vegetarians can always order a fruit plate." Especially on international flights, when a non-Western-style vegetarian meal is more likely to be served, a fruit plate can be a "sure bet" for some people. It can also be light and refreshing. On the other hand, the non-Western-style vegetarian meals can be delicious, too - maybe even better than the Western-style fare!"*

Here are some travel tips from the book,

*"At least 24 hours in advance of the flight, or at the time you make your reservation, call the airline reservations desk and check to see if a snack or meal is being served on your flight(s). If so, tell the clerk that you would like to request a special meal. Airlines offer a variety of special meal options. Depending upon the airline, there may be several meal options that are low in fat, vegetarian and nonvegetarian.*

*"Throughout the airline industry, the vegetarian meal (or, in airline lingo, the VGML) is likely to be vegan, free of dairy and egg. But vegans might still want to specify "no dairy, no eggs" when they place their request, just to make sure. Vegans are also advised to read food labels on packets of salad dressing and cookie wrappers, for instance, just to be sure they don't contain animal products. Those who prefer to have some dairy or egg with their meal may be able to specify a lacto-ovo-vegetarian meal (or DVEG).*

*"A fruit bowl or fruit plate is often available upon request. This is typically made with fresh, sliced fruit and can be a refreshing, light meal. Frequently, this option is fat-free. Sometimes, however, a fruit bowl includes a scoop of cottage cheese. Vegans may need to request "no dairy," just to be sure."*

Another idea is to bring some snacks of your own, especially if it is going to be a long flight.

THIS SUMMER, I'M GOING ON A THREE-WEEK TRIP TO JAPAN WITH MY JAPANESE CLASS. THERE WE WILL BE STAYING WITH JAPANESE FAMILIES ALL THREE WEEKS. IN JAPAN, THEY DON'T EAT MUCH RED MEAT, BUT THEY DO EAT FISH, AND I AM A VEGETARIAN. IT IS CONSIDERED RUDE TO NOT EAT EVERYTHING ON YOUR PLATE? WHAT SHOULD I DO?

We forwarded your question to a Japanese freelance writer, Hiroko Kato, who has written several articles for *Vegetarian Journal.* This was Hiroko's reply:

*"Hi there! I am a vegetarian living in Tokyo. I understand your situation, but believe you could survive three weeks in Japan.*

*"First, let me explain Japanese eating customs. As you suspect, the idea of vegetarianism is uncommon in Japan. In fact, it is probably worse than you think, as people here currently eat a lot of red meat and poultry; although we eat tofu and plenty of vegetables too. We have a tradition of Zen Buddhist vegetarianism (vegan actually), but unfortunately, the tradition is now limited to just Buddhists.*

*"Considering these situations, your host family might have little knowledge of vegetarianism. Therefore you need to explain in advance what vegetarianism is, what you would like to eat, as well as why you became vegetarian. They may feel a little bit of difficulty satisfying you, but it is not rude if you can communicate well with your host family.*

*"Your host family may have no idea how to cook a vegetarian meal without using any meat and fish. You can show them how to prepare foods the vegetarian way. Not only in the kitchen, you should also help by joining in grocery shopping. There are a variety of foods in Japanese supermarkets for vegetarians and it will be exciting for you to find new items there. However, it is almost impossible to find meat alternatives in Japan, such as those available in the US.*

*"Italian foods like pasta and Chinese foods like stir-fried vegetables with rice are easy to make vegetarian in Japan, too. The problem is authentic Japanese food. Because fish stock is used in almost every meal, you can't eat even a bowl of miso soup if you try to stick to the vegetarian way. Noodles like soba and udon come with soup or sauce containing fish stock. Speaking of miso soup, you can make it with kombu seaweed instead of fish stock or just cook it without any soup stocks. Soba and udon drizzled with soy sauce are also good.*

*"The great advantage of being vegetarian in Japan is tofu. You'll never find such high-quality fresh tofu in the US. There are plenty of soy products too, so you can request that you would like tofu dishes. Additionally many traditional Japanese sweets are vegan! I hope you like them.*

*"If you are vegetarian, I assume you know how to courteously deal with non-vegetarians. Do this in Japan, just as you do in the US. Moreover, it will be a great cultural exchange to tell your host family about your vegetarianism.*

*"I wrote the article about how to eat vegan food in Japanese restaurants in the May/June 2000 issue of* Vegetarian Journal *and am currently writing a web diary as a vegetarian living in Tokyo (members.aol.com/ochocok4/vegan.htm). Please check them!"*

Another of Hiroko's *Vegetarian Journal* articles can be found online at www.vrg.org/journal/vj2000jan/2000janmiso.htm.

# CHAPTER 9

# VEGGIE KIDS

Among the most frantic phone calls, letters, and e-mails we receive are from vegetarian parents and parents-to-be. They had known how to live as vegetarians themselves, but what does this mean for their infant or child just starting pre-school? We've been developing more and more materials for vegetarian children, trying to keep up with the growing demand. We've also received many e-mails from teenagers needing solid nutritional information to read and share with their parents. Many of us in the office can empathize with their quest for knowledge, having become vegetarian in our teens ourselves.

## WHAT TYPES OF RESOURCES AND ADVICE DO YOU HAVE FOR VEGETARIAN FAMILIES?

Among the brochures we offer are *Tips for Parents of Young Vegetarians, Raising Vegan Children, Vegan Pregnancy and Childhood, Traveling with Vegan Children,* reprint from <u>Pediatric Manual of Clinical Dietetics</u> chapter on *Nutrition Management of the Vegetarian Child,* and *Vegetarian Nutrition for Teenagers.* We also provide information regarding nutritional needs for children and related information in <u>Simply Vegan</u>, as well as a school foods packet to help parents introduce more vegetarian foods to their child's school. In July, 2000, VRG organized a parents' e-mail list with several hundred families participating. For information on how to sign-up go to the Raising a Vegetarian Family section of the VRG website (www.vrg.org/family).

For kids we offer our *I Love Animals and Broccoli* coloring book and shopping basket activity book. The coloring book comes with an optional lesson plan that is very popular with educators and those home-schooling their children. We've also published a storybook-cookbook for kids and their parents, <u>Leprechaun Cake and Other Tales</u> (see page 269).

Please visit the *Raising a Vegetarian Family* section of our website at www.vrg.org/family. Also see the *Veg Kids & Teens* section for additional information at www.vrg.org/family/kidsindex.htm.

## WHAT RESOURCES DO YOU HAVE FOR PREGNANT WOMEN?

We have some of our resources online, and others are available by mail. The following brochures are available online. To request a paper copy write, e-mail, or phone VRG.

*Vegan Pregnancy and Lactation* www.vrg.org/nutrition/pregnancy.htm
*Raising a Vegetarian Family* www.vrg.org/family/index.htm
*Feeding Vegan Kids* www.vrg.org/nutshell/kids.htm

There is a section on pregnancy and lactation in <u>Simply Vegan</u> (www.vrg.org/catalog/simplyvegan.htm). Please see page 245 of the appendix for a menu plan for vegan children.

## DO YOU HAVE ANY RECOMMENDATIONS FOR BOOKS ON VEGETARIAN OR VEGAN PREGNANCIES?

<u>Simply Vegan</u> is one of the standards for vegan nutrition information. Dr. Michael Klaper's, <u>Pregnancy, Children, and the Vegan Diet</u> is a very popular title with mothers-to-be. <u>The Vegetarian Way</u> would be another excellent resource. You might also wish to read <u>The Vegetarian Female</u> by Anika Avery-Grant, RD. See page 242 for additional titles that may be useful.

## IS THERE SUCH A THING AS VEGAN PRENATAL VITAMINS?

Some of the vitamins Freeda carries appear vegan. The vitamin D-2 (also called ergocalciferol) found in all of their multi-vitamins, including prenatal vitamins is from vegan sources. The product Freeda uses is derived from bacteria grown on wood pulp and then exposed to ultraviolet light. Vitamin D-3 (also called cholecalciferol) is only available from Freeda as plain vitamin D-3 (not in multi-vitamins). It's derived from lanolin, which is not a vegan source.

Freeda's contact information is 36 East 41st St., New York, NY 10017; (212) 685-4980; www.freedavitamins.com.

VRG recommends consulting a dietitian or health care professional before taking a prenatal vitamin.

## CAN I FEED MY INFANT ADEQUATELY WITH A SOY FORMULA?

*"If for any reason you choose not to breastfeed or if you are using formula to supplement breast feeding, there are several soy-based formulas available. These products support normal infant growth and development. Soy-based formulas are used by vegan families as the best option when breastfeeding is not possible. As of 2001, all soy formulas contain vitamin D derived from lanolin (sheep's wool). Some soy-based formulas (such as Parent's Choice ® and some store brands) may contain animal-derived fats, so check the ingredient label. Soy formulas are used exclusively for the first six months. Iron supplements may be indicated at 4-6 months if the formula is not fortified with iron.*

*"Soymilk, rice milk, and homemade formulas should not be used to replace breast milk or commercial infant formula during the first year. These foods do not contain the proper ratio of protein, fat, and carbohydrate, nor do they have enough of many vitamins and minerals to be used as a significant part of the diet in the first year."*
(Reprinted from <u>Simply Vegan</u>, pg 190).

# I'M CONCERNED ABOUT THE PHYTOESTROGENS IN SOY FORMULA. IS THIS SAFE TO FEED MY SON?

There has been somewhat of a controversy recently over the safety of soy infant formula and to a lesser extent, over the use of soyfoods by young children. The concern is that the biologically active isoflavones (also called phytoestrogens) in soybeans, while possibly being beneficial in adults, might have adverse effects in infants during the early developmental period. Isoflavone exposure in infants consuming soy formula is extremely high on a body weight basis, and so it is not unreasonable to consider what effect if any these phytoestrogens might have on infants. Short-term studies indicate that soy formula is perfectly safe and adequate for growth and development. Given that literally millions of infants have consumed soy formula during the past 30 years, the almost complete lack of any reports of ill effects, with the exception of allergic reactions, is striking and very much speaks to the safety issue. Of course, Asian children have been exposed to isoflavones in the form of soyfoods for centuries, but critics emphasize that it is the first few months of life which is the extremely sensitive period and during which isoflavones could potentially wreak havoc. They also believe that because Asians have consumed soy for centuries, their reaction to soy might be very different from Westerners. Furthermore, soy formula foes contend that the adverse effects of soy formula will not become manifest until the teenage years and beyond, perhaps by adversely affecting fertility or even sexual orientation. Unfortunately, there is little data on the health picture of adults who consumed soy formula as infants, although a recent study did find no unusual hormonal patterns in young children who were fed soy formula. Therefore, given the history of use, both soy formula and soyfoods appear to be safe products for use by infants and children, respectively.

Reed Mangels, PhD, RD

# CAN I MAKE MY OWN RICE MILK INFANT FORMULA?

The occasional reports of nutritional problems in vegan or vegetarian infants are often due to use of a homemade formula in the first year after birth. Products such as commercial or home-prepared soymilk, rice milk, nut or seed milk; non-dairy creamer; water-based cereal porridge; or mixtures of fruit or vegetable juices should not be used to replace breast milk or commercial infant formula for infants under one year. These foods do not contain the proper ratio of protein, fat, and carbohydrates nor do they have adequate amounts of many vitamins and minerals. In short, there is NO commercial rice milk for infants. Infants who are allergic to both cow's milk- and soymilk-based infant formulas and who are not being breast fed may require special formulas made from casein hydrolysate. This should be discussed with the infant's health care provider.

Reed Mangels, PhD, RD

## How do I get my kids to drink soymilk instead of cow's milk?

Try mixing (out of the children's sight) 1 part soymilk to 4 parts cow's milk and gradually increase the amount of soymilk and reduce the amount of cow's milk until they're drinking 100% soy. Get the kids involved. Purchase a number of different kinds of fortified soymilk and let them taste this "special" new milk and vote for their favorite. Be sure to choose a product with calcium added and serve it well chilled. My children don't like seeing flakes of calcium floating in their soymilk. If that's true for yours, shake it well before serving. Don't choose a reduced fat soymilk for young children. Regular soymilk is already close to lowfat cow's milk in terms of fat content; young children don't need to reduce fat further. Try not serving milk of any kind for a week and then when the taste of cow's milk is not so familiar, introduce soymilk again, calling it some fun name and not trying to say it's the same as cow's milk. Chocolate soymilk is certainly an option although it's rather high in sugar for everyday use. If they don't want to drink soymilk straight, try using it in smoothies or milkshakes, puddings, frozen desserts (one child of mine liked soymilk frozen until it was slushy; she'd eat it with a spoon), cream soups, baking, etc. Try flavoring it with a little bit of maple syrup for maple milk. Add a dash of almond or vanilla extract for almond milk or vanilla milk.

Reed Mangels, PhD, RD

## I am breastfeeding and it seems that whenever I eat vital wheat gluten (seitan) my daughter gets very fussy (gas?), crying and waking at night. Other

THINGS COULD BE GOING ON (TEETHING, GROWTH SPURT, ETC.), BUT IT SEEMS TO HAPPEN ESPECIALLY WHEN I HAVE EATEN VITAL WHEAT GLUTEN. I AM EXCLUSIVELY BREAST-FEEDING HER NOW, BUT WILL BE STARTING HER ON SOLIDS SOON. I WAS WONDERING IF YOU HAVE ANYTHING IN YOUR RESOURCES THAT COULD MAKE A CONNECTION FROM HER FUSSINESS TO THE WHEAT GLUTEN VIA BREASTMILK?

You're right, there are many things that could make a baby fussy that are not related to your diet. On the other hand, sometimes babies do react to something in the mother's diet. I'm assuming that you are eating other wheat products and have not noticed any particular reaction. Since gluten is the protein part of the wheat and is found in foods that contain wheat, I wouldn't expect her to react to wheat gluten if she does not react to wheat. Is there a spice or something else in the recipe used in the preparation of the wheat gluten that she could be reacting to?

These things are usually out-grown pretty quickly if they are diet-related so shouldn't be used to restrict the foods that she eats once she starts on solid food.

Reed Mangels, PhD, RD

## MY DAUGHTER IS RAISING HER INFANT SON ON A VEGAN DIET. SHOULD I BE WORRIED?

No. If she is providing adequate nutritional care he should be perfectly fine. To ease your mind and help you understand your daughter's dietary choices, you might want to read though the *Raising Vegetarian Family* section on the VRG website. You will find a long article on *Feeding Vegan Kids* at www.vrg.org/nutshell/kids.htm.

## HOW DO YOU DEAL WITH PEER AND FAMILY PRESSURE?

Often, explaining your choices about why you don't eat meat helps. If you are dealing with a person who doubts that a vegetarian or vegan diet is healthy for children, you might want to give the person some nutritional literature and

information. We have information such as this on our website at www.vrg.org/
family, or write, e-mail, or phone VRG to request paper copies be mailed.

Each child is different, and how, when, and what you explain will vary. Social
situations can be easy or hard, depending on the level of understanding and
respect on everyone's parts. For example, at children's parties, some vegan and
vegetarian parents have chosen to make a treat for all the kids to enjoy. That
way, the other children and parents see there is nothing "weird" about the way
your family eats. (We have some delicious party ideas, including vegan cake
recipes, online at www.vrg.org/journal/vj98sep/989party.htm).

For kids, it is possible that your friends might try and pressure you into eating
meat. In the long run, they will respect you more for standing firm in your ideals
instead of compromising them.

Talking to other vegetarian and vegan parents also helps, so on to the next
question...

### HOW CAN I MEET OTHER VEGETARIAN AND VEGAN PARENTS?

The Vegetarian Resource Group invites you to be a part of a network of vegetarian parents interested in exchanging ideas on various topics such as creating tasty
snacks for toddlers, the challenges of non-vegetarian family/friend gatherings,
how to talk with your child about vegetarianism, helping kids handle peer pressure, even shopping resources for leather/wool alternatives!

To learn more and to sign up, go to http://groups.yahoo.com/group/vrgparents.

(Note: At the beginning of 2001, there were close to 300 families participating
from around the globe.)

### CAN I MAKE MY OWN VEGAN BABY FOODS?

Sure! We have many articles with recipes in our Raising a Vegetarian Family section of the VRG website (www.vrg.org/family). They include:

"Wholesome Baby Foods from Scratch," by Karna S. Peterson, R.D., M.P.H.
With recipes for Cooked Leafy Greens, Basic Vegetable Recipe, Fresh Fruit,
Soybean Puree, Fresh Orange Sherbet, Homemade Fruity Gel, Knackbrod
(Swedish Hard Bread), and Carrot/Apple Mix.

"Avoiding the Baby Food Trap," By JoAnn Farb
With recipes for Green Potatoes, Quick-Browned Tofu , Chapati Roll-Ups, and
Tofu bagel spread.

"Healthy Fast Food for Pre-Schoolers," by Lisa Rivero
With recipes for Simple Peanut Butter/Tahini Sauce, Sweet Albert Sauce,
Banana Pudding Sauce, Quick Carrot Sauce, Orange Raisin Sauce, and Sweet
Potato Fig Sauce.

## MY VEGETARIAN CHILD IS HAVING A HARD TIME EATING AT SCHOOL. WHAT CAN I DO TO ENCOURAGE THE SCHOOL TO INCORPORATE MORE VEGETARIAN FOODS FOR THE KIDS?

This will depend on the school, their school lunch system, and also the willing-
ness of the administration and food service to make a few changes. We have a
school foods packet that can be mailed upon request. It offers resources, advice,
and information to share with the school officials.

The most important aspect is to be educated about vegetarianism AND school
foods policies BEFORE you start talking to the administration. If it is a school
receiving United States Department of Agriculture (USDA) reimbursement you
will face tighter restrictions and regulations. The packet explains some of these.
The USDA "Healthy School Meals Resource System" webpage offers more information: www.nal.usda.gov/fnic/schoolmeals.

Please refer to the United States Department of Agriculture (USDA) publication,
Toolkit for Healthy School Meals: Recipes and Training Materials, as well as the
Community Nutrition Action Kit that accompanies the toolkit. These are the current USDA tools for nutrition education and healthy meal preparation in the
schools. Your school food service department should already have copies from
the USDA. Please see page 244 in the appendix for information about the
Toolkit and additional information about school meals.

Once the changes reach the food service level, you will also want to make sure they have the resources, recipes, and understanding of vegetarian food service. If you have a veg-friendly food service director, you could start there and have them plead your case to the administration. Also, find out if you have any vegetarian teachers who might be willing to help.

Our *Tips for Introducing Vegetarian Foods to Institutions* is very helpful. It is online at www.vrg.org/fsupdate/tipsintroinstitute.htm or write, phone, or e-mail for a paper copy.

## HOW SHOULD THE REQUEST TO ADD MORE VEGETARIAN MENU OPTIONS BE MADE? VERBALLY, WRITTEN, BY COMMITTEE, AT A SCHOOL BOARD OR PTA MEETING, ETC.?

This will depend on the school district. Each of those methods would be ways to start. You may wish to first approach a friendly teacher or the food service staff informally and gather information. This will give you an idea of how much of a battle it will become or if you already have a sympathetic ear.

## WHAT'S A REALISTIC TIMEFRAME IN WHICH A CHANGE LIKE THIS CAN BE MADE?

Some people working with their schools have seen small changes within a month or two. In some cases, if the ordering has been done for the school year, the changes won't be visible for a year. However, some cafeteria staff might get creative with what they have on hand.

## BUT WHERE DOES A SCHOOL GET VEGETARIAN INFORMATION AND PRODUCTS?

The issue of vegetarian products and foods comes down to the amount of money the school district has to spend. Much of the food a school serves is part of the government commodities program. There are distributors for products, such as veggie burgers, from which schools could order if the funding was available. Just remember that changes are often instigated by one person. Our quantity cook-book Vegan in Volume has a chapter on school foods. This chapter, *Feeding Frenzy - Cooking for Kids*, has a section titled *Understanding Federal School Food Lunch Guidelines*, as well as sections on menu ideas, recipes, and nutrition news for children. We also publish a quarterly food service newsletter, *Foodservice Update.*

## WOULD THESE METHODS/RULES BE DIFFERENT FOR A STUDENT IN A PRIVATE SCHOOL?

It is likely that there would be differences. It is usually easier to make the changes in a private school. They tend to have more control and are small enough to institute change. They want to keep parents happy and tend to have more flexibility with their budget.

Due to governmental guidelines, most schools being reimbursed (these include public and non-profit private schools) have to follow certain menu specifications.

These are several types of School Meal Systems in use:

  ✳NuMenus: a nutrient-based approach that enables schools to evaluate menus based on the overall nutritional composition of meals, rather than by food groups. Schools may find it easier or less expensive to use the other approaches. This menu system is less commonly used, but is easier to utilize when incorporating vegetarian foods.

  ✳Assisted NuMenus: a nutrient-based system using ready-made menus that have been provided to the school by another source.

  ✳Food Based Menus: is the old system, which calls for specified amounts from the traditional four food groups.

For additional information view www.nal.usda.gov/fnic/schoolmeals/Regulations/index.html.

AFTER READING THE ARTICLE ON YOUR SITE CALLED
"VEGETARIANISM IN EDUCATIONAL SETTINGS," I WAS
THINKING HOW WONDERFUL IT WOULD BE IF THERE WAS
SUCH A THING AS A VEGETARIAN SCHOOL, LIKE MIDDLE
SCHOOL OR HIGH SCHOOL. THAT WOULD ELIMINATE SO
MANY OF THESE CONCERNS THAT VEGETARIAN PARENTS
HAVE, LIKE THE SCIENCE CLASSES, SCHOOL TRIPS, LUNCH-
ES, ETC., NOT TO MENTION THAT THE KIDS WOULD BE
LEARNING IN A MUCH MORE SUPPORTIVE ENVIRONMENT.
DO YOU KNOW IF SUCH A SCHOOL EXISTS IN THE US?

There are a few places that tend toward those lines. The Farm School in
Summertown, Tennessee is a vegetarian private school (www.thefarm.org/
lifestyle/fs.html) that is part of The Farm community, a cooperative settlement
founded in 1971. Some schools run by the Friends (a Quaker group), Seventh-
day Adventists, and Waldorf schools may support vegetarian ethics. There is also
a school for troubled or at-risk youth in Maryland called The Maryland Salem
Children's Trust which serves only vegetarian meals in keeping with the school's
compassionate overview. It seems that in areas where you find enclaves of vegetarian parents, you will find more compassionate schools and teachers.

I WANT TO BECOME A VEGETARIAN BUT I HATE TOFU AND
BEANS. IS THERE ANYTHING ELSE I CAN EAT TO KEEP ME
HEALTHY? AND I FORGOT THAT I NEEDED TO STATE THAT
I AM ONLY 12 YEARS OLD. ALSO I LOOKED AT YOUR SITE
AND IT SAYS MOSTLY TOFU AND BEANS SO PLEASE DON'T
JUST SEND ME A PAGE OF YOUR SITE TO READ. (UNLESS
IT SAYS OTHER THAN TO EAT TOFU AND BEANS) THANKS
AGAIN!

If you go back to the webpage about Vegetarian Nutrition for Teenagers
(www.vrg.org/nutrition/teennutrition.htm) you will see that it does say "variety is
the key to a healthy vegetarian diet." So, even if you did like tofu and beans,
that's not all you should eat. For example, for your protein sources, you could eat
wholegrain breads, cereals, nuts, peanut butter, and soymilk. For your calcium
sources, you could eat broccoli, kale, or calcium fortified orange juice or soymilk.

Your diet should also include plenty of fruits and vegetables.

Also, if you want a vegetarian substitute for meat, your local grocery store might carry Chik Patties, a vegetarian product made by Morningstar. These are popular with vegetarian children and teenagers. There are also different types of vegetarian burgers at the supermarkets. Other products you might enjoy are Tofurky slices, vegan "bacon," and Lightlife Deli Slices and jerky. Some you'll like, some you won't be crazy about. You'll probably need to experiment.

One more thing: as you get older your tastes will change. So even if you don't like tofu and beans now, you might enjoy them when you're older. Try beans and tofu prepared in ways that you are not familiar with, such as a tofu dish at a Chinese restaurant or a bean dish from a Middle Eastern restaurant. Perhaps you just haven't tried them prepared in a way that you like.

I HAVE A 6-YEAR-OLD DAUGHTER WHO I AM PRETTY EASY WITH WHEN IT COMES TO DAIRY AND SWEETS OUTSIDE OF OUR HOME. (WE ARE VEGAN AT HOME.) WHEN MY DAUGHTER GOES TO MY PARENTS' HOUSE AND THEY ARE EATING MEAT, SHE BEGS THEM FOR CHICKEN OR, ON THANKSGIVING, TURKEY. EVERY TIME I TURNED MY BACK ON THANKSGIVING, SOMEONE WAS GIVING HER TURKEY, WHICH SHE BEGGED THEM FOR. I GOT REALLY UPSET AND YELLED AT THEM AND HER. AM I WRONG OR DO YOU THINK I SHOULD LET HER MAKE HER OWN DECISION AT THIS AGE? THAT IS WHAT MY FAMILY THINKS. PLEASE LET ME KNOW WHAT YOU THINK.

I don't have the magic answer for you but here are some suggestions. I do have 2 children, 7 and 4, who are being raised vegan. So far they've been good about obeying me on food at other peoples' houses but the younger one loves to pretend she is eating chicken, etc. Try to figure out what's going on with your daughter. Is she trying to get attention? Is she teasing you? Is this a power struggle? I don't know what you've told her about why you are vegan but you may want to discuss this again with her and let her tell you what she thinks about the whole thing. Share your feelings with her. Six seems awfully young to me to decide you are going to eat meat. As I write this, I think "well, if a 6 year old wanted to be vegetarian, I'd support it." I do think these are two different situations. There seems to me to be a moral imperative for becoming vegetarian and not for eating meat. I think you are within your rights as a parent to tell your daughter (before the next family gathering) that your family does not eat meat and that you expect her to not sneak meat. Speak personally, kindly but firmly to all members of the family and tell them that you do not want them to give your child meat. It's tough but I know that other families have done this with other foods (like sweets, candy, etc.).

Reed Mangels, PhD, RD

VRG also offers an e-mail list for parents. You might find the experiences of other vegetarian parents helpful. It is online at groups.yahoo.com/group/vrgparents.

## PLEASE SEND ME MORE INFORMATION ABOUT YOUR ANNUAL ESSAY CONTEST. I'M 17.

**SUBJECT:** 2-3 page essay on any aspect of vegetarianism. Vegetarianism is not eating meat, fish, and birds (for example, chicken or duck). Among the many reasons for being a vegetarian are beliefs about ethics, culture, health, aesthetics, religion, world peace, economics, world hunger, and the environment.
Entrants should base their paper on interviewing, research, and/or personal opinion. You need not be a vegetarian to enter. All essays become the property of The Vegetarian Resource Group.

### ENTRY CATEGORIES:
A. Ages 14-18.
B. Ages 9-13.
C. Ages 8 and under.

**PRIZES:** A $50 savings bond will be awarded in each category.

**DEADLINE:** Must be postmarked by May 1 for each current year of judging.

**SEND ENTRIES TO:** The VRG, PO Box 1463, Baltimore, MD 21203; FAX: (410) 366-8804; e-mail: vrg@vrg.org. Include your name, address, telephone number, age, grade, school, and teacher's name.

The essay requirements and lesson plans for educators can also be accessed online at www.vrg.org/essay/. Go to www.vrg.org/family/kidsindex.htm to read past winning essays.

## ALTHOUGH I HAD GRAND IDEALS OF AN ORGANIC, NATU-RAL FOODS EXISTENCE FOR MY KIDS, I REALISTICALLY NEED TO KNOW WHAT FAST FOODS WE CAN EAT.

We publish *Vegetarian Menu Options at Restaurants and Quick Service Chains.* This 32-page "guide to fast food" details which foods are vegetarian and vegan, as well as which appear vegetarian, but are not, and the cooking methods used. The complete guide is available for $4. There is a quick guide to what is available at major chains on page 198.

## MY 7-YEAR-OLD SON WANTS TO BE A VEGETARIAN. HE IS EVEN PASSING UP MCDONALDS! SO I, AS A MOTHER, NEED TO KNOW MORE ABOUT THIS. I PLAN ON MAKING THE WHOLE FAMILY EAT LESS MEAT, AND STILL COMPENSATE FOR MY SON. WHAT ARE SOME GOOD BOOKS FOR US TO READ? AND I DO STILL WANT TO LET HIM EAT FISH, BECAUSE I READ A LOT ABOUT THE NUTRIENTS THEY HAVE. IS THIS STILL OKAY?

We have a section on our website that might help soothe your fears. Our *Raising a Vegetarian Family* section of the website is at www.vrg.org/family. It has information, both nutritional and practical. *Feeding Vegan Kids* offers nutritional information and is at www.vrg.org/nutshell/kids.htm. Paper materials are also gladly provided - just write, phone, or e-mail a request.

As for cookbooks, there are several that are written specifically for families. We've found <u>Meatless Meals for Working People</u> to be very popular. Other possible titles include <u>Vegetables Rock!</u>, <u>Great Food for Great Kids Recipes,</u>

<u>Vegetarian Children</u>, <u>Raising Your Family Naturally</u>, <u>Kids Can Cook</u>, and <u>Feeding the Whole Family</u>. See page 242 for a list of suggested books for vegetarian families.

As for fish, although it is not vegetarian, that is up to you. However, a vegetarian diet, if balanced, should provide your son with all the nutrients he needs.

<hr/>

I HAVE A GRANDDAUGHTER WHO IS IN SECOND GRADE AND BECAME A VEGETARIAN WHEN SHE WAS FOUR AFTER SEEING THE MOVIE *BABE*. SHE IS FEELING ISOLATED AND I WOULD LIKE TO HOOK HER UP WITH A VEGETARIAN PEN PAL. I KNOW THERE USED TO BE SUCH A THING, BUT HAVEN'T SEEN ANYTHING RECENTLY, NOR CAN I REMEMBER WHO SPONSORED IT. CAN YOU HELP?

I think we can help a bit.

There is a vegetarian pen pal service in the United Kingdom and information about this is on the web at www.vegsoc.org/youth/penpals.html, or contact VC 21 Zone, Bronwen Humphreys, The Vegetarian Society, Parkdale, Dunham Road, Altrincham, Cheshire WA14 4QG.

There is another listing here: www.vegsource.com/talk/penpal/index.html

Here are a few webpages that might also be of interest:
* www.vegfamily.com (Veg Family)
* www.vrg.org/family/ (VRG Family section)
* www.vrg.org/links/#Youth (links to youth resources)

We have a vegetarian parents' list and if you would like to have your granddaughter send a brief message, I can forward it to the families on the list that might have children interested in writing her.

We can also provide your granddaughter with some of our children's materials, including our *I Love Animals and Broccoli Coloring Book* and *Shopping Basket*.

## BESIDES THE SOUP TO NUTS AND I LOVE ANIMALS AND BROCCOLI BOOKS, ARE THERE ANY RESOURCES FOR TEACHING PRESCHOOLERS ABOUT VEGETARIANISM?

Herb the Vegetarian Dragon, by Jules Bass and Debbie Harter, is a publication that seems popular among parents and kids. In the story, all the other dragons are meateaters except for Herb. Other themes in the story include peer pressure to eat meat and trying to live on a world with different types of creatures. Also, try The Race Against Junk Food, 'Twas the Night Before Thanksgiving, The Kind Wolf, and Babe.

You might find the listing of children's books from the May/June 1997 issue of *Vegetarian Journal* helpful. It is online at www.vrg.org/journal/vj97may/976vbook.htm. Write, phone, or e-mail to request a paper copy.

The International Vegetarian Union also offers a list of books suitable for children ages 4-8. This is online at www.ivu.org/books/reviews/children4-8.html.

# CHAPTER 10

# SOY

For many years, tofu was seemingly synonymous with vegetarian. However, soyfoods have recently gained in popularity and are becoming more widely accessible to the average consumer. Some hail soy as a miracle cure, while other accuse it of being a health threat. In this chapter, we've tried to cover some basic information about soyfoods, as well as address some of the controversy.

### I'M STILL NOT CLEAR ON SOY. IS IT A BEAN OR WHAT? HOW CAN I INCLUDE SOME SOY-BASED FOODS ON MY MENU? HOW CAN I "SELL" IT TO MY OMNIVORE CUSTOMERS, SO IT'S WORTH MY WHILE TO HAVE IT ON THE MENU?

Soy certainly is getting a lot of press these days; the FDA is allowing soy producers to list health claims on their soy products concerning the role of soy in reducing the risk of heart disease. The USDA is allowing school food services to substitute soy for meat in school meals. So, we're not surprised that you're getting more requests for soy foods (and we bet that your "omnivores" will be more than willing to sample new and exciting menu items). Soy comes from soybeans, and soybeans belong to the legume family, the same as lentils and peas. Fresh green soybeans (edamame in Japanese) can be steamed and eaten as a snack or used to add crunch to salads. Think of edamame as a bar snack, as a fun appetizer, or as a different side dish. Cooked soybeans are available canned, in green, black, and yellow. Use them to make a fast chili, bean soup, or addition to salad bars. You can purée soybeans to form the base of a dip for chips and veggies. Ask your purveyors about in-the-pod or shelled, frozen soybeans.

Soy has been around for at least 5,000 years. Amuse your customers with a little soy history, such as sailors and traders bringing soybeans with them as they traveled around the world as early as the 1400's. The first commercial soy crop was grown in 1829. During the Civil War, soldiers used soybeans as a substitute coffee and brewed a hot beverage from them. American farmers grow about two billion bushels of soybeans a year. Although there are no RDA's for soy, if someone asks, medical research suggests that 25 grams of soy protein a day may help to control cholesterol, slow bone thinning, and reduce the risk of heart disease and some cancers. Soymilk can be drunk on its own and can be readily substituted for cow's milk. Pour it over hot or cold cereal, use it for creamy sauces and salad dressings, and in cold smoothies or hot coffee beverages. Tofu, available in different textures and flavors, can be sliced cold and put into green or pasta salads or prepared hot in stir-fries, soups, and pastas. It can also be used as a pizza topping. Tempeh (fermented soy) is firm enough to grill or roast, and its smoky flavor makes it a good alternative to beef in sandwiches, chili, soups, and casseroles. TVP (textured vegetable protein) can be formed into burgers, loaves, and roasts or crumbled into sauces or soups. Good luck and think soy!

Nancy Berkoff, RD
VRG Food Service Advisor

## I'VE HEARD CONFLICTING OPINIONS ON THE USE OF SOY PRODUCTS TO RELIEVE HOT FLASHES AND OTHER DISCOMFORTS OF MENOPAUSE. WHAT DO YOU THINK?

Soy products contain substances called isoflavones, which are weak estrogens that can have hormonal effects. Rapid changes in hormone levels in menopause can lead to changes in temperature regulation and to hot flashes and night sweats. Soy isoflavones may help to reduce these discomforts by keeping blood estrogen levels from dropping as much as they typically do in menopause. When soy foods are added to women's diets, women report a modest decrease in the frequency (1, 2) and the severity (3, 4) of hot flashes and vaginal dryness, although this is not always seen (5). These effects appear to be smaller than those observed with conventional hormone replacement therapy. If you are experiencing symptoms and would prefer to avoid hormone replacement therapy, a trial of adding soy to your diet seems reasonable. However, we should note that it's too early to say that soy products can replace conventional therapy. On the positive side, they do appear to reduce risk of heart disease. On the negative side, they seem to stimulate breast cell multiplication in some women, which raises concerns about increased cancer risk (6, 7). In addition, soy products may or may not reduce bone loss associated with menopause.

1 Maturitas 1995. 21:189-195.
2 Obstet Gynecol 1998. 91:6-11.
3 Menopause 1997. 4:89-94.
4 Menopause 1999. 6:7-13.
5 J Nutr 2000. 130:671S.
6 Am J Clin Nutr 1998. 68 (Suppl):1431S.
7 Cancer Epidem Bio Prev 1996. 5:785.

## I AM INTERESTED IN USING SOY AS A NATURAL ESTROGEN REPLACEMENT IN MY DIET. MY QUESTION IS THIS: IS THE ESTROGEN IN SOY HEAT-SENSITIVE - I.E., IN COOKING, DOES IT HOLD UP UNDER COOKING TEMPERATURES? IS THERE RESEARCH TO BACK THIS UP?

Soy works for some women to control symptoms like hot flashes. It does not work for everyone. Soy products appear to have a modest effect in terms of preventing osteoporosis which is less than the effect seen with estrogen therapy. This may or may not be a concern for you. Soy may also help reduce risk of heart disease, a condition which women are at greater risk for after menopause.

Here's a good website by Mark Messina which does discuss the use of soy products to replace estrogen: www.olympus.net/messina/answers.html#q17.

There are many reasons why a vegetarian diet is a good choice. Vegetarians have lower rates of obesity, heart disease, high blood pressure, diabetes, and some kinds of cancer. So, rather than just adding soy products to your diet, you may want to consider going vegetarian. The Vegetarian Resource Group has lots of helpful information.

With regard to your question on the effect of cooking on soy products, it appears that the amount of phytoestrogens (called isoflavones) in soy products is not reduced by cooking unless the food is burned. However, in some cases the chemical form of the isoflavone is changed. We do not yet know what effect this has on the usefulness of the isoflavones. We do know that the type of isoflavone found in fermented soy foods like miso and tempeh is different from the form found in other foods like soymilk, tofu, and soy flour; however, further research is needed in this area. Studies on the effect of soy on reducing symptoms of menopause like hot flashes have used soy flour or soy foods (presumably cooked) and positive results have been seen, suggesting that cooking does not markedly affect the ability of phytoestrogens from soy to reduce menopausal symptoms, at least in some women.

The reference for the effect of cooking on soy isoflavones is: Chemical modification of isoflavones in soyfoods during cooking and processing. *American Journal of Clinical Nutrition* 1998; 68 (suppl):1486S-1491S.

Reed Mangels, PhD, RD

## IS IT TRUE THAT EATING SOY PRODUCTS CAN SUPPRESS THE THYROID?

Soybeans are among a number of foods that contain compounds called goitrogens. These interfere with thyroid function and in extreme cases could cause an enlarged thyroid or goiter which is a sign of thyroid insufficiency. However, research indicates that boosting iodine intake (iodine is a mineral needed for normal thyroid function) prevents this goitrogenic effect. It also appears that heating soy - which is a part of the process in making all soyfoods - eliminates the goitrogenic effects.

Some of the concern dates back to the 1950s when several cases of goiter occurred in infants fed soy formulas that weren't fortified with iodine. However these formulas were based on soy flour while today's soy infant formulas are based on soy protein isolate. Soy protein isolate has been shown to be less goitrogenic than soy flour. Also, the formulas used today are fortified with iodine. As a result, there haven't been any cases of goiter in babies fed today's soy infant formulas. However, in babies who have a rare congenital disease that requires treatment with synthetic thyroid hormone, those who consume soy infant formula do need increased doses of this hormone.

Research shows that fiber supplements also increase the amount of thyroid medication needed by people who are hypothyroid. Soy may act in the same way, by decreasing the absorption of thyroid hormone. This is not a reason for healthy people to stop eating soyfoods. In recent research, eating isoflavone-rich soyfoods didn't affect thyroid function in premenopausal women, post-menopausal women, or men. (Isoflavones are one of the compounds in soy that are being studied for possible goitrogenic effects.)

Most evidence suggests that eating soyfoods doesn't pose any risk for healthy people. However, it could be a problem for those whose intake of iodine is marginal and there is some evidence that vegans have lower iodine intakes than meat eaters. Therefore, it is very important for vegans who consume soyfoods to make sure that they are getting enough iodine. Using moderate amounts of iodine-fortified salt is the easiest way to do this, although iodine supplements are available as well. For people who are taking thyroid medication, it is certainly possible that soy could raise medication needs and this is something that should be monitored by a physician. Those with a history of thyroid problems should have their thyroid function monitored regularly, whether or not they consume soyfoods.

Virginia Messina, MPH, RD

## WHAT'S THIS I HEAR ABOUT TOFU MAKING PEOPLE SENILE?

Reprinted from *Vegetarian Journal* September/October 2000 "Scientific Update" by Reed Mangels, PhD, RD -

*"A recent study of Japanese men living in Hawaii found that those who ate tofu 2 to 4 times per week when they were around 45-65 years old had higher rates of mental deterioration (low brain weight, Alzheimer's disease, poorer cognitive function) in their later years when compared with men who ate less tofu (White, et al). Results were similar for the wives of the men, although the women were not asked how much tofu they ate; researchers assumed if their husbands ate tofu, the wives did also. Male subjects who ate the most tofu in midlife had a 1.6 to 2-times higher risk of impaired brain function, compared to those who ate less tofu. The authors of this study speculated that isoflavones were responsible for the apparent adverse effect of tofu consumption. It is possible that other unknown factors impacted brain function and that tofu consumption was*

*associated with those factors and was not itself the risk factor. A study of older Japanese women living in the Seattle area found that tofu intake over a two-year period did not affect cognitive function (Rice, et al). However, two years may be too short a time to observe a significant effect on function.*

*"At this point, dietary changes should not be made as a result of the one study showing brain changes associated with tofu consumption. There may be other factors in these subjects or their diets that could have influenced the results. Hopefully, additional research will clarify many of these issues."*

White LR, Petrovitch H, Ross GW, et al. 2000. Brain aging and midlife tofu consumption. *J Am Coll Nutr* 19: 242-255.
Rice MM, Graves AB, McCurry SM, et al. 2000. Tofu consumption and cognition in older Japanese American men and women. *J Nutr* 130 (suppl 3): 676S.

<hr>

**I JUST READ YOUR ARTICLE ABOUT THE PROCESSING OF TVP. MY QUESTION IS, ARE THE OTHER SOY PRODUCTS QUESTIONABLE TOO? I RECENTLY REVIEWED AN ARTICLE ABOUT SOY. CAN YOU RESPOND TO SOME OF THE FOLLOWING STATEMENTS BASED ON WHAT I READ IN THE ARTICLE?**

(All responses from Reed Mangels, PhD, RD)

**Statement:** Soybeans contains phytic acid (phytates) that block the body's uptake of essential minerals like calcium, magnesium, iron and zinc, and they are very resistant to phytate reducing techniques such as long, slow cooking. Only after a long period of fermentation (tempeh and miso) are phytate and antinutrient levels of soybeans reduced, making their nourishment available to the human digestive system. The high levels of harmful substances remaining in precipitated soy products leave their nutritional value questionable at best, and in the least, potentially harmful.

**Response:** Yes, soybeans contain phytates which interfere with absorption of minerals. However, I think this is a grossly exaggerated concern. Whole grains and other dried beans also contain phytates. Should we eliminate all of these foods? Soybeans are high in phytic acid but this does not mean that their use completely prevents us from absorbing any of the minerals listed above. Iron absorption from soy tends to be fairly poor, but soy is also high in iron to begin with so there is some compensation for reduced absorption. Vitamin C containing foods eaten along with soy products counteract the effects of phytate. Calcium absorption from soy (including from whole soybeans) is quite good despite the presence of phytic acid. Soy products are not an outstanding source of zinc but that alone is not a reason to avoid use of soy products. Fermentation of soy products (tempeh, miso) reduces their phytate content.

**Statement:** Soybeans contain potent enzyme inhibitors that block uptake of trypsin and other enzymes that the body needs for protein digestion. Normal cooking does not deactivate these harmful anti-nutrients.

**Response:** Raw soybeans contain enzyme inhibitors that interfere with the digestion of protein. However, raw soybeans are not usually eaten. Cooking deactivates these inhibitors and cooking is used in the production of all soyfoods. Cooking/processing does not destroy all of the enzyme inhibitors in soyfoods so that, generally, they do contain small amounts of these inhibitors. There is no evidence of which I'm aware of problems associated with these very low levels of inhibitors. Additionally, some of these inhibitors become inactivated when they come in contact with gastric juices. Finally, some of these enzyme inhibitors have been hypothesized to actually have anticancer effects.

**Statement:** Soybeans contain hemagglutinin, a clot promoting substance that causes red blood cells to clump together. These clustered blood cells are unable to properly absorb oxygen for distribution to the body's tissues, and cannot help in maintaining good cardiac health. Although the act of fermenting soybeans does deactivate both trypsin inhibitors and hemagglutinin, precipitation and cooking do not. Even though these enzyme inhibitors are reduced in levels within precipitated soy products like tofu, they are not altogether eliminated.

**Response:** Heat inactivates these hemagglutinins as does fermentation. Most of us don't eat raw soybeans. The amount of these hemagglutinins in soyfoods seems to be pretty low and almost nonexistent in some soy products such as meat substitutes. Again, I haven't seen evidence that these present a problem for people who eat soy.

**Statement:** The results of recent studies on soybeans' effect on human health have been largely underwritten by various factions of the soy industry. The primary claims about soy's health benefits are based purely on bad science. They provided several examples.

**Response:** Define "bad science." Research has been published in recognized peer-reviewed journals using methodology that is generally accepted as appropriate.

**Statement:** Some researchers speculate that the inactive B-12 found in fermented soy products may actually serve to block the body's B-12 absorption.

**Response:** Key word here is speculate. Evidence is needed to substantiate this type of statement. Tempeh, a fermented soy product is not considered to be a reliable source of vitamin B-12. If it does contain any vitamin B-12 analogues (they look like vitamin B-12, but can block absorption), this should only have a small, if any, effect on someone eating a varied diet.

**Statement:** The processes which render the soybean edible are also the processes which render it inedible. Alkaline solution is used in the fermenting process and then the mixture is heated. This process destroys most, but not all, of the anti-nutrients. It also has the effect of denaturing the proteins of the beans so they become very difficult to digest and greatly reduced in effectiveness. The alkaline solution produces a carcinogen, lysinealine, and reduces the already low cysteine content within the soybean. Cysteine plays an essential role in liver detox, allowing our bodies to filter and eliminate toxins. Without proper amounts of cysteine, the protein complex of the soybean becomes useless.

**Response:** Protein digestion from soyfoods is actually pretty good - better than 90%. So I'm perplexed as to how the conclusion was reached that protein in soy become difficult to digest. Soy is lower in cysteine in proportion to other essential amino acids when compared to the amino acid needs of humans. However, use of soy products and other foods certainly provide more than adequate amounts of cysteine. Soy is a good protein source.

## I'M CONFUSED. ONE MINUTE ALL I HEAR ABOUT IS SOY'S BENEFITS AND THE NEXT IT IS BEING TREATED LIKE A TOXIN. WHAT GIVES?

There were several good articles explaining both sides of this conflict. One was done by Laura Lane for CNN and is titled "How Good Is Soy?" If you go to the CNN website and use the search feature it should be easily accessible. The other was "Mad About the Soy," by Suzannah Oliver, and can be accessed on the Fox News website at www.foxnews.com/health/101000/soy.sml. For a more scientific resource, refer to the Loma Linda University *Vegetarian Nutrition & Health Letter* article "Is Soy Safe to Eat?" (September 2000). The articles all come to the conclusion that there is not enough evidence yet to prove that you should exclude soy foods from your diet.

# CHAPTER 11

# VEGAN CONCERNS

The reasons people become vegan vary. In many cases it is because of the plight of farm animals, whether slaughtered immediately or eventually. This chapter addresses concerns and questions we've had posed to us, which tend to focus on the animal rights aspects. We've also included information to help others understand why vegans avoid certain products.

For further information about veganism, read, Becoming Vegan, by Brenda Davis, RD, and Vesanto Melina, MS, RD, Simply Vegan, by Debra Wasserman and Reed Mangels, PhD, RD, Vegan: The New Ethics of Eating, by Eric Marcus, and *Why Vegan?* by Vegan Outreach.

## WHY DON'T VEGANS DRINK MILK OR EAT EGGS?

The decision to become vegan often stems from ethical, health, and/or environmental reasons. Some vegans feel that consumption of dairy and egg products supports the meat industry. Once the animals that provide eggs and milk are too old or are no longer productive, they are slaughtered for meat. The dairy industry creates an excess of calves born because they need the dairy cows to keep lactating. These calves are raised for veal, leather, and other products. Male chicks are also seen as unnecessary excess and are routinely killed. The conditions that these animals are raised in are of concern for many vegans.

Many vegans choose this lifestyle to promote a more humane and caring world. They know they are not perfect, but believe they have a responsibility to try to do their best, while not being judgmental of others.

To read more request a copy of *Vegan Diets in a Nutshell* from VRG or go to www.vrg.org/nutshell.vegan.htm.

Another excellent introduction to vegan ethics is *Why Vegan?*, by Vegan Outreach. It goes into detail about the ethical issues involved. *Why Vegan?* is accessible at www.veganoutreach.org/whyvegan. You can also contact Vegan Outreach at 211 Indian Dr., Pittsburgh, PA 15238.

<hr />

## WHAT ARE THE CONCERNS ABOUT USING FREE-RANGE EGGS?

There are eggs marketed as "free-range" and "humanely-raised." However, the conditions the hens are kept in may be quite similar to chicken houses. There is no uniform standard of care, and ultimately the hens are killed for meat, once past their egg-laying prime.

<hr />

## I AM LOOKING FOR A BOOK OR SOME INFORMATION THAT MIGHT TELL OF SOME OF THE MORE HIDDEN PLACES ANIMAL PRODUCTS ARE USED, SUCH AS FILM PROCESSING, GELATIN, AND OTHER THINGS OF THIS SORT.

Are you looking beyond food ingredients? Unfortunately, there is no one definitive guide. VRG does research related to this topic and some of our information is contained in this book. Some ingredient lists mix food, cosmetic, and industrial ingredients together, but each has different standards. Some of the best information about "hidden" ingredients often comes from meat producers. See page 37 for a list of various animal-derived ingredients in everyday products.

Common places to find animal ingredients include shoes, candles, film, soap, and other personal care products. There are other ordinary places that are so ubiquitous that they are difficult to spot, such as horsehair in plaster walls, animal glue in old furniture, casein in paint, and leather-bound books.

Truthfully, there is no such thing as a pure vegan. We would drive ourselves crazy trying to aspire to living 100% free of animal products. We must keep the ideal and work toward the world we want to live in, while realizing that each of us does the best we can. There are things we can easily avoid, such as cheese, omelets, milkshakes, fur, and leather. This is a choice we, as vegans, make. Regrettably, animal products are so pervasive that often we cannot avoid animal-derived substances that are in our furniture, car engines, asphalt, and magazines. Everyone will draw the line in different places. Avoid what you can and find positive ways to try and create change. As more people become vegan, this can slowly change.

## WHAT'S WRONG WITH SILK?

Many vegans choose not to consume anything from an animal, including insects. Especially when the insect is killed as part of the production methods.

Modern silk is the product of a domesticated silkworm (Bombyx mori). According to Dr. John Dingle, "The Bombyx genus of silkworms has co-evolved with the mulberry tree genus (Morus)...It is estimated that 1500 silkworms eat approximately 250kg leaves and produce 1 kg silk." Once the cocoons reach the size necessary for harvesting (4-5 weeks), they are steamed "for 3 minutes to kill the pupa."

For additional information go to :
* www.animal.uq.edu.au/staff/jgd/silk_and_silkworm_production.htm
* www.vegansociety.com/info/info19.html
* www.vegsoc.org/info/clothing.html#sil

## WHAT ABOUT WOOL?

Due to modern domestic husbandry of wool bearing sheep, they must be shorn. Their coats are so heavy and thick that they would not be able to survive the summer heat without shearing. Wild species of sheep do not need to be sheared. Different regions of the world produce different types of wool. Sheep bred in the UK tend to produce a coarse wool, while Merino sheep, bred in Spain and

Australia, produce a fine wool that is used in clothing. "Mulesing" is performed in an effort to control "flystrike," a dangerous condition where blow flies lay eggs in the soft tissue of sheep, most commonly the anus and surrounding area. The following is a description from the Agriculture of Western Australia website,

> "Mulesing involves surgical removal of wool-bearing skin from the crutch area, and is best done at lamb marking, or following shearing or crutching of weaners. When the cuts heal, the natural bare area around the vulva and anus is stretched and enlarged. This reduces dampness caused by sweating, urine and faecal staining, and so minimizes susceptibility to flystrike."

If the wound is not carefully monitored in the weeks after the operation, the lambs become even more susceptible to flystrike. According to the Codes of Practice, Welfare of Animals (Australia), tail docking and castration can be performed without anaesthetic.

As with dairy cows and egg-laying hens, when the wool production of the sheep declines, the ewe is sent to slaughter. The lambs born to these sheep are also sold for meat.

## WHY DON'T VEGANS CONSUME HONEY?

Many vegans choose not to consume anything from an animal, including insects. For some of the issues surrounding honey, please read "Busy Bees," by Caroline Pyevich, from the November/December 1996 issue of *Vegetarian Journal.* Write, phone, or e-mail to request a copy, or view it online at www.vrg.org/journal/vj96nov/bee.htm.

## WHY DON'T VEGANS WEAR LEATHER?

Reprinted with permission from *The Animals' Agenda*, PO Box 25881, Baltimore, MD 21224; (410) 675-4566;www.animalsagenda.org.

## The Skin Off Their Backs
## By Elliot L. Gang

The use of animal skins as clothing dates back to our cave-dwelling ancestors, and while the business of producing leather has evolved since then, the ethics behind the practice haven't. Last year more than 37 million beef and dairy cattle were slaughtered primarily for meat, not hides. But the pervasive use of leather increases the number of cattle killed, and tanning is destructive to the environment.

Much of the value of cattle comes from offal or byproducts, including hide, tallow, and bone. The National Cattlemen's Beef Association (NCBA) claims that "[u]se of by-products keeps beef prices to consumers lower than they otherwise would be. Hides are the single most valuable by-product." Although cattle hide is used to make glue, gelatin, and "pet" treats, almost all the economic value of hide comes from its use in leather production. Government and industry figures put the worth of the hide at about 6-7 percent of the value of the live animal, or just over $2 billion a year in the United States. To put these figures in perspective, in the article, "Winning the War for the West" (*Atlantic Monthly*, July 1999), Perri Knize estimated that "on average, ranchers make only a two percent return on their operations, and many don't do that well. They would be better off liquidating their assets and putting them in a passbook savings account." USDA figures give an estimated average rancher profit of 6-8 percent in mid-1999 (not including capital replacement costs). Clearly, a loss of 6-7 percent in earnings would drive some ranchers out of business, and cause many more to scale back their cattle raising operations.

Specialty and "exotic" leathers are made from a variety of unfortunate animals, including pigs, sheep, goats, horses, bison, emus, and ostriches. Wild animals killed for leather include boars, deer, elephants, kangaroos, water buffaloes, whales, zebras, eels, sharks, seals, walruses, frogs, crocodiles, lizards, snakes, and turtles. Alligators are both hunted and raised commercially for their skins; in 1995, approximately 200,000 were killed in the United States. Many of the wild animals killed for exotic leathers are poached, and some species are threatened or endangered. There are few reliable figures for the sale of specialty leathers, but estimates run into the billions of dollars.

The United States dominates the world cattle hide market. Almost half of the hides produced in America are exported, and last year's exports netted $960 million. The process of turning raw hides into leather products takes a toll on both the environment and human health. The Environmental Protection Agency (EPA) notes common hazardous waste products found at tanning facilities include aniline dyes, chromium salts, corrosive sludge and liquids, volatile organic compounds, and sulfides. Many aniline dyes and volatile organic compounds used in leather tanning are toxic and carcinogenic. Exposure to these wastes is an occupational hazard for tannery workers. Toxic waste disposal, the release of inadequately treated wastewater, and leaching from contaminated soil results in ground, water, and air pollution. Long-term exposure to chromium in drinking water can cause liver, kidney, and nerve damage. Occupational exposure to the chemicals is linked to high rates of testicular and other cancers in tannery workers. Surrounding communities also show elevated cancer rates, including leukemia.

The production of leather is energy intensive, even if the energy costs of raising cattle are ignored. The basic process involves stripping the hide from the carcass, cleaning it with a salt and bactericide solution, and soaking it for cleaning and rehydration. Then sulfides and calcium hydroxide are used to remove the hair and make removing all the flesh easier. The hide is then treated with more chemicals (often sulfides), neutralized, and pickled (usually with a sulfuric acid solution) to allow tanning agents to penetrate the skin. Then it is tanned using chromium salts and wrung out to dry before being sorted and further processed based upon its ultimate use.

But today, the use of leather most often boils down to choice rather than necessity. Nonleather materials are becoming better produced and more mainstream. Improved synthetics, including microfibers, are cheaper and more comfortable than past materials. And although the production of synthetics also involves some degree of environmental pollution, there is far greater damage from animal agriculture.

## BUT DOWN DOESN'T INVOLVE KILLING THE BIRD, DOES IT?

Some of the feathers come from slaugtered birds and some come from birds that are live plucked. Removing feathers from live geese and ducks is traumatic and painful. The birds are often injured in the struggle. The birds are plucked two to three times a year until ultimately slaughtered.

According to the United States Department of Agriculture, "When these birds are slaughtered, they are first stunned electrically. After their throats are cut (by hand, for geese) and the birds are bled, they are scalded to facilitate removal of large feathers. To remove fine pinfeathers, the birds are dipped in paraffin wax. Down and feathers, a very valuable by-product of the duck and goose industry, are sorted at another facility." (Safety of Duck and Goose, FSIS Consumer Education and Information). This would apply to down produced in the US; China, Hungary, and Poland are the major producers.

For additional information contact United Poultry Concerns, Inc. at PO Box 150, Machipongo, VA; (757) 678-7875; www.upc-online.org. They have a web-page about down production at www.upc-online.org/livepluc.html. Also see The International Vegetarian Union webpage on vegan clothing concerns: www.ivu.org/faq/clothing.html.

# CHAPTER 12

# UNIQUE QUESTIONS

This chapter addresses the questions that make my day as a researcher. These are the ones that I had never thought of and that caused me to scratch my head, wondering where I was going to find an answer. Digging for the answers often leads to even more questions! These are the ones that show that we, as vegetarians, are constantly questioning our surroundings and wondering how we can improve upon accepted convention.

### I LOVE TO FEED THE BIRDS IN MY YARD, BUT IS THERE A VEGETARIAN SUET AVAILABLE?

Pre-made vegetable suet is more common to England where it is used in pies and pastries. It would easily be found there at grocery stores and the like. In the US, you might want to try an English specialty store.

Vegetable suet can be easily melted and mixed with seeds, but is more difficult to mold than beef suet. It can be smeared on trees, packed into pine cones, or rough bark strips. In warmer weather, the suet can melt and stick to the birds' feathers, reducing the bird's ability to maintain body heat. It is best to use when the average temperature is near or below freezing.

Birdseed suet can be made by mixing vegetable shortening/suet, peanut butter, oatmeal, and birdseed. Check a bird-watching guide for recipes and suggestions.

## IS TATTOO INK VEGAN?

This information comes from Seth Cefari, a Baltimore tattoo artist with over 10 years of experience.

*The inks are metal-based, for example red iron oxide, titanium etc. The vehicle which disperses the inks can be different things such as soap grain alcohol. The only thing that may not be vegetarian is glycerine (which can be vegetable-or animal-derived). This is not ink, but rather what might be used in the process of getting the ink from the gun to your body. This would be a question to ask the person tattooing you because they should know what is used in the vehicle that disperses the ink.*

To get back to your question, the inks themselves should be vegan.

## IS THERE ANY PALEO RECORD OF GARLIC CONSUMPTION?

I couldn't find a reference that old, but I did find some history here:
www.garlicfestival.com/Rx/worldhistory.html
www.web-holidays.com/garlic/history.htm
www.gerlados.com/historygarlic.htm

According to one site, there are references to garlic as far back as 1500 BC, in Egypt, where it was said to help a variety of ailments.

## HOW DO I GET RID OF INSECTS WITHOUT KILLING THEM?

According to the Natural Food Garden, by Patrick Lima, a great insect repellent that won't kill the bugs is a homemade mixture. Lima recommends blending a few peeled garlic bulbs, a small onion, and a tablespoon of cayenne peeper in a quart of water. Next add any pungent herbs such as peppermint, cedar leaves, wormwood, or coriander (cilantro). Let the mixture steep for an hour or more. Strain through a cloth and transfer to a spray bottle. You can spray the mixture anywhere you see the bugs and chances are they will not return to that area.

NEXT SEMESTER, I WILL BE IN COSTA RICA DOING LEAD-
ERSHIP TRAINING IN THE LOCAL DEAF COMMUNITY. I
RECENTLY READ ABOUT AN ACTIVITY I WOULD LIKE TO USE
WITH THE "BUDDING LEADERS" (AND MORE-EXPERIENCED
LEADERS) THAT I WILL BE WORKING WITH — THE PROBLEM
IS, IT CALLS FOR USING EGGS. AS A VEGAN, I WOULD LIKE
TO DEVISE A VEGAN ALTERNATIVE THAT WOULD RETAIN
THE SPIRIT AND PURPOSE OF THE ACTIVITY.

IN THE ACTIVITY, GROUPS ARE GIVEN AN EGG, SOME POP-
SICLE STICKS, SOME STRAWS, AND SOME TAPE. EACH
GROUP IS ASKED TO USE THE STICKS, STRAWS, AND TAPE
TO CREATE A BASKET OR CRATE DESIGNED TO PROTECT
THE EGG FROM BEING BROKEN, EVEN IF DROPPED FROM A
HEIGHT OF FIVE FEET. AT FIRST I THOUGHT OF USING
EMPTY GLASS BOTTLES, BUT THEN I REJECTED THIS IDEA
FOR TWO REASONS — FIRST, SOME GLASS BOTTLES ARE
THICK AND PRETTY STURDY DESPITE BEING MADE OF
GLASS SO, UNLIKE EGGS, EVEN SOME UNPROTECTED BOT-
TLES MIGHT NOT ALWAYS BREAK FROM A FALL AT A
HEIGHT OF FIVE FEET AND, SECOND, IF THEY DO BREAK,
THE RESULTING SHARDS OF GLASS WOULD BE A LOT MORE
DANGEROUS THAN BROKEN EGG SHELLS.

DO YOU HAVE ANY SUGGESTIONS FOR MATERIALS I CAN
USE OTHER THAN EGGS THAT WOULD BE 1) FRAGILE/EASI-
LY BROKEN; 2) PREFERABLY SMALL — IT PROBABLY ISN'T
IMPORTANT THAT THEY BE THE EXACT SAME SIZE AS
EGGS; 3) CHEAP AND EASY TO OBTAIN, NO MATTER WHERE
I AM (I WOULD PROBABLY HAVE TO OBTAIN MOST OF MY
MATERIALS WHILE IN COSTA RICA); AND 4) VEGAN!

This was one of our more unusual inquiries. The usual egg replacers, such as
bananas and Ener-G, just aren't going to work this time!

We had a bit of a VRG brainstorm and came up with the following suggestions:
Light bulbs (you could use some that have burned-out, which should be readily
available). They are made of glass, so you might want to wrap them in tape,

gauze, plastic wrap, or another material to keep the glass from shattering.

Another posibility would be to make "eggs" using some paper-mache and a balloon. You would need to weight them somehow, to make them a bit more fragile, or increase the height. Perhaps a combination of the two would work. Additional suggestions are: tomatoes (or other fragile fruits/veg), kiwi fruit, water balloons, chalk, and crackers.

***

## As a vegan, I was horrified to find out recently that at least some watercolor paper also has sizing made from animal gelatin! Does anyone know if this is true of ALL paper made commercially, or if it's possible to find some that doesn't have any sizing at all?

Paper sizing can be made from soap, gelatin, fatty acids and glycerides, and casein.

According to the Winsor & Newton website, *"Sizing is the reduction of absorbency in the sheet. Without it color could not be drawn across the sheet as it would blot immediately. Many brands of watercolor papers are both 'internally' and 'externally' sized. Internal sizing reduces the absorbency of the fibre itself by chemically bonding to it. External sizing is a layer of gelatine on the surface of the paper, resulting in the watercolor film laying on the surface, looking brighter and allowing it to be sponged off if desired by the painter. Gelatine gives a harder surface which also allows scraping and rubbing without damaging the paper itself. External sizing is also known as gelatine surface sizing."* (www.winsornewton.com)

Daniel Smith Artist Materials claims to produce paper sizing that is made of cellulose fibers and cornstarch. For more information, go to www.danielsmith.com/papermaking.html or contact Daniel Smith Artist Materials (800) 426-6740. Gum rosin and fumaric acid, both of which are vegan, are also commonly used. It is one of those ingredients you won't be able to determine unless you find a paper company that specifies the origin of their sizing.

A CUSTOMER OF MINE HAS A SEVERE ALLERGY TO MSG AND WONDERED IF IT WAS NATURALLY OCCURRING. I LOOKED IN MY VARIOUS REFERENCE BOOKS AND FOUND MENTIONS OF SEAWEED AND SOYBEANS AS NATURALLY OCCURRING SOURCES OF MSG. DO YOU HAVE ANY IDEA HOW MUCH MSG IS FOUND IN SOYBEANS? WOULD A PRODUCT LIKE SOYMILK OR TOFU HAVE ENOUGH TO CAUSE AN ALLERGIC REACTION? I ALSO WONDERED IF NATURALLY OCCURRING MSG WAS LESS LIKELY TO CAUSE A REACTION THAN CHEMICALLY PRODUCED MSG?

MSG is the abbreviation for monosodium glutamate - a compound that is added to foods to enhance flavor. It's made up of sodium, water, and the amino acid glutamate. Virtually every food that contains protein contains glutamate. As far as I know, MSG must be added to foods; only the glutamate is naturally occurring. Glutamate is found naturally in foods in two forms bound to other amino acids in protein and in "free" form. Some people who have a reaction to added MSG have also been reported to have symptoms from foods which contain high levels of "free" glutamate such as tomatoes, Parmesan cheese, and mushrooms, especially shiitake mushrooms. Some food ingredients which contain free glutamate include autolyzed yeast extract, hydrolyzed vegetable protein (HVP), hydrolyzed protein, hydrolyzed plant protein, plant protein extract, potassium glutamate, and textured protein.

The amount of free glutamate found in the food seems to be more important than whether it is naturally occurring or not. Soybeans are not especially high in total glutamate compared to other plant proteins.

Reed Mangels, PhD, RD

⟨❖⟩

## DOES BONE CHINA REALLY HAVE BONES IN IT?

According to our research, bone china was, and still is, made with bone ash. Bone china was created in England in the mid-18th century. England was trying to compete with Chinese porcelain, and bone china was one of the new pottery types invented. It required a much lower firing temperature than porcelain and had similar translucent qualities. To this day England is a leading manufacturer of bone china.

Bone ash is added to the clay body to create whiteness, translucency, and strength. The content of bone ash required in bone china varies around the world, but it is generally 25 to 50% of the composition of the clay body. British standards specify a minimum content of 35%, and in the US, standards specify a minimum of 25%. Formulations of bone china are generally 50% bone ash, 25% kaolin (China clay), and 25% feldspar (mineral). The bones are processed with 1150-degree heat, and rendered into a fine powder. Many manufacturers see the end-product as being free of animal material because it has been burned away.

According to Spode, a pottery company based in England and one of the world's leading manufacturers of bone china, they do not know of a substitute for animal-based bone ash that meets their quality requirements. Paul Bridgett, who has worked for Royal Doulton (UK) and Pfaltzgraff (USA), and is currently employed by English China Clays International (ECC), stated, "I believe I am safe in saying that ALL commercial bone china currently for sale is produced using animal bone by-products." ECC is the world's largest producer of kaolin, and advises tableware manufacturers around the world.

During the course of our research, we learned of a mineral-derived bone ash, produced from the mineral apatite. This synthetic form of bone ash is known as dicalcium phosphate. The low calcium content in dicalcium phosphate causes the color in the final product to degrade, so it is considered unsuitable for mass use. Mr. Bridgett knew of a " 'synthetic bone' being used in Japan, but this, too, originates from animal bone."

Something interesting of note: A.R.T. Studio Clay has recently discontinued selling imported English natural bone ash because of the "mad cow" scare in Britain. They also sell synthetic bone ash, and said their customers prefer it.

On the bright side, fine china, porcelain, and stoneware should be made without bone ash. Fine china uses feldspar instead of bone ash; porcelain is fired at extremely high temperatures and traditionally should not be made with bone ash; stoneware consists of kaolin, ball clay, feldspar, and flint. However, according to Spode, small amounts of bone ash are often used in ceramics made in Asia, including the Far East.

# CHAPTER 13

# QUESTIONS ABOUT VRG

## WHAT IS THE VEGETARIAN RESOURCE GROUP?

The Vegetarian Resource Group (VRG) is a non-profit organization dedicated to educating the public on vegetarianism and the interrelated issues of health, nutrition, ecology, ethics, and world hunger. In addition to publishing the *Vegetarian Journal*, VRG produces and sells cookbooks, as well as other books, pamphlets, and article reprints that are subject-related.

Our health professionals, activists, and educators work with businesses and individuals to bring about healthy changes in your school, workplace, and community. Registered dietitians and physicians aid in the development of nutrition-related publications and answer member or media questions about the vegetarian and vegan diet. The Vegetarian Resource Group is a non-profit educational organization. Financial support comes primarily from memberships, contributions, and book sales.

For more information write, phone, e-mail or visit the VRG website at www.vrg.org/nutshell/about.htm.

❦

## DO YOU HAVE A LIST OF TABLING MATERIALS, BROCHURES, AND BOOKS?

We sure do. It is included on page 248 of the appendix. It is also online at www.vrg.org/nutshell/materials.htm.

## How do I become a member of VRG?

Membership to The Vegetarian Resource Group is $20 a year. Prices for one-year membership in Canada and Mexico are $32, and $42 for all other countries. With your membership you will receive the 36-page bi-monthly *Vegetarian Journal.*

The various levels of membership for one year include: $20 (Member), $30 (Contributor - also comes with a copy of Vegan Handbook), and $50 (Supporter - also comes with a copy of Vegan Handbook and Meatless Meals for Working People). These offers are only good in the US.

To become a member online, go to www.vrg.org/journal/subscribe.htm. You can also send a check or money order to The Vegetarian Resource Group, PO Box 1463, Baltimore, MD 21203, or call (410) 366-8343, Monday-Friday, 9 a.m.-5 p.m. EST, to order using a Visa or MasterCard.

## Can you send me a free sample copy of *Vegetarian Journal*?

Since we don't accept paid advertising to subsidize printing and mailing costs, we are not able to mail out free copies of the *Journal.* However, you are able to access many years of past articles on our website at www.vrg.org/journal. If you would like a sample copy mailed to you, they are $3.

## What publications does the VRG offer?

### VRG publishes the following books:
Conveniently Vegan, Leprechaun Cake and Other Tales, The Lowfat Jewish Vegetarian Cookbook, Meatless Meals for Working People, VJ Guide to Natural

Foods Restaurants in the US and Canada, No Cholesterol Passover Recipes, Simple, Lowfat, & Vegetarian (temporarily out of print), Simply Vegan, Vegan Handbook, Vegan Meals for One or Two, and Vegan in Volume

## And these periodicals:
*Vegetarian Journal, Vegetarian Journal's Foodservice Update Newsletter, VRG News* (monthly e-mail newsletter)

## How much would it cost to have you send me 6 of your "I Love Animals and Broccoli" coloring books?

We generally send out materials when a self-addressed stamped envelope is included with the request. However, if you are able, we ask that you help cover publishing costs, which are roughly 10-15 cents per brochure. If you would like to make a larger donation, it would be greatly appreciated. For material requests such as this, contact us at vrg@vrg.org or call (410) 366-8343 (Monday to Friday, 9 am to 5 pm EST).

## Where can I find information about the VRG Message Checks? What about a VRG credit card?

The checks are created by Message!Checks, and the design reads "Be Kind to Animals, Don't Eat Them" across the front. Message!Checks was founded in 1985 to help support organizations working for the environment, animal issues, social issues, and more. A portion of every order placed goes directly to the VRG. The checks are printed on recycled paper (20% post-consumer) with soy-based inks. The Message!Products website is www.messageproducts.com. VRG is listed under the animal rights section. We can also send you a paper order form. Write, phone, or e-mail us at vrg@vrg.org with your request, and be sure to include your mailing address.

We also have applications for the VRG MBNA credit card and will gladly mail you one. VRG receives money each time the card is used.

# Services The VRG Provides

## ACTIVIST ASSISTANCE
Providing speakers and referrals for speakers
Advisors for local and national groups and individuals about organizing and
  publishing
Working with ethnic and minority groups, especially the Latino, Jain, and Jewish
  communities
Working with international vegetarian groups
Answering questions from companies, activists, the media, and consumers
Providing materials for tabling
Maintaining a list of vegetarian groups
Discounts on books and *Vegetarian Journal*
Video loan
Tips for activists

## BUSINESS
Providing a decal for restaurants indicating vegetarian meals available
Developing booklets for supermarkets and companies
Conducting polls on the number of vegetarians in the US and vegetarian meals
  ordered, which is helpful for marketing and business planning
Restaurant guide listing veg friendly restaurants
Listing companies which have vegetarian and vegan products for use in institutions
Reviewing books and products in *Vegetarian Journal, Foodservice Update,* and
  on the VRG website
Assisting, promoting, and consulting for vegetarian food companies

## COOPERATION WITH OTHER PROFESSIONAL AND
## CONSUMER GROUPS AND NON-PROFIT AGENCIES
Meals on Wheels
USDA NutriTopics
The American Dietetic Association
Mid Atlantic Publishers Association
Member Maryland Association of Non-Profit Organizations

## FOOD SERVICE
Assisting, promoting, and consulting for vegetarian food companies
Recipes and Information for food services
Conducting polls on the numbers of vegetarians
Answering questions from companies, activists, the media, and consumers

*Vegetarian Journal's Foodservice Update Newsletter*
Listing companies which have vegetarian and vegan products for use in institutions
Exhibits and presentations at food service conferences

## GOVERNMENTAL POLICY
Testifying about governmental regulations
Research on how policy is made

## INTERNET
Providing access to many of our materials and a wealth of vegetarian
    information on the VRG website <www.vrg.org>
Linking to other groups, companies, and businesses promoting vegetarianism
E-mail newsletter - VRG-News
Vegetarian game
Answering e-mail and bulletin board questions
College-level online course for vegetarian nutrition and cooking

## MEDIA
Resource for radio, tv, print, and electronic media
Media spokespeople

## MEMBER AND CONSUMER SERVICES
*Vegetarian Journal* magazine
Periodic dinners and potlucks
Developing a meal plan for the Meals on Wheels program
Answering questions via e-mail, phone, and mail
VRG Message Checks
VRG MBNA Visa/Mastercard credit card
Audrey Fluke and Ruth E. Caring Awards
Maintaining a database to aid individuals in finding dietitians or doctors familiar
    with vegetarian/vegan diets
Volunteer opportunities, both local and long-distance

## NUTRITION EDUCATION
Maintaining a database to aid individuals in finding dietitians or doctors familiar
    with vegetarian/vegan diets
Working with ethnic and minority groups, especially the Latino, Jain, and Jewish
    communities
Providing speakers and referrals for speakers
Educating health professionals

Nutrition education materials
Assisting, promoting, and consulting for vegetarian food companies
Developing booklets for supermarkets and companies
Answering questions from companies, activists, the media, and consumers
Booths at fairs and conferences

## PROFESSIONAL DEVELOPMENT
Educating health professionals
Providing speakers and referrals for speakers
Consulting and assisting professional groups
Presentations, abstracts, and exhibitions at professional conferences
Internships

## PUBLICATIONS
*Vegetarian Journal* Magazine
*Foodservice Update Newsletter*
Books: Simply Vegan, Conveniently Vegan, Leprechaun Cake, Lowfat Jewish
Vegetarian Cookbook, Meatless Meals for Working People, VJ Guide to Natural
Foods Restaurants in the US and Canada, No Cholesterol Passover Recipes,
Simple, Lowfat, & Vegetarian (temp. out of print), Vegan Handbook, Vegan
Meals for One or Two, Vegan in Volume
Brochures and Booklets (including *Raising Vegan Children, The Guide to Food
Ingredients, The Guide to Fast Food,* and *A Shopper's Guide to Leather
Alternatives*)
E-mail Newsletter - *VRG News*

## RESEARCH
Polls on the numbers of adult and teen vegetarians
Research on how policy is made
Food ingredients
Consumer products
Fast food chains
Leather alternatives

## STUDENT RESOURCES
Essay contest and lesson plan
Teen nutrition information
Speaker referral
Resources for teens
Exhibits and presentations at education conferences

Assisting in the organization of youth activist groups
Internships

## TRAVEL INFORMATION

VJ Guide to Natural Foods Restaurants in the US and Canada
Travel Bulletin Board on VRG website
City Guides, both local and national
Vegetarian Vacation Guide
Travel resources on VRG website

THE VEGETARIAN RESOURCE GROUP is a non-profit organization which educates the public about vegetarianism, and the interrelated issues of health, nutrition, ecology, ethics, and world hunger.

For more information write to The Vegetarian Resource Group, PO Box 1463, Baltimore, MD 21203 or call (410) 366-8343. You can also visit the website at www.vrg.org or e-mail vrg@vrg.org.

# APPENDIX

# Quick Glance at Vegetarian Menu Items at Restaurant and Quick Service Chains

## This section is excerpted from VRG's 32-page guide (see page 269).

**Note:** Suppliers and ingredients are ever changing. When you are purchasing foods, an exact guarantee of the ingredients is probably not possible. In many cases we've labeled items as vegetarian when there could be a few "maybe" ingredients, such as mono- and diglycerides and/or natural flavors. We know that many vegetarians do not eat cheese made with animal rennet, but for the purposes of this chart, we've included some cheeses that may contain this animal derivative. Also, some foods are listed as vegetarian per the ingredient statement, however they may share a cooking surface with meat. Everyone draws the line as to what he or she will eat in a different place. We've done our best to provide as much information as possible to allow people to make informed decisions. You may want to read our 32-page guide for more complete details about the menu items (available for $4 from The Vegetarian Resource Group, PO Box 1463, Baltimore, MD 21203; 410-366-8343; www.vrg.org).

*If you have food allergies, please contact the individual restaurants for their allergen statement. Ingredients change frequently and often egg and dairy are masked by other ingredients, such as "natural flavors."

## ARBY'S
**Vegetarian:** baked potatoes (plain, broccoli and cheddar), apple and cherry turnovers, mozzarella cheesesticks, jalapeño bites, croutons, croissants, blueberry muffins, biscuits, all buns, all milkshakes, green peppers and onion mix, margarine/butter blend, sauces/dressings (honey mustard, tartar sauce, tangy southwest sauce, Thousand Island), hot chocolate drink mix
**Vegetarian (no egg/dairy):** garden salad, side salad, liquid margarine, marinara sauce, sauces (Arby's sauce, barbeque sauce, barbeque dipping sauce), turnovers appear vegan (cooking methods unknown, sugar)
**Non-vegetarian:** sour cream (gelatin), potato products such as jalapeño baked potato, homestyle fries, curly fries, potato cakes are cooked in same oil as meats

## BOJANGLES'
**Vegetarian:** creamy coleslaw, macaroni and cheese, multi-grain roll, all of the biscuits

**Vegetarian (no egg/dairy):** marinated coleslaw, Cajun pinto beans, green beans, corn on the cob
**Non-vegetarian:** hash browns (Botato Rounds), seasoned fries (animal shortening used)

## BOSTON MARKET
**Vegetarian:** apple pie, brownies, chocolate chip cookies, cinnamon apples, oatmeal raisin cookie, cornbread, split top bun, white roll, coyote bean salad, penne pasta salad, red bliss potato salad, fruit salad, potato salad, green bean casserole, green beans, honey glazed carrots, penne marinara, tomato bisque soup, butternut squash, coleslaw, mashed potatoes
**Vegetarian (no egg/dairy):** chunky cinnamon applesauce, cranberry walnut relish, fruit salad, steamed vegetables, zucchini marinara, apple cobbler, tossed salad (sans croutons and dressing)
**Non-vegetarian:** According to Boston market, the following may contain animal-derived enzymes: black beans and rice, broccoli and red peppers, Caesar salad, buttered corn, honey wheat and white roll, macaroni and cheese, Mediterranean pasta salad, new potatoes, Jumpin' Juice squares, squash casserole, rice pilaf, creamed spinach, stuffing, tortellini salad, gravies

## BURGER KING
**Vegetarian:** croissants, sauces (King Sauce, tartar sauce, honey mustard dipping sauce), ranch dressing, bagels, Dutch apple pie, Spicy Bean Burger (in UK and Ireland)
**Vegetarian (no egg/dairy):** French fries
**Non-vegetarian:** Snickers ice cream bar (gelatin), sweet and sour dipping sauce (anchovies)

## CHI-CHI'S
**Vegetarian:** chile con queso, cheese nachos, vegetable fajita, vegetable quesadilla, Mexican fried ice cream, apple chimi
**Vegetarian (no egg/dairy):** chips and salsa, dinner salad (without cheese), refried beans (without cheese), guacamole
**Non-vegetarian:** Spanish rice (chicken fat), enchilada sauce (chicken fat)

## CHURCH'S FRIED CHICKEN
**Vegetarian:** corn on the cob, fried okra, mashed potatoes, coleslaw, biscuits
**Vegetarian (no egg/dairy):** corn on the cob (without butter)
**Non-vegetarian:** French fries (beef fat), white and brown gravies (chicken/beef fat), fried pies (animal protein), Cajun rice (animal protein), collard greens (animal protein)

## DENNY'S

**Vegetarian:** pancakes, eggs, French toast, waffles, omelet, hashed browns, cold cereals, garden salad, Boca Burger, mozzarella sticks, onion rings, seasoned fries, baked/mashed potato, cottage cheese, green beans, baby carrots, corn, dressings (bleu cheese, French, Thousand Island, Caesar, creamy Italian, ranch), honey mustard sauce, chocolate silk pie, cheesecake pie, cheese pizza, sugar cone, dinner roll

**Vegetarian (no egg/dairy):** oatmeal fixins' (raisins, brown sugar, sliced banana), juice, English muffin, grits, applesauce, fresh fruit, frozen strawberries, jelly (all flavors), nut and fruit topping, fruit syrups, baked potato topped with salsa, marinara sauce, sautéed mushrooms, grilled onions and peppers, barbecue sauce, guacamole, vegetable plates, seasoned fries, mashed potatoes, sauerkraut, dressings (light Italian, reduced French, Oriental dressing, oil and vinegar), light rye bread, bagel, boule bread

**Non-vegetarian:** lemon meringue pie (gelatin), rice pilaf (chicken broth), regular French fries (beef fat)

## DUNKIN' DONUTS

**Vegetarian:** donuts, bagels (may contain sugar, l-cysteine, and honey), cookies, cream cheeses, muffins, cinnamon bun, Dunkacinno, Omwich made without meat

## EL POLLO LOCO

**Vegetarian:** honey glazed carrots, spinach-flavored and tomato-flavored tortillas, BRC burrito, Orange Bang, Pina Colada Bang

**Vegetarian (no egg/dairy):** flour tortillas, BRC burrito without cheese, pinto beans, corn-on-the-cob, cucumber salad, spiced apples, guacamole, hot sauce, salsa, Italian dressing

**Non-vegetarian:** BBQ baked black beans (ham), Crispy Green Beans (bacon), instant stuffing (chicken), chicken gravy (chicken), Baja Glaze (chicken), Caesar dressing (fish, gelatin), light sour cream (gelatin), raspberry marble cheesecake (gelatin), cranberry walnut cheesecake (gelatin), Lime Parfait (gelatin)

## JACK IN THE BOX

**Vegetarian:** biscuits, croissants, seasoned curly fries, hash browns, stuffed jalapenos, buttermilk dipping sauce, croutons, double fudge cake

**Vegetarian (no egg/dairy):** pita bread, potato wedges, syrups (grape, strawberry, cappuccino), sauces (hot, taco, teriyaki, barbecue, sweet and sour, soy), malt vinegar packet, salsa, apple turnover

**Non-vegetarian:** egg roll (pork), secret sauce (anchovies), cheesecake (gelatin)

# KFC
**Vegetarian:** bread, corn on the cob, coleslaw, mashed potatoes without gravy, macaroni salad, cornbread, biscuits
**Vegetarian (no egg/dairy):** three-bean salad
**Non-vegetarian:** chocolate parfait (lard), the following contain meat/meat flavoring: green beans, greens, red beans and rice, barbecue baked beans, gravy

# KRISPY KREME
**Vegetarian:** due to unspecified glycerine and sorbitan monostearate, we are not certain if they are vegetarian or non-vegetarian

# LITTLE CAESARS
**Vegetarian:** pizza cheeses
**Vegetarian (no egg/dairy):** dough, tomato sauce, Crazy Sauce, Crazy Bread

# LONG JOHN SILVER'S
**Vegetarian:** dressings (fat-free ranch, ranch, Caesar, Thousand Island), sandwich buns, coleslaw, corn cobbettes
**Vegetarian (no egg/dairy):** rice, corn cobbettes without butter
**Non-vegetarian:** green beans (meat flavoring)

# MCDONALD'S
**Vegetarian:** honey mustard sauce, breakfast sauce (on Breakfast Burrito), McSalad Shaker salads, garden salad without dressing, shakes, granola, apple pies, ice cream, strawberry topping, hot caramel topping, ice cream cones, McDonaldland cookies, chocolate chip cookies, birthday cakes, Egg McMuffin (made without meat), hotcakes, grape jam and strawberry preserves, breakfast burrito (made without meat), cinnamon roll, margarine
**Vegetarian (no egg/dairy):** bagels, green chilies, burrito mild sauce
**Non-Vegetarian:** French fries (beef flavoring), Big Xtra! Seasoning (beef fat/extract), Caesar dressing (anchovies), Red French Reduced Calorie dressing (anchovies), low fat yogurt (gelatin), biscuit dressing (animal derived flavoring), hash browns (animal derived flavors)

# PIZZA HUT
**Vegetarian:** honey mustard sauce, creamy cucumber dressing,
**Vegetarian (no egg/dairy):** Thin 'n Crispy crusts, regular pizza sauce, spaghetti marinara sauce, pasta, Italian and French dressings, dessert pizza crust, cherry topping, and icing
**Non-Vegetarian:** White Pasta sauce (chicken flavor/fat), Fajita sauce (chicken/chicken fat), Taco Bean sauce (beef), Creamy Caesar dressing (anchovies)

## POPEYE'S
**Vegetarian:** corn on the cob, coleslaw
**Vegetarian (no egg/dairy):** corn on the cob (without butter)
**Non-vegetarian:** biscuits (beef tallow), onion rings (beef tallow)

## SUBWAY
**Vegetarian:** wheat sub (contains honey), all bread products, cheese sub, Gardenburger, VeggieMax, soy turkey sub (available at select locations), soy cheese, all cookies, fat-free ranch, fat-free french, sauces (Southwest Ancho, horseradish, honey mustard)
**Vegetarian (no egg/dairy):** Veggie Delight Salad, Italian roll, Boca Burger, soy turkey sub without soy cheese, Fruizle smoothie, Italian dressing
**Non-Vegetarian:** Asiago Caesar dressing (anchovies)

## TACO BELL
**Vegetarian:** bean taco (prepared w/o sour cream), Chalupa shell, Gordita flat-bread, tostada shells, pizza shells, taco salad tortilla chips, Veggie Fajita Wrap, 7-Layer Burrito, country gravy, tostada, Mexican Pizza (made without meat), Taco salad (made without meat), Kid's Meal (bean burrito, nachos, drink), Country Breakfast burrito (made without sausage), Breakfast Quesadilla, guacamole
**Vegetarian (no egg/dairy):** bean burrito (made without cheese), bean taco (made without cheese - specially prepared), seasoned rice, tortillas and tortilla chips (flour, wheat, and corn), Veggie Fajita Wrap without cheese, pinto beans, sauces (red, mild, hot, salsa, green, pico de gallo), tostada without cheese, Cinnamon twists, Border Ices
**Non-Vegetarian:** sour cream (gelatin)

## WENDY'S
**Vegetarian:** dressings (fat-free French, reduced fat/reduced calorie Hidden Valley Ranch, bleu cheese, reduced fat/reduced calorie Garden Ranch Sauce), sauces (honey mustard, sweet and sour, barbeque), kaiser and sandwich buns, breadsticks, croutons, cottage cheese, pasta salad, potato salad, liquid margarine
**Vegetarian (no egg/dairy):** French fries, deluxe garden salad, side salad, dressings (French, reduced fat/reduced calorie Italian), applesauce, banana strawberry glaze, taco chips
**Non-Vegetarian:** Italian Caesar dressing (anchovies), reduced fat/ reduced calorie Caesar vinaigrette (anchovies)

# Quick Guide to Helpful Websites

## NUTRITION INFORMATION:

The Vegetarian Resource Group: www.vrg.org/nutrition

The American Dietetic Association: www.eatright.org

The American Dietetic Association Vegetarian Nutrition Dietetic Practice Group: www.eatright.org/dpg/dpg14.html

## RECIPES:

VRG: www.vrg.org/recipes and www.vrg.org/journal/index.htm#Recipes

FatFree.com: www.fatfree.com

International Vegetarian Union (IVU): www.ivu.org/recipes

Veggies Unite: www.vegweb.com

## NEW VEGETARIANS:

VRG: www.vrg.org/nutshell/nutshell.htm

## ANIMAL RIGHTS AND WELFARE:

Animal Protection Institute (API): www.api4animals.org

Animal Rights Resource Site (ARRS): www.animalconcerns.org

Farm Animal Reform Movement (FARM): www.farmusa.org

Farm Sanctuary: www.farmsanctuary.org

Friends of Animals (FOA): www.foa.org

Humane Society of the US (HSUS): www.hsus.org

People for the Ethical Treatment of Animals (PETA): www.peta-online.org

## VEGETARIAN ORGANIZATIONS:

The Vegetarian Resource Group (VRG): www.vrg.org

International Vegetarian Union (IVU): www.ivu.org

North American Vegetarian Society (NAVS): www.navs-online.org

**Vegetarian Society of the UK (VSUK):** www.vegsoc.org

**Vegan Outreach:** www.veganoutreach.org

## Children and Parents:

**The Vegetarian Resource Group (VRG):** www.vrg.org/family

**The Vegetarian Resource Group Parents' List:**

groups.yahoo.com/group/vrgparents

**Vegetarian Baby:** www.vegetarianbaby.com

## Products and Mail Order:

**VRG:** www.vrg.org/links/products.htm

## Food Ingredients and Nutritional Content:

**VRG:** www.vrg.org/nutshell/faqingredients.htm

**US Dept. of Agriculture (USDA):**

www.nal.usda.gov/fnic/cgi-bin/nut_search.pl

## Vegetarian Restaurants:

**VRG:** www.vrg.org/catalog/guide.htm and
www.vrg.org/links/restaurant.htm

**VegDining:** www.vegdining.com

**VegEats:** www.vegeats.com/restaurants

**HappyCow:** www.happycow.net

Excerpted from *Online Resources for Vegetarians* by The Vegetarian Resource Group (www.vrg.org/nutshell/online.htm).

# Protein Content of Selected Vegan Foods

**Excerpted from <u>Simply Vegan</u>, by Debra Wasserman and Reed Mangels, PhD, RD (pages 142-143)**

| Food | Amount | Protein (grams) | Protein (g/100 cal) |
|---|---|---|---|
| Tempeh | 1 cup | 31 | 9.5 |
| Seitan | 4 ounces | 15-31 | 21.4-22.1 |
| Soybeans, cooked | 1 cup | 29 | 9.6 |
| Veggie dog | 1 link | 8-26 | 13.3-20 |
| Veggie burger | 1 patty | 5-24 | 3.8-21.8 |
| Lentils, cooked | 1 cup | 18 | 7.8 |
| Tofu, firm | 4 ounces | 8-15 | 10-12.2 |
| Kidney beans, cooked | 1 cup | 15 | 6.8 |
| Lima beans, cooked | 1 cup | 15 | 6.8 |
| Black beans, cooked | 1 cup | 15 | 6.3 |
| Chickpeas, cooked | 1 cup | 15 | 5.4 |
| Pinto beans, cooked | 1 cup | 14 | 6.0 |
| Black-eyed peas, cooked | 1 cup | 13 | 6.7 |
| Vegetarian baked beans | 1 cup | 12 | 5.2 |
| Quinoa, cooked | 1 cup | 11 | 3.5 |
| Soymilk, commercial, plain | 1 cup | 3-10 | 3-12 |
| Tofu, regular | 4 ounces | 2-10 | 2.3-10.7 |
| Bagel | 1 medium (3 oz) | 9 | 3.7 |

| Food | Amount | Protein (grams) | Protein (g/100 cal) |
|---|---|---|---|
| Peas, cooked | 1 cup | 9 | 3.4 |
| Textured Vegetable Protein (TVP), cooked | 1/2 cup | 8 | 8.4 |
| Peanut butter | 2 Tbsp. | 8 | 4.1 |
| Spaghetti, cooked | 1 cup | 7 | 3.4 |
| Spinach, cooked | 1 cup | 6 | 11.0 |
| Soy yogurt, plain | 6 ounces | 6 | 6 |
| Bulgur, cooked | 1 cup | 6 | 3.7 |
| Sunflower seeds | 1/4 cup | 6 | 3.3 |
| Almonds | 1/4 cup | 6 | 2.8 |
| Broccoli, cooked | 1 cup | 5 | 10.5 |
| Whole wheat bread | 2 slices | 5 | 3.9 |
| Cashews | 1/4 cup | 5 | 2.7 |
| Almond butter | 2 Tbsp | 5 | 2.4 |
| Brown rice, cooked | 1 cup | 5 | 2.1 |
| Potato | 1 medium (6 oz) | 4 | 2.6 |

Sources: USDA Nutrient Database for Standard Reference, Release 12, 1998 and manufacturers' information.

The recommendation for protein for adult male vegans is around 63-79 grams per day; for adult female vegans it is around 50-63 grams per day.

# Calcium Content of Selected Vegan Foods

Excerpted from <u>Simply Vegan</u>, by Debra Wasserman and Reed Mangels, PhD, RD (page156)

| Food | Amount | Calcium (mg) |
| --- | --- | --- |
| Soy or ricemilk, commercial, calcium-fortified, plain | 8 ounces | 150-500 |
| Collard greens, cooked | 1 cup | 357 |
| Blackstrap molasses | 2 Tbsp | 342 |
| Tofu, processed with calcium sulfate* | 4 ounces | 200-330 |
| Calcium-fortified orange juice | 8 ounces | 300 |
| Commercial soy yogurt, plain | 6 ounces | 250 |
| Turnip greens, cooked | 1 cup | 249 |
| Tofu, processed with nigari* | 4 ounces | 80-230 |
| Kale, cooked | 1 cup | 179 |
| Okra, cooked | 1 cup | 176 |
| Soybeans, cooked | 1 cup | 175 |
| Sesame seeds | 2 Tbsp | 160 |
| Bok choy, cooked | 1 cup | 158 |
| Tempeh | 1 cup | 154 |
| Mustard greens, cooked | 1 cup | 152 |
| Figs, dried or fresh | 5 medium | 135 |
| Tahini | 2 Tbsp | 128 |
| Almonds | 1/4 cup | 97 |

| Food | Amount | Calcium (mg) |
|------|--------|--------------|
| Broccoli, cooked | 1 cup | 94 |
| Almond butter | 2 Tbsp | 86 |
| Soymilk, commercial, plain | 8 ounces | 80 |

*Read the label on your tofu container to see if it is processed with calcium sulfate or nigari.

Note: Oxalic acid, which is found in spinach, rhubarb, chard, and beet greens is often said to bind with calcium and reduce absorption. These foods should not be considered good sources of calcium. Calcium in other green vegetables, like kale, collard greens, Chinese mustard greens, and Chinese cabbage flower leaves is well absorbed. Fiber appears to have little effect on calcium absorption except for the fiber in wheat bran which does have a small effect. (Simply Vegan, page 157)

The recommended level of calcium for adults age 19 through 50 years is 1000 milligrams per day. An intake of 1200 milligrams of calcium is recommended for those age 51 years and older.

Sources: Composition of Foods. USDA Nutrient Data Base for Standard Reference, Release 12, 1998. Manufacturer's information.

# Iron Content of Selected Vegan Foods

Excerpted from Simply Vegan, by Debra Wasserman and Reed Mangels, PhD, RD (pages 164-165)

| Food | Amount | Iron (mg) |
| --- | --- | --- |
| Soybeans, cooked | 1 cup | 8.8 |
| Blackstrap molasses | 2 Tbsp | 7.0 |
| Lentils, cooked | 1 cup | 6.6 |
| Tofu | 4 oz | 0.7-6.6 |
| Quinoa, cooked | 1 cup | 6.3 |
| Kidney beans, cooked | 1 cup | 5.2 |
| Chickpeas, cooked | 1 cup | 4.7 |
| Lima beans, cooked | 1 cup | 4.5 |
| Pinto beans, cooked | 1 cup | 4.5 |
| Veggie burger, commercial | 1 patty | 1.1-4.5 |
| Black-eyed peas, cooked | 1 cup | 4.3 |
| Swiss chard, cooked | 1 cup | 4.0 |
| Tempeh | 1 cup | 3.8 |
| Black beans, cooked | 1 cup | 3.6 |
| Bagel, enriched | 3 oz | 3.2 |
| Turnip greens, cooked | 1 cup | 3.2 |
| Prune juice | 8 oz | 3.0 |
| Spinach, cooked | 1 cup | 2.9 |
| Beet greens, cooked | 1 cup | 2.7 |
| Tahini | 2 Tbsp | 2.6 |

| Food | Amount | Iron (mg) |
| --- | --- | --- |
| Raisins | 1/2 cup | 2.2 |
| Cashews | 1/4 cup | 2.0 |
| Figs, dried | 5 medium | 2.0 |
| Seitan | 4 oz | 2.0 |
| Bok choy, cooked | 1 cup | 1.8 |
| Bulgur, cooked | 1 cup | 1.7 |
| Apricots, dried | 10 halves | 1.6 |
| Potato | 1 large | 1.4 |
| Soy yogurt | 6 oz | 1.4 |
| Tomato juice | 8 oz | 1.4 |
| Veggie hot dog | 1 hot dog | 1.4 |
| Almonds | 1/4 cup | 1.3 |
| Peas, cooked | 1 cup | 1.3 |
| Green beans, cooked | 1 cup | 1.2 |
| Kale, cooked | 1 cup | 1.2 |
| Sesame seeds | 2 Tbsp | 1.2 |
| Sunflower seeds | 1/4 cup | 1.2 |
| Broccoli, cooked | 1 cup | 1.1 |
| Brussels sprouts, cooked | 1 cup | 1.1 |
| Millet, cooked | 1 cup | 1.0 |
| Prunes | 5 medium | 1.0 |
| Watermelon | 1/8 medium | 1.0 |

Sources: USDA Nutrient Data Base for Standard Reference, Release 12, 1998. Manufacturer's information.

The RDA for iron is 10 mg/day for adult men and for post-menopausal women and 15 mg/day for pre-menopausal women.

# Daily Values*

**Excerpted from <u>Simply Vegan</u>, by Debra Wasserman and Reed Mangels, PhD, RD (page 203)**

| | |
|---|---|
| Protein (for adults and children 4 or more years of age) | 50 gm |
| Fat | Less than 65 gm |
| Saturated Fat | Less than 20 gm |
| Cholesterol | Less than 300 mg |
| Total Carbohydrate | 300 gm |
| Fiber | 25 gm |
| Sodium | Less than 2400 mg |
| Potassium | 3500 mg |
| Vitamin A | 5000 IU |
| Vitamin C | 60 mg |
| Thiamin | 1.5 mg |
| Riboflavin | 1.7 mg |
| Niacin | 20 mg |
| Calcium | 1000 mg |
| Iron | 18 mg |
| Vitamin D | 400 IU |
| Vitamin E | 30 IU |
| Vitamin B6 | 2 mg |
| Folacin | 0.4 mg |
| Vitamin B12 | 6 mcg |
| Phosphorus | 1000 mg |
| Iodine | 150 mcg |
| Magnesium | 400 mg |
| Zinc | 15 mg |
| Copper | 2 mg |
| Biotin | 0.3 mg |
| Pantothenic acid | 10 mg |

* a term that appears on food labels. It is used to compare the amount of fat, fiber, vitamins, minerals, and other nutrients in a food to the amounts which should be consumed each day.

# A Senior's Guide To Good Nutrition
## by Suzanne Havala, M.S., R.D.

### Introduction to Diet and Aging

Relatively little is known about how the nutritional needs of older people differ from those who are younger. Although many people enjoy a generally healthy and vital old age, age-related health problems do increase with advancing years and often have an effect on eating habits.

The science of gerontology, or the study of normal aging, is still quite new, and science is giving us new insights into aspects of aging that in the past have been accepted as "normal." While there is a similar pattern of changes that takes place among all humans as they age, these changes can occur at different rates in different individuals. We do not know how much of this difference is due to genetic make-up, and how much is due to lifestyle factors such as diet.

There is abundant evidence to show that an optimal level of nutrition can extend the lifespan and improve the quality of life. A large body of research examining the health of vegetarians, who typically consume a diet that is lower in calories, saturated fat, and protein, and higher in fiber and phytochemicals than nonvegetarians, shows that vegetarians suffer from less heart disease, obesity, high blood pressure, diabetes, and some forms of cancer. Vegetarians also tend to live longer than nonvegetarians.

Good eating habits throughout life can help to promote physical and mental well-being. For older people, eating right can help to minimize the symptoms of age-related changes that, for some, can cause discomfort or inconvenience. Although the aging process affects some people differently from others, everyone can benefit from eating a well-planned vegetarian diet.

### Do Seniors Have Special Nutritional Needs?

Very little is known about how the aging process affects the body's ability to digest, absorb, and retain nutrients such as protein, vitamins, and minerals. Therefore, little is known about how the nutritional needs of older people differ from those of younger adults. Recommended nutrient intakes for seniors are currently extrapolated from those of younger adults.

One point that is generally agreed upon, however, is that older people tend to take in less energy, or calories, than younger people. This may be due, in part, to a natural decline in the rate of metabolism as people age. It may also reflect a decrease in physical activity. If the total intake of food decreases, it follows that intakes of protein, carbohydrate, fat, vitamins, and minerals also decrease. If calorie intake is too low, then intakes of necessary nutrients may also be low.

Many other factors can affect the nutritional needs of older people and how successfully they meet those needs, including their access to food. For instance, some of the changes that take place as people age can affect the kinds of foods they can tolerate, and some can affect their ability to shop for or prepare food. As people age, problems such as high blood pressure or diabetes become more common, necessitating certain dietary modifications. Digestive system problems become more common, and some people may have trouble chewing or swallowing.

Generally, current dietary recommendations for adults also apply to older people. These are summarized in the following chart:

# Limit:
sweets
regular coffee and tea
greasy or fatty foods
alcohol
oil, margarine, and "junk" foods
other added fat
salt

## Eat plenty of:
fruits
whole grain breads and cereals
vegetables

## Drink plenty of fluids, especially water

## Who Should Be Concerned About Their Diet?

Young or old, it pays to eat well and understand some nutrition basics. For starters, since food intake usually declines with age, it may be increasingly important for older people to make sure that what they do eat is nutritious. There may be less room in the diet for sweets and other "empty calorie" foods, which provide little in the way of nutrition in exchange for the calories they contribute to the diet. Eat fewer snack chips and commercially made cakes and cookies, and do your best to limit soft drinks, candy, and alcohol.

A sensible program of exercise, such as walking, may also be wise. People who are physically active have an easier time controlling their weight while still taking in more calories than those who are sedentary. The higher the calorie intake, the more likely a person is to obtain all the nutrients he or she needs.

A simple way to assess your own diet is to keep a written log or diary of everything that is eaten over a period of a few days to two weeks. Include some details about how foods were prepared, and be sure to make a note about portion sizes. Then compare the results to the general guidelines above. Write down ideas for improvement in areas that need some attention.

## Should I Take Supplements?

With few exceptions, vitamin and mineral supplements are rarely necessary for people who eat a varied diet and enough food to meet their energy needs. In fact, taking large doses of some vitamins and minerals may cause imbalances in body stores of others, and some are toxic at high levels. Your best bet is to get the nutrients you need from whole foods, without the use of a supplement, unless otherwise directed by your dietitian or physician.

## How Can My Diet Help Me?

Digestive system problems are the most frequent source of discomfort for older people. Sometimes these problems cause people to avoid foods that would otherwise be a healthy addition to the diet. For instance, flatulence or intestinal gas may prompt some individuals to forgo certain vegetables such as cabbage or beans, which are good sources of vitamins, minerals, and fiber. In other cases, adding more of certain types of foods can reduce the severity of some problems. Let's take a look at how a well-planned diet can help with a variety of common complaints.

## Constipation

Constipation can result from not drinking enough fluids and by eating a diet that is too low in fiber or bulk. Certain medications, including antacids made with aluminum hydroxide or calcium carbonate, can also cause this problem, and it can be made worse by the habitual use of laxatives.

There are several things that people can do to prevent constipation from occurring. Including a liberal amount of whole grain breads and cereals in the diet, as well as plenty of vegetables and fruits, is a start. Eating dried fruits such as prunes or figs, or drinking prune juice, may also help, since they have a natural laxative effect for many people. Drinking plenty of fluids is very important, and water is the best choice. Most people should drink six to eight glasses of water or other fluids each day. Foods that are high in fat, such as many sweets, meats and high fat dairy products, oils and margarine, or fried foods should be limited. These foods are very calorie dense and may displace foods that would otherwise provide needed fiber in the diet. Decreasing the consumption of fatty foods may also lessen the need for antacids. Don't forget, too, that a regular routine of exercise is effective in promoting good muscle tone and preventing constipation.

## Gas and Heartburn

Many people experience general abdominal discomfort after eating, which may include belching, intestinal gas or flatulence, bloating, or burning sensations. These complaints have many causes, including overeating, eating too many high-fat foods, alcohol, or carbonated beverages, swallowing too much air when eating, lying down to rest immediately after eating, and taking certain drugs or aspirin. Switching to a diet that is high in fiber may also cause some flatulence at the start, although it usually lessens as the body adapts to the increased fiber intake.

One way to help relieve problems such as these is to eat smaller, more frequent meals over the course of the day instead of eating one or two larger meals. Avoiding fatty foods, alcohol, and carbonated beverages is a good idea, too. It may also be helpful to eat slowly and to chew food thoroughly before swallowing. If heartburn is a problem, avoid reclining immediately after meals, or if you do so, keep the back elevated to at least 30 degrees so that you are not lying flat on your back. Regular exercise can also help to minimize trouble with intestinal gas.

## Chewing and Swallowing Problems

These may occur for a variety of reasons. For people who have trouble chewing foods, it may be helpful to cut food into small pieces and to allow extra time to chew food at a comfortable, unhurried pace. Cooking some fruits and vegetables may also be helpful and necessary for some. Poorly fitting dentures should be checked by a dentist and possibly replaced.

Drinking plenty of fluids can alleviate some swallowing problems if the throat or mouth is dry, which may be caused by certain medications or may simply be related to commonly-occurring changes that accompany the aging process. Lozenges or hard candies may be helpful in keeping the mouth moist. It may be necessary to ask your physician about whether or not a particular medication may be contributing to the problem.

## What If I Have to Follow a Special Diet?

The older people get, the more likely it is that they will develop medical problems that require a special, or therapeutic, diet. People who develop diabetes, high blood pressure, and heart disease, for instance, may have special considerations in meal planning. Most conditions, however, benefit from a diet that is high in fiber from whole grains, fruits, and vegetables, and low in animal products. Well-planned vegetarian diets can help to control blood sugar levels. By limiting fat, salt, and sugar, vegetarian diets can also be useful in controlling high blood pressure, heart disease, and other conditions. However, since individuals vary in their needs, those who must follow a special diet should consult a registered dietitian for more detailed recommendations and help with meal planning.

Many people also wonder if diet can help to treat conditions such as arthritis and osteoporosis. At present, no conclusive evidence exists to recommend one kind of diet over another for the treatment of arthritis. However, a lowfat vegetarian diet may be helpful in promoting normal weight, which, in turn, may help reduce or prevent some symptoms of arthritis.

The risk for osteoporosis is influenced by many factors, including diet. Diets that are excessively high in protein and sodium can accelerate the loss of calcium from bones. Vegetarian diets tend to be moderate in protein content and, when care is taken to avoid processed foods, they can be lower in sodium as well. Including plenty of greens and other calcium-rich foods in the diet will help to ensure an adequate intake of calcium.

One of the most common surgical procedures for older people is cataract surgery, and there is a considerable amount of research being conducted presently on the relationships between diet and the incidence of cataracts and macular degeneration.

## What If I Have No Appetite?

Depression because of changes in living conditions, loss of companions, certain medications, and complications in preparing meals can all result in a loss of interest in food. Sometimes eating smaller, more frequent "mini-meals" can help. It may also be a good idea to seek out meals in a social context. For instance, local vegetarian societies may have regular organized potluck dinners or restaurant outings that provide an opportunity to make new friends and enjoy a meal in the company of others.

Some common nutrition-related problems that older people encounter, and suggestions for dealing with them, are summarized in the following chart:

## Common Problems and Suggested Solutions

| | |
|---|---|
| **Flatulence or gas, burning sensation, heartburn** | Eat smaller, more frequent meals. |
| **Belching or bloating** | Avoid alcohol, carbonated beverages, and high fat foods such as some sweets, meats, oils and margarine, and high-fat dairy foods. Eat slowly and chew foods well. Avoid lying down after meals. If you do, keep head and back elevated at a 30-degree angle. |
| | Consider reducing aspirin intake. Ask physician to check medications. |
| **Difficulty chewing** | See dentist if problem is poorly fitting dentures. Cut food into small pieces and chew food at a comfortable, unhurried pace. |
| | Cook some vegetables and fruits to soften. |
| **Difficulty swallowing** | Ask physician to check medications. Drink plenty of water. Use lozenges or hard candies to keep throat moist. |
| **Constipation** | Eat liberal amounts of whole grains as well as vegetables and fruits. Try dried fruits such as prunes |

217

or figs, or drink prune juice.

Drink 6 to 8 glasses of fluid, especially water, each day.

Limit greasy or fatty foods such as high-fat dairy foods, oils and margarine, fried foods, high fat sweets and meats.

Limit use of antacids.

Get into a regular routine of exercise, such as walking.

**High blood sugar**            Limit sweets and alcohol.

See a registered dietitian for help with planning a high-fiber, high-carbohydrate diet.

**High blood pressure**         Limit salty foods.

See a registered dietitian for help in planning a heart-healthy diet.

**Heart disease**               See a registered dietitian for help in planning a diet low in saturated fat.

**Loss of appetite**            Eat small, frequent meals or snacks.

Also, see **Handy Hints for Quick Meals** on the following page.

## How Can I Make Preparing Meals a Little Easier?

Some older people may find meal planning is more burdensome if shopping or preparing meals is difficult. Arthritis, for instance, or impaired hearing or poor eyesight may make it hard to drive to the grocery store, to read food labels or package instructions, or to open bottles and handle cooking utensils. It may also be difficult to maintain the motivation to cook for only one or two people.

For all these reasons, it may be necessary for meals to be simple, quick, and convenient to prepare. Ready-to-eat, whole grain breakfast cereals are a nutritious meal or snack anytime, as are quick-cooking hot cereals like oatmeal, which can be cooked in a microwave oven. Fresh fruit is also convenient, but canned fruits, packed in their own juice or water, will keep for months in the cupboard and can also make a simple snack. Whole grain breads, bagels, and lowfat muffins can be kept in the freezer and individual servings taken out as needed. Other good freezer and cupboard staples include bags of mixed, plain frozen vegetables, whole grain crackers, peanut butter, canned beans such as pinto beans or black-eyed peas, and jars of vegetable salads such as three-bean or beet salad.

It also makes sense, for those who are able to do more extensive cooking, to fix enough of a recipe so that some can be frozen in small batches to be reheated at a later date. For example, bean chili, vegetable lasagna, some casseroles, whole grain cookies, lowfat muffins, or pancakes all freeze well and can be stored in small containers that can be reheated in a conventional or microwave oven.

A summary of some handy hints for quick meals follows:

## Handy Hints for Quick Meals

**Cupboard staples**

Ready-to-eat, whole grain breakfast cereals; quick-cooking whole grain cereals such as oatmeal; canned fruit packed in own juice; whole-grain crackers; nut butters; canned beans such as pintos or black-eyed peas; jars of vegetable salads such as beets or three-bean, low-sodium vegetarian soups; aseptically-packaged (long-life) containers of soy milk; popcorn; dried fruit.

**Freezer staples**

Frozen fruit pieces such as strawberries or raspberries; whole grain breads or muffins (to take out as needed); bags or boxes of plain, mixed frozen vegetables; fruit juice concentrate.

| | |
|---|---|
| **Make-aheads**<br>(to be frozen in small<br>batches and reheated<br>at a later date) | Bean chili; vegetable lasagna;<br>vegetable and bean soups; whole<br>grain-and-vegetable casseroles;<br>whole grain cookies, lowfat<br>muffins, or pancakes. |
| **Also keep on hand** | Flour tortillas; salsa and chutneys; fresh fruit. |
| **Shopping tips** | Split bags of fresh vegetables,<br>such as carrots, celery, and<br>onions, or heads of lettuce, with<br>a friend to reduce the amount of<br>spoiled food that has to be thrown away.<br><br>Shop with a list, and keep a list on-going at home. |

## Does Eating Well Have To Be Expensive?

For some elderly people, a limited income or limited access to transportation to a grocery store can complicate meal planning. So, good planning can not only be efficient, it can also be economically helpful as well. Foods prepared from scratch at home are usually less expensive than packaged mixes and frozen entrées, for example, and the cook has more control over what ingredients are used, also. For example, salt or fat in a recipe can be reduced when food is prepared at home, or whole wheat flour can be substituted for refined white flour.

Wise food choices can help save money. Buying in bulk, whether an item is on special or not, can be cheaper than buying small containers of food, although storage space must be available. If a person has access to food outlet stores, substantial savings can be had on things such as baked goods or breads. If freezer space is available, trips to an outlet can be less frequent. Coupon clipping, especially for brands that are usually purchased anyway, can save as much as 10% off food bills. Many stores offer double or triple the face value of the coupon. On the other hand, store brands of certain items can be much cheaper than name brands, even after coupon discounts, and often with little detectable difference in quality. Paper goods, canned goods, jams and jellies, and breakfast cereals are just a few examples of items which may have store brand or generic options.

There are certain food items that tend to be relatively costly and also should be limited for health reasons for most people. Sweets, especially prepared desserts such as cakes, pies, and cookies, and junk foods such as chips and other fried snacks, snack cakes, and some candies can be fairly expensive. High-fat dairy foods such as cheese and ice cream are relatively expensive, and for non-vegetarians, meat is typically the costliest item on the grocery list.

Desserts can be prepared at home, with alterations in the recipe to make them more nutritious, and money can be saved. Junk food snacks can be replaced with less expensive snacks such as air-popped plain popcorn, mixtures of dry cereals, bagels, whole grain muffins, or seasonal fresh fruit. If cheese is eaten, buy small quantities and use it sparingly. Add a sprinkling of grated cheese to salads or on top of a casserole or sandwich, rather than using it as a more prominent ingredient. Meatless meals, incorporating mixtures of vegetables, whole grains, and legumes such as canned or rehydrated beans and lentils, are economical and healthful, not to mention delicious.

## What Food Assistance Programs are Available for Seniors?

Food assistance programs, such as food stamps, can increase buying power for people who are eligible. Food delivery programs, such as Meals-on-Wheels, are also available for people who are housebound or have difficulty getting around or preparing meals. Congregate meal programs are available in some areas, where older people can meet in a central location to enjoy a meal in the company of others, and transportation is frequently provided to the meal site.

It is usually necessary to ask if vegetarian meal options can be made available, and the ability of food service personnel to accommodate the vegetarian's needs may vary from site to site or city to city. If there is difficulty in obtaining vegetarian meal options, contact the local vegetarian society. They may be able to refer the problem to a local dietitian-member for assistance. Find out if others are interested in lowfat vegetarian meal options. Quantity recipes are available from The Vegetarian Resource Group and other organizations, and these can be provided to food service directors or dietitians who may be able to incorporate them into menus.

Meal delivery programs may be organized by community nonprofit organizations or health and social service agencies such as hospitals, churches, nursing homes, and visiting nurses associations. To determine who is eligible, call these organizations directly. Otherwise, people can be referred by another family member, a physician, a visiting nurse, or a social worker.

Grocery delivery service is also available at stores in some communities. For people who have trouble finding transportation to the grocery store, or for those with physical limitations, a list can be phoned in to a local grocery store and someone will deliver the purchases to the home.

## Summing It All Up

A well-planned vegetarian diet is health-supporting for all ages. While age-related changes affect different people in different ways, a good diet can help to overcome or reduce symptoms of certain problems that may become more common with age.

## Sample Meal Plan

**Breakfast**
6 oz. orange juice
1 cup cooked oatmeal with
1/4 cup chopped raisins and dates
6 oz. soymilk

**Snack**
1 banana
1 slice whole grain toast with
2 teaspoons peanut butter

**Lunch**
1 cup vegetarian chili
1/2 fresh green pepper, sliced
1 corn muffin * (* see recipe on next page)
water

**Snack**
2 bagel halves with apple butter
6 oz. soymilk

**Dinner**
1-1/2 cups spinach salad with onions,
        mushrooms, and cherry tomatoes
2 tablespoons no-oil dressing
1 cup cooked spaghetti topped with
1/2 cup tomato-basil sauce
Chunk of Italian bread
2 chilled, canned peach halves
water

**Snack**
3 cups plain popcorn
6 oz. apple juice

*14% fat    14% protein    72% carbohydrate    30 grams of fiber*

## Recipe Suggestion

This recipe originally appeared in <u>Simply Vegan</u> (see page 265) by Debra Wasserman and Reed Mangels, PhD, RD.

1 cup cornmeal
1 cup whole wheat flour
1 tablespoon baking powder
1/4 cup oil
1 cup soy milk
1/3 cup molasses or maple syrup

Preheat oven to 375 degrees. Mix ingredients together in bowl. Pour batter into lightly oiled 8-inch round pan. Bake for 20 minutes.

Variation: Prepare same batter; however, pour batter into lightly oiled muffin tins and bake at the same temperature for the same amount of time. Children will especially enjoy these muffins.

Total calories per serving: 299     Fat: 11 grams     Protein: 6 grams
Carbohydrates: 46 grams     Iron: 3 mg     Calcium: 161 mg     Sodium: 29 mg
Dietary Fiber: 2 gm

Suzanne Havala, MS, RD is a nutrition advisor for The Vegetarian Resource Group.

Reprinted from *Meatless Menu Alternatives for Seniors,* The Vegetarian Resource Group.

# Eat Better, Perform Better
## Sports Nutrition Guidelines for the Vegetarian
## By Enette Larson, M.S., R.D.

## EATING TO EXERCISE AND COMPETE

Active individuals often wonder what, and even if, they should eat before a workout - especially when hunger seems to strike just around workout time - or when the race or tennis match begins too early to consider eating beforehand. Experienced athletes may remember eating the wrong food at the wrong time and wondering why they felt awful or performed poorly. Can the timing and choice of foods consumed close to and during a workout really make a difference in how you perform? Following a good diet with adequate amounts of energy, carbohydrates, protein, vitamins, and minerals is critical for optimal performance. No one performs their best by starting a workout hungry or with low glycogen (carbohydrate) stores or after eating the wrong types of food too close to exercising. Also, failing to replace depleted carbohydrates, protein, and fluids after a workout can decrease performance in the days that follow. Because the recommendations for food and fluid intake before, during, and after exercise vary somewhat with different sports activities, this article will cover guidelines for all types and levels of vegetarian athletes.

## FUELING UP BEFORE - THE PRE-EVENT MEAL

The purpose of eating prior to a workout or competition is to provide the body with fuel and fluid. The idea is to choose foods which will prevent hunger, provide additional carbohydrate fuel, and minimize possible intestinal complications. Generally, the meal should be consumed far enough in advance to allow for stomach emptying and intestinal absorption. A good rule of thumb is to limit the pre-event meal to about 800 calories, and give yourself one hour before the workout for each 200 calories you eat. For example, 5 pancakes, syrup, a banana, and juice would be eaten about 4 hours before a workout. A smaller 200 calorie meal such as a bowl of cereal or a bagel and juice would be eaten between 1 and 2 hours before starting. Meal timing is especially important in activities such as running, aerobic dancing, and swimming, and less critical in sports such as cycling. Athletes who have a "nervous stomach" before competition may find liquid meals such as blenderized fruit shakes with tofu or soy yogurt easier to tolerate. The pre-event meal should contain fluid and foods that are high in carbohydrates, and low in fat, protein, salt, simple sugars, and concentrated fiber. Cereal with sliced bananas and skim milk or juice, pancakes with fresh fruit topping, oatmeal with fruit, a baked potato topped with soy yogurt and vegetables, and tofu spread on bread with fruit are good examples. Too much protein, fiber, and fat in the pre-event meal can lead to heartburn, nausea, diarrhea, or constipation in certain individuals.

**Adequate fluid intake is the single most important recommendation for all types of exercise.**

## SUPPLEMENTING - INTAKE DURING THE EVENT

Replacing both fluid and carbohydrate during exercise is important. What and how much to replace depends on the type, duration, and intensity of the exercise. Adequate fluid intake is the single most important recommendation for all types of exercise. The general recommendation is to drink 1/2 to 1 cup of water every 10 to 20 minutes. In a hot environment, when perspiration is especially heavy, drinking up to 2 cups of water every 15 minutes may be necessary to replace fluid losses. Adequate hydration enables the active body to regulate its temperature effectively and allows for good circulation and muscle function.

Carbohydrate replacement is necessary in events lasting longer than 90 minutes and may even be beneficial during high intensity exercise of shorter duration. This applies to both continuous events like cycling, running, and hiking, and sports with intermittent activity like soccer and weight training. Under these conditions, consuming carbohydrates during exercise increases both the time and the intensity the athlete is able to exercise before becoming exhausted. Researchers believe that carbohydrate feedings delay fatigue by providing additional fuel for the working muscle and preventing blood sugar from dropping[1]. A carbohydrate intake of approximately 30 to 80 grams per hour[2] (1 to 3 large bananas or 15 to 60 ounces of a 6 to 7% fluid replacement beverage) are recommended for delaying fatigue during prolonged strenuous exercise.

## REFUELING - THE POST-EVENT MEAL

The meal following a workout is nutritionally the most important meal for aiding recovery from exercise and maintaining the ability to train the following days. Fluid, carbohydrate, and protein intake after exercise is critical, especially after heavy exercise. A high carbohydrate intake is required to replace depleted muscle glycogen stores. Delivery of a protein source may also aid in repairing and rebuilding damaged muscle tissue and replenishing the amino acid stores. Collective evidence indicates that exercise significantly alters protein metabolism, especially as the exercise becomes more prolonged and more strenuous.[3] Since the body begins to replace its depleted stores and repair any microscopic damage to muscle fibers almost immediately after exercise, provision of these depleted nutrients in the post-event meal may accelerate recovery.

Researchers investigating the role of carbohydrate in exercise performance suggest that consuming a carbohydrate source starting 15 to 30 minutes after exercise, followed by additional carbohydrate feedings, will optimize muscle glycogen replacement.[4] Delaying the ingestion of carbohydrates by several hours slows down the rate at which the body is able to store glycogen. For the casual exerciser, this means packing a piece of fruit, fruit juice, or a fluid replacement beverage for a post-workout snack, and then eating a mixed high carbohydrate and protein meal (such as pasta with lentil spaghetti sauce or tofu, vegetables, and rice) shortly thereafter. For the heavily training endurance athlete, a meal containing both a good source of protein and 100 grams of carbohydrate is recommended, followed by additional carbohydrate feedings every 2 to 4 hours.

# Guidelines for Planning The Pre-event Meal

|  | Protein (Grams) | Carbohydrate (Grams) |
|---|---|---|
| **200 CALORIES** | | |
| 2 Starch Servings | 6 | 30 |
| 1 Fruit Serving | 0 | 15 |
| **Total** | **6** | **45** |
| | | |
| **400 CALORIES** | | |
| 3 Starch Servings | 9 | 45 |
| 1 Fruit or Vegetable | 0-2 | 5-15 |
| 1 cup Fruit Juice or 4 oz. Tofu | 0-7 | 2-45 |
| **Total** | **9-18** | **52-105** |
| | | |
| **600 CALORIES** | | |
| 4 Starch Servings | 12 | 60 |
| 2 Fruit or 6 Vegetables | 0-12 | 30 |
| 1 cup Fruit Juice or 4 oz. Tofu | 0-7 | 2-45 |
| 1 tsp. Preserves or Syrup | 0 | 13 |
| **Total** | **12-31** | **105-148** |
| | | |
| **800 CALORIES** | | |
| 5 Starch Servings | 15 | 75 |
| 3 Fruit or 6 Vegetables | 0-12 | 30-45 |
| 1 cup Fruit Juice or 4 oz. Tofu | 0-7 | 2-45 |
| 1 tsp. Preserves or Syrup | 0 | 13 |
| **Total** | **15-34** | **120-178** |

ONE STARCH SERVING:

1/3 cup cooked rice, legumes, sweet potato
1/2 cup corn, potato, cooked cereal, pasta (cooked)
3/4 cup ready-to-eat cereal
3/4 cup winter squash
1 slice bread, 6-inch tortilla, 4-inch pancake
1/2 bagel, bun, English muffin, 6-inch pita bread

ONE FRUIT SERVING:                    ONE VEGETABLE EXCHANGE:
1 average piece fruit                 1/2 cup non-starchy vegetable
1/2 banana or mango
1/2 cup fruit, canned fruit, or fruit juice
2 TB raisins, 3 prunes, 7 apricot halves

*Note: The fat content of the pre-competition meal can vary with food choices. Select foods that contain no more than 2 grams of fat per serving. Any more than this will increase both the calories and the fat composition of the pre-exercise meal greater than that recommended.*

## FASTING - A DETRIMENT TO PERFORMANCE

Research shows that meal skipping and fasting can be detrimental to performance. An overnight fast depletes sugars stored in the liver (liver glycogen) and can contribute to light-headedness and the early onset of fatigue.[5] A high carbohydrate meal before exercise increases the carbohydrate available for the exercising muscle which provides benefit during both prolonged endurance exercise and high-intensity exercise. Starting any exercise session hungry or light-headed, keeps you from performing your best. If time or calories are a factor, eat a small high-carbohydrate snack (banana, bagel, cereal, vegan "energy bar") about an hour and a half before exercise or drink a glass of a fluid replacement beverage about 10 minutes prior to exercise.

## FIBER - A HELP OR A HINDRANCE?

Vegetarian diets are generally high in both soluble and insoluble fiber. A small amount of soluble fiber before or during exercise may be beneficial by preventing rapid highs and lows in blood sugar. However, some athletes are sensitive to fiber before exercise,[6] especially major competitions. If you experience stomach or intestinal cramps, or diarrhea before exercise, limiting high fiber foods such as legumes, whole grain products, bran products, and dried fruit in the meal preceding exercise may eliminate this distress. Sensitive athletes may need to reduce their fiber intake 24 to 36 hours before competition. Regular meal times and bowel habits also prevent exercise-induced intestinal complications.

It is also important to consider that adequate fiber intake is easily met and often exceeded by vegetarian athletes who have high calorie intakes. Sometimes, trying to eat a high calorie diet containing excess fiber can cause discomfort. Cyclists, for example, participating in a simulated Tour de France had difficulty maintaining adequate energy intake of 8,000 to 10,000 calories when whole grains and high fiber food were selected.[7] Those athletes with high calorie intakes should not be overly concerned about fiber and should select a variety of high carbohydrate foods that both contain fiber and are low in fiber (white bread, pasta, white rice, potatoes without skin, and fruit juice).

## CONCLUSIONS AND PRACTICAL IMPLICATIONS

Maintain an overall diet high in complex carbohydrates and low in fat. Eating a well-balanced diet containing adequate amounts of calories, protein, vitamins, and minerals is critical for optimal performance.

Choose pre-exercise meals that work well for you, including complex carbohydrates and fluids. Limit fat, protein, salt, and simple sugar. Before major competitions, don't shock your body by introducing unfamiliar foods.

Fasting or meal skipping before exercise can impair performance. Wait approximately 1 hour for every 200 calories you consume before exercise. Drink plenty of fluids during exercise. If exercise lasts longer than 90 minutes, eat or drink 30 to 80 grams of carbohydrate per hour to prolong performance time.

To aid recovery from exercise, consume a high-carbohydrate snack within 30 minutes after exercise and follow with a mixed high carbohydrate and protein meal.

If you experience stomach or intestinal complications during exercise, your pre-exercise meal may have been too high in fat or fiber.

## SELECTED REFERENCES

1. Coyle EF, Coggan AR, Hemmert MK and Ivy JL. "Muscle glycogen utilization during prolonged strenuous exercise when fed carbohydrate." J Appl Physiol 61:165-172, 1986.

2. Murray R, Paul GL, Seifert JG and Eddy DE. "Responses to varying rates of carbohydrate ingestion during exercise." Med Sci Sports Exerc 23:713-718, 1991.

3. Paul G. "Dietary protein requirements of physically active individuals." Sports Medicine 8:154-157, 1989.

4. Coyle EF. "Carbohydrates and athletic performance." Gatorade Sport Science Exchange 1(7), 1988.

5. Hultman E. "Nutritional effects on work performance." Am J Clin Nutr 49:949-957, 1989.

6. Rehrer NJ, vanKemenade MC, Meesler TA, Saris WHM and Brouns F. "Nutrition in- to GI complaints among triathletes." Med Sci Sports Exerc 22:s107, 1990.

7. Brouns F and Saris WHM. "Diet manipulation and related metabolic changes in competitive cyclists." American College of Sports Medicine Annual Meeting, 1990.

This article is by Enette Larson, MS, RD and is excerpted from Vegan Handbook, edited by Debra Wasserman and Reed Mangels Ph.D., R.D.

# Why is Wine so Fined?
## By Caroline Pyevich

Although wine usually contains only grapes, yeast, and a small amount of sulfites, which are added and created during fermentation, the processing of wine introduces small amounts of substances which may be of concern to vegetarians and vegans.

Every wine is different and no uniform formula exists for producing wine. The taste of a wine is a reflection of where its grapes were grown. The soil gives the wine its flavor, which is why wines produced in certain areas have a distinctive flavor. Winemakers may choose not to extensively process their wine in order to retain some of these natural qualities.

A clarifying or fining agent makes wine clear by removing proteins from the wine. The agents eventually settle out of the wine. Different proteins serve as clarifying agents depending upon both the type of wine and the desired flavor. Lab trials determine both the clarifying agent and quantities used. The fining agents have an opposite polarity to that of the wine. Therefore, the agents solidify with the protein and they remain in the wine, although they can be removed.

Some clarifiers are animal-based products, while others are earth-based. Common animal-based agents include egg whites, milk, casein, gelatin, and isinglass. Gelatin is an animal protein derived from the skin and connective tissue of pigs and cows. Isinglass is prepared from the bladder of the sturgeon fish. Bentonite, a clay earth product, serves as a popular fining agent.

Organic agents are more likely to be used in the clarification of premium wines. Premium wines are typically those which cost more than $7 a bottle and are produced from grapes grown in desirable locations. According to Bouchaine Vineyard, twenty-five percent of the premium wines produced in the United States are clarified with an organic protein.

Egg whites from chicken eggs are used for red wine clarification and are removed before the wine is bottled. The egg whites are not specially processed or separately distributed for the wine industry. They are regular, store-bought eggs or farm eggs. Two or three egg whites can clarify a 55-gallon barrel of wine.

Winemakers in France (Burgundy) commonly utilize egg whites in their production because they can use the whites of the eggs after the yolks have already been added to their foods. Egg whites generally clarify more expensive wines (above $15 a bottle) or French wines which are expected to age.

Large producers of wine in the United States do not usually use egg whites as a fining agent, and they may implement potassium caseinate as a substitute for eggs. Whole milk and casein are two other possible fining agents in some red wines.

Gelatin can clarify either white or red wine. Gelatin pulls suspended material out of wine, and less expensive wines may use this material. One ounce of gelatin can clarify 1,000 gallons of wine.

Gelatin serves as a finishing agent in some wine and beer. A finishing agent adds a "final touch" to the quality and clarity of the wine without making any radical change in its flavor. Gelatin may also be used in addition to another fining agent and is removed after the clarification process.

Although the clarifying agents for red wine are animal products, many producers of red wine do not need to use any clarifying agent to remove tannins. (Tannins are naturally occurring compounds that precipitate proteins from a solution.) By pressing the wine at an early stage of the winemaking process, the tannins can be removed without the additional proteins.

Isinglass is used to fine selected white wine. Germany, which initially introduced this method, is one of the main countries that still uses this technique. Some American wineries use isinglass to clarify white wine or chardonnay, but this substance is not commonly incorporated in wine production. Activated carbon or bentonite are alternative clarifiers of white wine.

The most popular substance used to remove the proteins of domestically produced white wines is bentonite. It is a silica clay which picks up the organic proteins left by the grapes. If left in the wine, these proteins would denature and form long molecular strands. This process would result in wine that is either hazy or has loose sediment floating in it. Therefore, bentonite acts as an agent to improve the cosmetic appearance of the wine for the consumer. Bentonite is used to fine most inexpensive wines. Two to three pounds of bentonite clarifies 1,000 gallons of wine.

Several other fining agents exist. Sparkaloid, a diatomaceous earth, clarifies white and red wine. Italian wine may be fined with either eggs, milk, or blood. Although blood of large mammals may serve as a clarifier in some Old Mediterranean countries, its use is forbidden in wine from either the United States or France.

Both the clarifying agents and the removed proteins coagulate on the bottom of the wine tank or barrel. They are then removed through either a settling process or a cellulose fiber filter. The ingredient list of a wine will not state the clarifier as an ingredient because it is removed from the final product. Calling or writing to a particular wine company may be the best way to discover which fining agent they use.

Wine may also be filtered to remove impurities. A wine can be filtered and not clarified, or clarified and not filtered. A wine marked "unfiltered" has not passed through a filtering substance, such as a plastic micropore filter. "Unfined" wines have not had a clarifying agent passed through them. Even though a wine label may state it is unfined, this may not always be the case. According to one California winery, some companies may mark a bottle of wine "unfined" as a marketing technique because no one avidly scrutinizes the wine producers to verify these claims.

Kosher wines may be more likely to avoid the use of the animal-based clarifying agents, but not all do so. The Union of Orthodox Jewish Congregations (OU) stated that all of their Kosher certified American-made wines do not currently use either gelatin, isinglass, or egg whites. They cannot vouch for the status of the international Kosher wines.

The Orthodox Union also claimed that a wine could theoretically be certified as Kosher if it contained egg whites or if the gelatin were completely removed from the final product. They did not reveal any general rule for certifying wine as Kosher and claimed that each certification agency may use different criteria for certifying wine. Star-K, another certification organization, also showed no aversion to the use of egg whites.

Kof K claimed that Kosher wine is not clarified with either gelatin or isinglass in America. Egg whites, a Kosher item, would be a permissible agent. Kof K mentioned that paper is sometimes used to clarify Kosher wine, as the paper adheres to the impurities. Kosher wine is a specialty item and is produced directly for the Kosher market.

(Reprinted from January/February 1997 issue of *Vegetarian Journal*)
See page 75 for sources of vegan wines.

# Handy Guide to Food Ingredients

**This section is excerpted from VRG's 28-page <u>Guide to Food Ingredients</u> (see page 269).**

*Classification of Commercial Ingredients*

**Vegetarian** means that the ingredient does not contain products derived from meat, fish, or fowl. It may include sources from eggs or dairy. Insect *secretions*, such as honey, are also classified as vegetarian.

**Vegan** means that the item contains no animal products whatsoever.

**Non-vegetarian** means that the ingredient (or substance used to process the ingredient) is derived from meat, fish, or fowl.

**Non-vegetarian** can apply to substances, such as proteins or amino acids, derived from animals (including insects), when the collection of those substances necessitated the intentional death of that animal.

In some cases, a few manufacturers told us that they use vegetarian sources. However, we cannot say with certainty that all manufacturers of a given ingredient produce that ingredient in the same way. Thus, we have classified these ingredients as **typically vegetarian, typically vegan, typically non-vegetarian,** or **may be non-vegetarian.** The classification depends on the degree to which we may conclude from man-ufacturers' information that a given ingredient may be vegetarian or vegan. Note that a vegetarian or vegan ingredient may have been tested on animals.

## Vegetarian

acid casein
albumen
beeswax
calcium caseinate
carbohydrate
casein
cysteine
cystine
honey
L-cysteine
L-cystine
lactalbumin
lac-resin
lactose
royal jelly
shellac
Simplesse
sodium caseinate
Sucanat Granulated
   with Honey

## Vegan

Accent
acesulfame K
acesulfame potassium
acetic acid
acid calcium phos-
   phate
acrylate-acrylamide
   resin
acrylic acid
activated charcoal

agar
agar-agar
algin
alginate
alginic acid
alum
aluminum ammonium
annatto
annatto extract
annatto seed
apple acid
arabic
ascorbic acid
aspartame
autolyzed yeast
   extract
baking powder
baking soda
beet sugar
bentonite
benzoyl peroxide
BHA
BHT
bicarbonate of soda
bioflavinoids
Brewer's yeast
bromelain
bromolin
butanoic acid
butylated hydroxy-
   anisole
butylated hydroxy-
   toluene

butyric acid
*n*-butyric acid
calcium biphosphate
calcium carbonate
calcium phosphate
calcium phosphate
   monobasic
calcium phosphate
   dibasic
calcium phosphate
   tribasic
calcium propionate
calcium sulfate
calcium sulfate
   anhydrous
candelilla wax
caramel color
carboxymethyl-
   cellulose
carnauba wax
carob bean gum
caroid
carrageenan
caustic soda
cellulose gum
charcoal
Chile saltpeter
chondrus extract
citric acid
CMC
cocoa butter
colophony
corn gluten

corn gluten meal
cream of tartar
cyanocobalamin
DevanSweet
diatomaceous earth
dicalcium phosphate
    dihydrate
distilled vinegar
Equal
erythorbic acid
essential oil
ethanol
ethyl alcohol
ethyl vanillin
fumaric acid
gluten
grain alcohol
grain vinegar
guar flour
guar gum
guaran
gypsum
hesperidin
hexadienic acid
hexadienoic acid
hydrogen peroxide
Irish moss
isoascorbic acid
Japanese isinglass
kieselguhr
light oil
lime
locust bean gum

maleic acid
malic acid
malt
malt extract
malt sugar
maltodextrin
maltol
maltose
mannitol
methyl paraben
methyl-$p$-hydroxy-
    benzoate
mineral oil
molasses
monocalcium phos-
    phate
monosodium gluta-
    mate
MSG
natural sugar
nonnutritive sweetener
norbixin
Nutrasweet
nutritional yeast
oleoresin
papain
paprika
paraffin
plaster of Paris
polyacrylomite
polydextrose
polyethylene
potash alum

potassium acid tartrate
potassium bitartrate
potassium hydrogen
    tartrate
potassium sorbate
potassium sulfate
precipitated calcium
    phosphate
1,2-propanediol
propanoic acid
propanoic acid,
    calcium salt
propionic acid
propylene glycol
resin
rice syrup
Rochelle salts
rosin
rutin
saccharin
soda ash
soda lye
sodium acid carbonate
sodium ascorbare
sodium benzoate
sodium benzosulfi-
    mide
sodium bicarbonate
sodium carbonate
sodium carboxy-
    methylcellulose
sodium hydrogen
    carbonate

sodium hydroxide
sodium isoascorbate
sodium nitrate
sodium potassium
    tartrate
sodium tartrate
sorbic acid
sorbic acid, potass-
    ium salt
sorbistat
sorbitan
spirit vinegar
St. John's bread
Sucanat
succinic acid
Sunette
tartaric acid
textured soy flour
textured soy protein
textured vegetable
    protein (TVP)
tricalcium phosphate
turbinado sugar
turmeric
tumeric
TVP
unmodified food
    starch
unmodified starch
vanilla
vanilla extract
vanillin
vinegar

vinegar, distilled
vital wheat gluten
vitamin B-12
vitamin C
vitamin P complex
washed raw sugar
wheat gluten
wheat isolate
white distilled vinegar
white oil
white vinegar
xantham gum
yeast autolyzates
zein
Zest

## Non-Vegetarian

carmine
carminic acid
cochineal
dripping
gelatin
Hi-Vegi-Lip
hydrogenated tallow
isinglass
keratin
lard
lard oil
pancreatin
pancreatic extract
pepsin
pork fat
pork oil

rennet
rennin
suet
tallow
tallow flakes
trypsin
tyrosine

## Typically Vegetarian

acidulant
alanine
albumin
alpha tocopherol
antidusting agent
antioxidant
arginine
artificial flavor
aspartic acid
beta-carotene
biotin
butyl lactate
calciferol
calcium panto-
    thenate
caproic acid
caprylic acid
carotenoid
cholecalciferol
coenzyme
color
corn sugar
curing agent

dextrose

drying agent

ethyl lactate

fermentation aid

foaming agent

fructose

fructose syrup

fruit sugar

glucose

glutamic acid

glycine

hexanoic acid

n-hexanoic acid

high fructose corn
   syrup

humectant

hydroscopic agent

isomerized syrup

lactase

lactic acid

leavener

leavening agent

lecithin

levulose

levulose-bearing syrup

malting aid

moisture-retaining
   agent

moisture-retention
   agent

natural sugar

n-octanoic acid

pickling agent

Provitamin A

sodium pantothenate

surface-finishing agent

tocopherol

vitamin B factor

vitamin D

vitamin D-2

vitamin D-3

vitamin E

water-retaining agent

wax

whey

whipping agent

## Typically Vegan

amylase

antimicrobial agent

antispoilant

artificial coloring

chelating agent

dough conditioner

dough strengthener

firming agent

lactoflavin

maple sugar

maple syrup

natural coloring

niacin

niacinamide

nicotinic acid

nicotinamide

nutritive sweetener

pantothenic acid

d-pantothenamide

phenylalanine

preservative

pyridoxal

pyridoxamine

pyridoxine

pyridoxine hydro-
   chloride

pyridoxol hydro-
   chloride

reducing agent

riboflavin

riboflavin-5-
   phosphate

sequestering agent

sorbitol

stabilizer

thickener

texturizer

thiamin

thiamine

thiamine hydro-
   chloride

thiamine mononitrate

thiamine mononitrite

vitamin

vitamin B-1

vitamin B-2

vitamin B-3

vitamin B-5

vitamin B-6

vitamin B-6 hydro-
   chloride

yeast food

## May be Non-Vegetarian

activated carbon
adipic acid
amino acid
anticaking agent
capric acid
clarifier
clarifying agent
n-decanoic acid
diglyceride
disodium inosinate
emulsifier
enzyme
fat
fatty acid
fining agent
flavor enhancer
folacin
folic acid
free-flow agent
glyceride
glycerin
glycerine
glycerol
hexanedioic acid
magnesium stearate
modified food starch
modified starch
monoglyceride
natural flavor

n-octadecanoic acid
oil
Olean
Olestra
palmitic acid
polyoxyethylene
    (20) sorbitan
    monooleate
polyoxyethylene
    (20) sorbitan
    monostearate
polysorbate
polysorbate 60
polysorbate 80
processing aid
protease
protein
pteroyl glutamic acid
retinol
sodium steoroyl
    lactylate
sodium stearoyl-2-
    lactylate
stearic acid
sucrose polyester
surface acting agent
surface-active agent
surfactant
vitamin A
vitamin A acetate
vitamin A palmitate
vitamin A propionate
wetting agent

wine

## Typically Non-Vegetarian

calcium stearate
cane sugar
colorose
n-hexadecanoic acid
inversol
invert sugar
invert sugar syrup
lipase
myristic acid
cis-9-octadecenoic acid
oleic acid
palmitic acid
refined sugar
sucrose
sugar
sugar syrup, invert
n-tetradecanoic acid

# Suggested Reading

## Suggested Reading - Cookbooks

### Cookbooks published by The Vegetarian Resource Group:
Conveniently Vegan
Leprechaun Cake and Other Tales
The Lowfat Jewish Vegetarian Cookbook
Meatless Meals for Working People
No Cholesterol Passover Recipes
Simply Vegan
Vegan Handbook
Vegan Meals for One or Two
Vegan in Volume

The following are cookbooks that have stood the test of time, as well as ones that offer recipes for specific dishes and styles of cooking.

Bates, Dorothy R., and Colby Wingate. Cooking with Gluten and Seitan. Summertown: The Book Publishing Company, 1993.

Bates, Dorothy R. The TVP Cookbook. Summertown: The Book Publishing Company, 1991.

Gentle World. The Cookbook for People Who Love Animals. 7th ed. Maui: Gentle World, Inc., 1992.

Golbitz, Peter. Tofu & Soyfoods Cookery. Summertown: The Book Publishing Company, 1998.

Grogan, Bryanna Clark. Nonna's Italian Kitchen: Delicious Home-Style Vegan Cuisine. Summertown: The Book Publishing Company, 1998.

Grogan, Bryanna Clark. The (Almost) No-Fat Holiday Cookbook: Festive Holiday Recipes. Summertown: The Book Publishing Company, 1995.

Hagler, Louise, and Dorothy R. Bates ed. The New Farm Vegetarian Cookbook. 3rd ed. Summertown: The Book Publishing Company, 1989.

Hagler, Louise. Tofu Cookery. 2nd ed. Summertown: The Book Publishing Company, 1991.

Hurd, DC, MD, Frank J., and Rosalie Hurd, BS. Ten Talents. 2nd ed. Collegedale: The College Press, 1985.

Jackson, Ann. Cookin' Southern. Summertown: The Book Publishing Company, 2000.

People for the Ethical Treatment of Animals. Cooking With PETA. Summertown: The Book Publishing Company, 1997.

Salloum, Habeeb. Classic Vegetarian Cooking from the Middle East and North Africa. New York: Interlink Publishing Group, Inc., 2000.

Schinner, Miyoko Nishimoto. Japanese Cooking Contemporary & Traditional: Simple, Delicious, and Vegan. Summertown: The Book Publishing Company, 1999.

Schumann, Kate, and Virginia Messina, MPII, RD. The Vegetarian No-Cholesterol Barbecue Cookbook. New York: St. Martin's Press, 1994.

Sobers, Yvonne McCalla. Delicious Jamaica: Vegetarian Cuisine. Summertown: The Book Publishing Company, 1996.

Stepaniak, Joanne. The UnCheese Cookbook. Summertown: The Book Publishing Company, 1994.

Tucker, Eric, and John Westerdahl, MPH, RD, CNS. The Millenium Cookbook. Berkeley: Ten Speed Press, 1998.

The Book Publishing Company offers many vegetarian and vegan cookbooks. Contact them at P.O. Box 180, Summertown, TN 38483.

# Suggested Reading - Vegetarian Families

Bates, Dorothy, and Suzanne Havala, MS, RD. Kids Can Cook. Summertown: Book Publishing Company, 2000.

Crist, Vonnie Winslow, and Debra Wasserman. Leprechaun Cake and Other Tales. Balitmore: The Vegetarian Resource Group, 1995.

Gross, Joy and Karen Freifeld. Raising Your Family Naturally. Secaucus: Lyle Stuart Inc., 1983.

Klaper, Michael, MD. Pregnancy, Children, and the Vegan Diet. 4th Ed. Umatilla: Gentle World Inc., 1987.

Krizmanic, Judy. A Teen's Guide to Going Vegetarian. Middleborough: Penguin Books USA Inc., 1994.

Lair, Cynthia. Feeding the Whole Family. 2nd Ed. San Diego: LuraMedia Inc., 1994.

Pierson, Stephanie. Vegetables Rock!. New York: Bantam Books, 1999.

Robbins, Meyera. Great Food For Great Kids Recipes. Studio City: Michael Wiese Productions, 1994.

Shandler, Michael, and Nina Shandler. The Complete Guide and Cookbook for Raising Your Child as a Vegetarian. New Canaan: Keats Publishing, Inc., 1981.

Wasserman, Debra, and Reed Mangels, PhD, RD. Simply Vegan. 3rd ed. Baltimore: The Vegetarian Resource Group, 2000.

Yntema, Sharon K. Vegetarian Children. Ithaca: McBooks Press, 1987.

# Suggested Reading - Travel

Bourke, Alex, and Alan Todd. Vegetarian Britain. London: Vegetarian Guides Ltd., 1998.

Bourke, Alex. ed. Vegetarian Europe. London: Vegetarian Guides Ltd., 2000.

Bourke, Alex, and Paul Gaynor. Vegetarian France. London: Vegetarian Guides Ltd., 1998.

Bourke, Alex, and Paul Gaynor. Vegetarian London. London: Cruelty-Free Living, 1998.

Civic, Jed and Susan. The Vegetarian Traveler. Burdett: Larson Publications, 1997.

Geon, Bryan. Speaking Vegetarian: The Globetrotter's Guide To Ordering Meatless in 197 Countries. Greenport: Pilot Books, 1999.

Frost, James Bernard. The Artichoke Trail. Edison: Hunter Publishing, Inc., 2000.

Lacy, Jo. ed. Viva! Guide to Vegetarian Brighton. Brighton: Viva!, 1998.

Shumaker, Susan, and Than Saffel. Vegetarian Walt Disney World and Greater Orlando. Morgantown: Vegetarian World Guides, 2000.

Shumaker, Susan, and Than Saffel. "It's A Veg World After All." Vegetarian Times. Feb. 1998: 71-78.

The Vegetarian Resource Group. Vegetarian Journal's Guide to Natural Foods Restaurants in the US and Canada. Baltimore: The Vegetarian Resource Group, 1998.

Zipern, Elizabeth, and Dar Williams. The Tofu Tollbooth. Woodstock: Ceres Press/Ardwork Press, 1998.

# School Foods Information
## by Nancy Berkoff, RD

When working with schools following USDA school meal guidelines, we suggest utilizing the Toolkit, as it was designed by the USDA
specifically for this purpose and meets the requirements of the USDA.

For example, commodity ingredients are incorporated into many of
the recipes. Commodities are no-cost or low-cost food ingredients available
to the schools through the federal government. Use of commodity foods
helps schools operate within their budgets and to serve healthy meals to the
largest number of children. Common vegetarian commodities include
canned beans, peanut butter, canned fruit, staple items such as flour and
corn meal, dried fruit, frozen fruit and vegetables, and dairy products such
as cheese and butter. Commodities vary in availability from year to year
and from region to region. The school food service director is expected to
take advantage of the commodities program whenever possible.

Please refer to the United States Department of Agriculture
(USDA) publication, **Toolkit for Healthy School Meals: Recipes and
Training Materials,** as well as the **Community Nutrition Action Kit**
that accompanies the toolkit. These are the current USDA tools for nutrition education and healthy meal preparation in the schools. Your school
food service department should already have copies from the USDA. If
you need additional copies of the **Community Nutrition Action Kit**,
they may be obtained for free from the USDA by calling (703) 305-1624
or writing to: USDA, 3101 Park Center Dr., Room 802, Alexandria, VA
22302. Copies of the **Toolkit for Healthy School Meals** can be purchased from the National Food Service Management Institute for $25.
Their telephone number is (800)-321-3054.

The **Toolkit for Healthy School Meals** notebook contains
quantity recipes with several lacto-ovo vegetarian (no meat, fish or fowl,
but including dairy, honey, and eggs) and vegan (no meat, fish, fowl,
dairy, eggs or honey) options. The recipes include nutritional analyses,
identify the component of the meal for which they can be used, and
include photographs of many of the selections, giving serving suggestions.

# Feeding Schedule For Vegan Babies Ages 4-12 Months

|  | 4-7 mos* | 6-8 mos | 7-10 mos | 10-12 mos |
|---|---|---|---|---|
| **MILK** | Breast milk or soy formula. | Breast milk or soy formula. | Breast milk or soy formula. | Breast milk or soy formula (24-32 ounces). |
| **CEREAL & BREAD** | Begin iron-fortified baby cereal mixed with breast milk or soy formula. | Continue baby cereal. Begin other breads and cereals. | Baby cereal. Other breads and cereals. | Baby cereal until 18 mos. Total of 4 svgs (1 svg=1/4 slice bread or 2-4 TB cereal). |
| **FRUITS & VEGETA-BLES** | None | Begin juice from cup: 2-4 oz vit C source. Begin mashed vegetables & fruits. | 4 oz juice. Pieces of soft/cooked fruits & vegetables. | Table-food diet. Allow 4 svgs per day (1 svg=2-4 TB fruit & vegetable, 4 oz. juice). |
| **LEGUMES & NUT BUTTERS** | None | None | Gradually introduce tofu. Begin casseroles, pureed legumes, soy cheese, & soy yogurt. | 2 svgs daily each about 1/2 oz. Nut butters should not be started before 1 year. |

* Overlap of ages occurs because of varying rate of development.

Reprinted from Simply Vegan, pages 192 and 194. Also available online at www.vrg.org/nutrition/pregnancy.htm

## Diet Plans for Vegan Children

# TODDLERS AND PRESCHOOLERS (AGE 1-4)

| FOOD GROUP | NUMBER OF SERVINGS |
|---|---|
| Grains | 6 or more servings. A serving is 1/2 to 1 slice of bread; 1/4 to 1/2 cup cooked cereal, grain, or pasta; 1/2 to 1 cup ready-to-eat cereal. |
| Legumes, Nuts, Seeds | 2 or more servings. A serving is 1/4 to 1/2 cup cooked beans, tofu, tempeh, or TVP; 1-1/2 to 3 ounces of meat analog; 1 to 2 Tbsp. nuts, seeds, or nut or seed butter. |
| Fortified soymilk, etc. | 3 servings. A serving is 1 cup fortified soymilk, infant formula, or breast milk. |
| Vegetables | 2 or more servings. A serving is 1/4 to 1/2 cup cooked, or 1/2 to 1 cup raw vegetables. |
| Fruits | 3 or more servings. A serving is 1/4 to 1/2 cup canned fruit, 1/2 cup juice, or 1/2 medium fruit. |
| Fats | 3-4 servings. A serving is 1 tsp. margarine or oil. |

Reprinted from Simply Vegan, pages 192 and 194. Also available online at www.vrg.org/nutrition/pregnancy.htm

## Diet Plans for Vegan Children

# SCHOOL-AGED CHILDREN

| FOOD GROUP | NUMBER OF SERVINGS |
|---|---|
| Grains | 6 or more servings for five to six-year-olds; 7 or more for seven to twelve-year-olds. A serving is 1 slice of bread; 1/2 cup cooked cereal, grain, or pasta; or 3/4 to 1 cup ready-to-eat cereal. |
| Legumes, Nuts, Seeds | 1-1/2 to 3 servings for five to six-year-olds; 3 or more for seven to twelve-year-olds. A serving is 1/2 cup cooked beans, tofu, tempeh, or TVP; 3 ounces of meat analog; or 2 Tbsp. nuts, seeds, nut or seed butter. |
| Fortified soymilk, etc | 3 servings. A serving is 1 cup fortified soymilk. |
| Vegetables | 2 or more servings for five to six-year-olds; 3 or more for seven to twelve-year-olds. A serving is 1/2 cup cooked or 1 cup raw vegetables. |
| Fruits | 2 to 4 servings for five to six-year-olds; 3 or more for seven to twelve-year-olds. A serving is 1/2 cup canned fruit, 3/4 cup juice, or 1 medium fruit. |
| Fats | 4 servings for five to six-year-olds; 5 for seven to twelve-year-olds. A serving is 1 tsp. margarine or oil. |

247

# VRG Publications, Resources, and Tabling Materials

Many of our brochures are available for a self-addressed stamped envelope or can be accessed for free online. The brochures available online at www.vrg.org are underlined below. Others can be requested by writing The Vegetarian Resource Group, PO Box 1463, Baltimore, MD 21203 USA or calling (410) 366-8343 Monday through Friday 9-5 (EST). You can also email vrg@vrg.org for more information. For ordering information on the reprints, periodicals, and books, please visit the *"Ordering from The Vegetarian Resource Group"* page on the website at www.vrg.org/catalog/order.htm or call (410) 366-8343 Monday through Friday 9-5 (EST) for more information or to place an order over the phone with a Visa or Mastercard.

## Animal Rights
What is Animal Rights?
Activist News
Animal Rights Booklet

## Basic Info
Vegetarianism in a Nutshell
Vegetarian Nutrition for Teenagers
Heart Healthy Eating Tips
Vegan Diets in a Nutshell
The American Dietetic Association Position Paper: Vegetarian Diets
Starting a Vegetarian Group
What is Animal Rights?
51 Projects of the VRG
*Also see the Nutshell portion of the VRG website and the nutrition section in Simply Vegan.*

## Catalogs
Activist Catalog
Wholesale Catalog
Professional Catalog

## Children
Raising Vegan Children
Traveling with Vegan Children
Food Experience Projects for Young
  Children
I Love Animals and Broccoli
  Coloring Book
I Love Animals and Broccoli
  Shopping Basket
Leprechaun Cake and Other Tales
Lesson Plan for I Love Animals
  and Broccoli
Guide to Fast Food
Pediatric Manual of Clinical
  Dietetics, Veg. Nutrition Chapter
Vegan Nutrition in Pregnancy and
  Childhood

## Core Brochures for Tabling
Vegetarianism in a Nutshell
Vegetarian Nutrition for Teenagers
Heart Healthy Eating Tips
Vegan Diets in a Nutshell
The American Dietetic Association
  Position Paper: Vegetarian Diets
Vegan Nutrition in Pregnancy and
  Childhood
Vegetarian Journal

## Diabetes
Dietary Exchange list
Diabetes and a Vegetarian Diet

## Educational
Food Experience Projects for Young
  Children
I Love Animals and Broccoli
Coloring Book
I Love Animals and Broccoli
  Shopping Basket
I Love Animals and Broccoli
  Activity Book
Leprechaun Cake and Other Tales
Lesson Plan for I Love Animals
  and Broccoli
VRG Annual Essay Contest
Lesson Plan for Essay Contest
Vegetarian Game

## Environment
Vegetarianism and the
  Environment
Vegetarian Journal articles on:
    Aquaculture
    Pesticides
    Water Usage on Chicken Farms
    Waste from Farms

## Food Ingredients
Guide to Food Ingredients
What's in Your Cheese?
Why is Wine So Fined?
Sugar and Other Sweeteners
Busy Bees

## Food Service
Vegetarian Journal's Foodservice
  Update Newsletter
Colleges and Camps Serving
  Vegetarian Options
Tips for Introducing Veg. Food into
  Institutions
Quantity Recipe Packet
Major League Ballparks

Hospital Survival Guide
Guide to Fast Food
Guide to Food Ingredients
School Foods Packet
Quantity Product Listing
Catering letter
Food For the Masses (VT)
Vegan in Volume (book)
*Also see the Foodservice section of the VRG website.*

## Fund Raising
VRG Visa/Mastercard info
Message!Check info
Special Activist offer
51 Projects of the VRG

## Internet
Online Resources for Vegetarians
www.vrg.org

## Japanese
Vegetarianism in a Nutshell in Japanese
Vegan Diets in a Nutshell in Japanese
About The VRG in Japanese

## Jewish
The Lowfat Jewish Vegetarian Cookbook (book)
No Cholesterol Passover Recipes (book)
Guide to Vegetarian Restaurants in Israel (book)
Jewish Vegetarians' Newsletter
No Schmaltz! Video

## Latino
Guide to Latin America
Vegetarianism in a Nutshell in Spanish
Vegetarian Teens in Spanish
Heart Healthy Tips in Spanish

## Meal Plans
Vegan Meal Plan
28 Day Meal Plan
Meals on Wheels 4 Week Menu Plan

## Misc.
Bumper Stickers
Postcards
Buttons
Magnets
T-Shirts
Envelope Stickers

## Misc. Articles
Humans are Omnivores

## Nutrition
Vegetarianism in a Nutshell
The American Dietetic Association Position Paper: Vegetarian Diets
Vegetarian Nutrition for Teenagers
Heart Healthy Eating Tips
Vegan Diets in a Nutshell
Vegetarian Food Pyramid
Iron Chapter from Simply Vegan
Protein Chapter from Simply Vegan
Calcium Chapter from Simply Vegan

Vitamin B12 in the Vegan Diet
   from Simply Vegan
*Also see the Nutrition portion of
the VRG website.*

## Organizing/Activism
What is Animal Rights?
Starting a Vegetarian Group
Forming a Student Group
Speaking to Classes about
   Vegetarianism
Animal Rights Booklet
Activist News

## Out of Print
Healthy Holidays
Vegetarian Journal Reports
Vegetarianism for Working People

## Parents
Vegetarianism in a Nutshell
Vegan Nutrition in Pregnancy and
   Childhood
Tips for Parents of Young
   Vegetarians
Raising Vegan Children
Traveling with Vegan Children
The American Dietetic Association
   Position Paper: Vegetarian Diets
Soy Formula from Simply Vegan
Vegetarian Nutrition for Teenagers
Guide to Fast Food
School Foods Packet
Pediatric Manual of Clinical
   Dietetics, Veg. Nutrition Chapter
Parents E-mail List
*Also see the Raising a Vegetarian*

*Family portion of the VRG website
and the nutrition section in Simply
Vegan.*

## Periodicals
Local Events Flyer (Maryland)
Vegetarian Journal
Vegetarian Journal's Foodservice
   Update Newsletter
VRG News

## Polish
Vegetarian Nutrition for Teenagers
   in Polish

## Poll Information (# of Vegetarians in US)
1994 Adult Poll
1997 Adult Poll
2000 Adult Poll
1995 Teen Poll
2001 Teen Poll
1999 Dining out Poll

## Recipes & Cooking Tips
Vegetarianism in a Nutshell
30 Day Menu for Those Who Don't
   Like to Cook
Thanksgiving Treasures
Holiday Recipes (old)
Sandwich Ideas (old)
*Also see the Vegetarian Recipes,
Catalog and Vegetarian Journal
portion of the VRG website, as well
as our list of books below.*

## Seniors
Heart Healthy Eating Tips
Vegan Diets in a Nutshell
Vegetarianism in a Nutshell
A Senior's Guide to Good Nutrition
Meatless Menu Alternatives for
   Seniors (Meals on Wheels)

## Sports/Athletes
Major League Ballparks
Sports Nutrition Article
Article on Jane Black, Champion
Vegan Weightlifter

## Students
Vegetarian Nutrition for Teenagers
Starting a Vegetarian Group
Forming a Student Group
Living Your Ethics
VRG Annual Essay Contest
School Foods Packet
Speaking to Classes
Colleges and Camps Serving
   Vegetarian Options
Online Resources for Vegetarians
Veggie Viewpoint: Eating at College
Vegetarian Game

## Teens
Vegetarianism in a Nutshell
VRG Annual Essay Contest
Vegetarian Nutrition for Teenagers
Guide to Fast Food

## Travel
Major League Ballparks
Vegetarian Vacation Guide

Guide to Fast Food
City Guides (Los Angeles, Anaheim,
   Chicago, Baltimore, Atlanta)
Maryland Dining Guide
The VJ Guide to Natural Foods
   Rest. in the US & Canada (book)
*Also see the Travel portion of the
VRG website.*

## Veganism
Vegan Diets in a Nutshell
Guide to Food Ingredients
Vegan Meal Plan
Vegetarian Journal
Simply Vegan

## Videos/Visual Aids
No Schmaltz! Video
Shopping for Health (4 videos)
Slide Show

## VRG Books
Conveniently Vegan
Guide to Vegetarian Restaurants in
   Israel
Leprechaun Cake and Other Tales
The Lowfat Jewish Vegetarian
   Cookbook
Meatless Meals for Working People
VJ Guide to Natural Foods Rests. in
   the US and Canada
No Cholesterol Passover Recipes
Simple, Lowfat, & Vegetarian
   (temp. out of print)
Simply Vegan
Vegan & Vegetarian FAQ
Vegan Handbook

Vegan in Volume
Vegan Meals for One or Two
Vegetarian Journal Reports
*Also see the Catalog portion of the VRG website.*

## VRG Booklets
Guide to Fast Food
Guide to Food Ingredients
I Love Animals & Broccoli Activity Book
Guide to Leather Alternatives
Quantity Recipe Packet

## VRG Carries These Books (We also have access to most vegetarian books currently in print, please inquire.)
Authentic Chinese Cuisine
Becoming Vegan
Burgers 'n Fries 'n Cinnamon Buns
CalciYum!
Cookbook For People Who Love Animals
Cookin' Southern
Cooking Vegetarian
Cooking with PETA
Cooking with Gluten and Seitan
Delicious Jamaica
Ecological Cooking
European Veggie Guide
Fabulous Beans
Flavors of India
Incredibly Delicious
Japanese Cooking Contemporary and Traditional
Lean and Luscious and Meatless

Life After Beef
Lighten Up!
Meatless Burgers
Millenium Cookbook
Natural Lunchbox
New Farm Vegetarian Cookbook
Nonna's Italian Kitchen
Oats, Peas, Beans & Barley Cookbook
Pasta - East to West
Peaceful Palate
Pregnancy, Children & the Vegan Diet
Race Against Junk Food
Shopping for Health
Simple Soybean & Your Health
Soups On!
Soup to Nuts Coloring Book
Table for Two
Taste of Mexico
Tofu Cookery
Tofu & Soyfoods Cookery
Tofu Tollbooth
The TVP Cookbook
Uncheese Cookbook
Vegan Nutrition: Pure and Simple
Vegan Vittles
Vegetarian Cooking For People w/Allergies
Vegetarian Europe
Vegetarian Sourcebook
Vegetarian Traveler
Vegetarian Way

# BIBLIOGRAPHY

## Chapter 1 Most Frequently Asked Questions

"Is it Kosher?" Kosher Quest. Online. 3 Mar. 2000.

"Marshmallows and Gelatins." Kashrus Conscience. Online. 26 Jan. 2001.

Mushell, Avroho, Rabbi. "Getting into the Thick of Things, Which Gelatin is Kosher?" Kashrus Magazine. Feb. 2001: 22-27.

Regenstein, Joe M. and Carrie E. Regenstein. "The Kosher Dietary Laws And Their Implementation in the Food Industry." Viewpoint. Sept./Oct. 1989: 29.

## Chapter 2 Vegetarianism in Daily Life

Akers, Keith. A Vegetarian Sourcebook. 2nd ed. Denver: Vegetarian Press, 1989.

Animal Protection Institute. What's Really in Pet Food. Sacramento: Animal Protection Institute, 1997.

Berthold-Bond, Annie. Clean & Green. New York: Ceres Press, 1990.

"Cats - A Vegetarian Diet." Vegetarian Society of the UK. Online. 15 June 1999.

"Dairy and Poultry Statistics." USDA-NASS Agricultural Statistics 1998. Online. 17 Dec. 1999.

Davis, Brenda, RD, and Vesanto Melina, MS, RD. Becoming Vegan. Summertown: The Book Publishing Company, 2000.

"Dogs - A Vegetarian Diet." Vegetarian Society of the UK. Online. 15 June 1999.

Eiznitz, Gail. Slaughterhouse: The Shocking Story of Greed, Neglect, and Inhumane Treatment Inside the US Meat Industry. New York: Prometheus Books, 1997.

"How do I know it's Kosher?" OU.ORG. Online. 30 Jan. 2001.

"Information Sheet: Alcohol." Vegetarian Society of the UK. Online. 30 Jan. 2001.

Luban, Rabbi Yaakov. "To 'D' or Not To 'D'." Kosher at OU.ORG. Online. 30 Jan. 2001.

Melina, Vesanto, RD, Brenda Davis, RD, and Victoria Harrison, RD. Becoming Vegetarian. Summertown: The Book Publishing Company, 1995.

The National Anti-Vivisection Society. Personal Care for People Who Care. 10th ed. Chicago: The National Anti-Vivisection Society, 2000.

"Poultry Slaughter Report: Apr. 2000" US Department of Agriculture. Online. 17 Jan. 2001.

"The Schwartz Collection on Judaism, Vegetarianism, and Animal Rights." Online. 27 June 2000.

Spencer, Colin. The Heretic's Feast. Hanover: University Press of New England, 1995.

"Sports and Physical Activity." International Vegetarian Union. Online. 28 Mar. 2000.

"Statistics of Hog, Cattle, and Sheep." USDA-NASS Agricultural Statistics 1998. Online. 17 Dec. 1999.

"The Schwartz Collection on Judaism, Vegetarianism, and Animal Rights." Online. 27 June 2000.

"21st Century Vegetarian: Setting Standards." London Vegetarian Society. Online. 6 Dec. 2000.

"Vegan Contraception." The Vegan Society. Online. 17 Jan. 2000.

"World Meat Situation in 1999 and Outlook for 2000." U.N. Food and Agriculture Organization. Online. 16 Feb. 2000.

## Chapter 3 Nutrition

"Contact ADA." American Dietetic Association. Online. 7 Feb. 2001.

Craig, Winston, PhD, RD. "Can Type 2 Diabetics Be Managed Effectively with a Vegetarian Diet?" Issues in Vegetarian Dietetics. Winter 1999: 1,8.

Davis, Brenda, RD. "Essential Fatty Acids in Vegetarian Nutrition." Issues in Vegetarian Dietetics. Summer 1998: 5.

Duncan, Kristine MS, RD. "Vegetarian Diets in the Treatment of Rheumatoid Arthritis." Issues in Vegetarian Dietetics. Autumn 1998: 1,5,6.

"Food, Nutrition, and the Prevention of Cancer: A Global Perspective." American Institute for Cancer Research. Online. 25 Jan. 2001.

Larson, D. Enette, MS, RD, LD. "Vegetarian Diet for Exercise and Athletic Training and Performing: An Update." Issues in Vegetarian Dietetics. Spring 1997: 1, 5-7.

Leonard, David, M.Ag. "Do Low-Carbohydrate Diets Really Improve Health?" Vegetarian Nutrition & Health Letter. May 1999: 1,2,4,8.

Messina, Virginia, MPH, RD, and Mark Messina, PhD. The Vegetarian Way. New York: Three Rivers Press, 1996.

Sekhon, Satnam, BHE, RDN. "Vegetarian Diets and Cancer Prevention." Vegetarian Nutrition Update. Winter 2001: 1.

## Chapter 4 Food Ingredients

Belitz, H. D., and W. Grosch. Food Chemistry. 2nd ed. Berlin: Springer-Verlag, 1987.

"Code of Federal Regulations: Title 21 - Food and Drugs." WAIS. Online. 1 Apr. 2000.

"General Motors will use Hormel animal protein product to make car parts." Fox Market Wire. Online. 31 Jan. 2001.

Hodgkin, Georgia, MS, RD. Diet Manual. 7th Ed. Loma Linda: The Seventh-Day Adventist Dietetic Association, 1990.

Igoe, Robert S., and Y.H. Hui. Dictionary of Food Ingredients. 3rd ed. New York: Chapman & Hall, 1996.

Schardt, David. "Glucosamine and Chondroitin: Joint Relief?" Nutrition Action Healthletter. Oct. 2000: 10.

Smith, John H. "The Basics of Making Cheese." The Scottish Dairy Association. Online. 28 Dec. 2000.

"Trader Joe's Rennet Products: West Coast." Trader Joe's. 3 Apr. 2000.

"Trader Joe's Rennet Products: East Coast." Trader Joe's. Jan. 2001.

"When Is a Cow More Than a Cow?" Telusplanet - JRoss. Online. 19 Mar. 2000.

Winter, Ruth, MS. A Consumer's Dictionary of Food Additives. 4th ed. New York: Crown Trade Paperbacks, 1994.

## Chapter 6 Vegetarian Products

McCartney, Linda. Linda's Kitchen. 3rd Ed. Boston: Bullfinch Press, 1995.

## Chapter 7 Cooking and Baking

The Guide to Cooking Schools. 13th ed. New York: Shaw Guides, 2000.

Nigro, Natalie and Shirley. Companion Guide to Healthy Cooking: A Practical Introduction to Natural Ingredients. Charlottesville: Featherstone & Brown, 1996.

Pickarski, Ron, OFM. Friendly Foods. Berkeley: Ten Speed Press, 1991.

## Chapter 8 Travel and Restaurants

Civic, Jed and Susan. The Vegetarian Traveler. Burdett: Larson Publications, 1997.

Geon, Bryan. Speaking Vegetarian: The Globetrotter's Guide To Ordering

Meatless in 197 Countries. Greenport: Pilot Books, 1999.

Shumaker, Susan, and Than Saffel. Vegetarian Walt Disney World and Greater Orlando. Morgantown: Vegetarian World Guides, 2000.

Shumaker, Susan and Than Saffel. "It's A Veg World After All." Vegetarian Times. Feb. 1998: 71-78.

Zipern, Elizabeth, and Dar Williams. The Tofu Tollbooth. Woodstock: Ceres Press/Ardwork Press, 1998.

**Chapter 9 Veggie Kids**
Avery-Grant, Anika, RD. The Vegetarian Female. Garden City Park: Avery Publishing Group, 1999.

Bass, Jules and Debbie Harter. Herb the Vegetarian Dragon. Bristol: Barefoot Books,1999.

Klaper, Michael, MD. Pregnancy, Children, and the Vegan Diet. 3rd Ed. Maui: Gentle World, Inc., 1997

**Chapter 10 Soy**
"How good is soy?" CNN. Online. 13 Dec. 2000

"Is Soy Safe to Eat?" Vegetarian Nutrition & Health Letter. Sept. 2000: 1-4.

Olivier, Suzannah. "Mad About Soy." Fox News. 10 Oct. 2000.

**Chapter 11 Vegan Concerns**
"Codes of Practice, Welfare of Animals - Sheep." Australian Capital Territory. Online. 5 Feb. 2001.

Davis, Brenda, RD, and Vesanto Melina, MS, RD. Becoming Vegan. Summertown: The Book Publishing Company, 2000.

Dingle, John, Dr. "Silk Information." School of Animal Studies, University of Queensland. Online. 19 Jan. 2000.

"Flystrike after mulesing." Agriculture Western Australia. Online. 20 Nov. 1997.

Gang, Elliot L. "The Skin Off Their Backs." The Animals' Agenda. 31 Oct. 1999.

"Information Sheet: Clothing." Vegetarian Society of the UK. Online. 7 Nov. 1999.

Klaper, Michael, MD. Vegan Nutition: Pure and Simple. Umatilla: Gentle World, Inc., 1987

"Live Plucking Geese and Eider Ducks for Down." United Poultry Concerns. Online.

Marcus, Erik. Vegan: The New Ethics of Eating. Ithaca: McBooks Press, 1998.

"Mulesing for flystrike control." Agriculture Western Australia. Online. 20 Nov. 1997.

Pyevich, Caroline. "Busy Bees." Vegetarian Journal. Nov./Dec. 1996: 18-21.

"Safety of Duck and Goose" USDA Food Safety and Inspection Service. Online. July 2000.

Vegan Outreach. Why Vegan? Pittsburgh: Vegan Outreach, 2000.

## Chapter 12 Unique Questions

Lima, Patrick. The Natural Food Garden. Rocklin: Prima Publishing, 1992.

"Winsor & Newton - Common Questions and Answers." Winsor & Newton. Online. 2000.

# INDEX

# Simply Vegan

## Quick Vegetarian Meals

**By Debra Wasserman & Reed Mangels, Ph.D., R.D.**

**The Bible of Veganism!**

The immensely popular **Simply Vegan** is much more than a cookbook. It is a guide to a non-violent, environmentally sound, humane lifestyle. It features over 160 vegan recipes that can be prepared quickly, as well as an extensive vegan nutrition section. The chapters cover topics on protein, fat, calcium, iron, vitamin B12, pregnancy and the vegan diet, and raising vegan kids. Additionally, there is a nutrition glossary, sample menus, and meal plans. This material is thoroughly researched, documented, and frequently cited by others.

There is also information on cruelty-free shopping by mail, including where to buy vegan food, clothing, cosmetics, household products, and books.

No vegan should be without this material!

**Available for $13. (224 pages)**

SEE PAGE 272 FOR ORDERING INSTRUCTIONS

# Vegetarian Journal

## In each bi-monthly issue you'll find:

**Nutrition Hotline**- answers to your questions about vegan and vegetarian diets.

**Low-fat Vegetarian Recipes**- quick and easy dishes, international cuisine, and gourmet meals.

**Food and Product Reviews**- such as our guides to non-dairy "milks" and vegetarian fast foods.

**Vegetarian Action**- projects by individuals and groups.

**Scientific Updates**- recent looks at scientific papers relating to vegetarianism

**Vegan Lifestyle Guides**- such as our "Shopper's Guide to Leather Alternatives."

The 36-page bimonthly **Journal** contains informative articles, delicious recipes, book reviews, notices about vegetarian events, product evaluations, hints on where to find vegetarian products and services, and more. All nutritional information in **Vegetarian Journal** is based on scientific studies. Our health professionals evaluate the current scientific literature and present it in a practical way which readers can easily apply to their own lives. In order to maintain an independent view, **Vegetarian Journal** does not accept paid advertising.

**$20 for one year subscription.**

# Vegan in Volume

## By Chef Nancy Berkoff, EdD, RD

This 272 page book has 125 quantity recipes for every occasion. Chef Nancy Berkoff offers help with catered events, weddings, birthdays, college food service, hospital meals, restaurants, dinner parties, and more. She shares her knowledge of vegan nutrition, vegan ingredients, menus for seniors, breakfast buffets, desserts, cooking for kids, and more.

**Available for $20. (272 pages)**

# Foodservice Update

The Vegetarian Resource Group publishes Foodservice Update, a quarterly newsletter devoted to food service. It is edited by Chef Nancy Berkoff, Ed.D., R.D. and Debra Wasserman.

**Subscriptions are $20 per year or $30 for one year of Foodservice Update and Vegetarian Journal.**

# The Lowfat Jewish Vegetarian Cookbook

**By Debra Wasserman**
Jewish people throughout the world traditionally have eaten healthy vegetarian meals. Enjoy these delicious recipes and share them with your family and friends.

There are over 150 lowfat international recipes, as well as breakfast, lunch, and dinner menus. We've included nutritional analysis for each recipe. There are 33 Passover dishes and Seder ideas, and also Rosh Hashanah dinner suggestions

All recipes are vegan and parve
**Available for $15. (224 pages)**

# No Cholesterol Passover Recipes

**By Debra Wasserman**
Featuring 100 Vegetarian Passover Dishes, the **No Cholesterol Passover Recipes** is a must for every home that wants to celebrate a healthy and ethical Passover. Enjoy eggless blintzes, dairyless carrot cream soup, festive macaroons, apple latkes, sweet and sour cabbage, knishes, vegetarian chopped "liver," no oil lemon dressing, eggless matzo meal pancakes, and much more.

All recipes are vegan and parve
**Available for $9. (96 pages)**

# Guide to Fast Food

This **Guide to Fast Food** lists the vegetarian and vegan menu items available at 80 chains. It also mentions the non-vegetarian items, such as fries made with beef fat, chicken broth in sauces, and gelatin in unexpected places.

**Available for $4. (32 pages)**

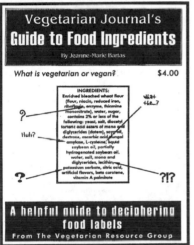

# Guide to Food Ingredients

This guide is very helpful in deciphering ingredient labels. It lists the uses, sources, and definitions of hundreds of common food ingredients. The guide also states whether the ingredient is vegan, typically vegan, vegetarian, typically vegetarian, typically non-vegetarian, or non-vegetarian.

**Available for $4. (28 pages)**

# Leprechaun Cake and Other Tales

**A Vegetarian Story-Cookbook**
A leprechaun in the kitchen, baby dragon down the block, friendly forest deer from South America, and the Snow Queen's Unicorn teach children about friendship, caring, and healthy cooking.

**Available for $10. (128 pages)**

# Vegan Handbook

### Edited by Debra Wasserman and Reed Mangels, Ph.D.,R.D.

Over 200 vegan recipes. Meal plans and menus, sports nutrition for vegetarians, senior's guide to good nutrition, 30 day menu for those who don't like to cook, guide to leather alternatives, vegetarian history, online resources, plus more.

**Available for $20. (256 pages)**

# Vegetarian Journal's Guide to Natural Food Restaurants in the U.S. and Canada

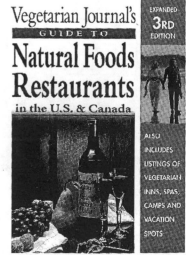

As people have become more and more health conscious, there has been a delightful proliferation of restaurants to meet the growing demand for healthier meals. Wonderful restaurants have opened up offering a wide and exciting variety of dining experiences. To help locate these places, there is now a single source for information on over 2,000 restaurants, juice bars, delicatessens, and more.

**Available for $16. (371 pages)**

# Conveniently Vegan

### By Debra Wasserman

Learn how to prepare meals with all the new natural foods products found in stores today. 150 healthy recipes using convenience foods along with fresh fruits and vegetables. Explore creative ideas for old favorites including Potato Salad, Stuffed Peppers, Quick Sloppy Joes, "Hot Dogs"and Beans, Lasagna, Chili, Bread Pudding, and Chocolate Pie. Menu ideas, food definitions, and product sources

**Available for $15. (208 pages)**

# Meatless Meals for Working People

### By Debra Wasserman and Charles Stahler

Enjoy 100 quick and easy vegan recipes, party ideas, and a spice chart. Includes information on what you can eat or should avoid at 80 fast food and quick service restaurant chains.

**Available for $12. (192 pages)**

# Join The Vegetarian Resource Group and Support Our Work!

Join at the contributor level of $30 and receive a one-year subscription to **Vegetarian Journal** (see 266) **and** a copy of **Vegan & Vegetarian FAQ**. This makes a great gift! Use or photocopy this page to take advantage of this special offer.

## Order additional copies of Vegan & Vegetarian FAQ for $15

Inquire about quantity discounts for stores and non-profit groups

---

# O R D E R   F O R M

Name _____

Address _____

City _____ State _____ Zip_____

Phone _____ E-mail _____

### Please list items and quantities:

___ _____ $_____

___ _____ $_____

___ _____ $_____

___ Check (payable to The VRG)

___ VISA/MC# _____

Exp. Date _____ Signature _____

\* All prices reflect FREE SHIPPING (US only). For orders under $25, please allow 4-6 weeks for delivery via media mail shipping. Orders $25 and over are sent via Fed Ex Ground or Priority Mail (1-6 days).

Mail to: The VRG, PO Box 1463, Baltimore, MD 21203, or call (410) 366-8343 with a Visa or Mastercard. Order and join online at www.vrg.org. Please e-mail vrg@vrg.org if you have any questions.